Sex and Gender in Pop/Rock Music

The Blues Through the Beatles to Beyoncé

Walter Everett

BLOOMSBURY ACADEMIC

NEW YORK • LONDON • OXFORD • NEW DELHI • SYDNEY

BLOOMSBURY ACADEMIC
Bloomsbury Publishing Inc
1385 Broadway, New York, NY 10018, USA
50 Bedford Square, London, WC1B 3DP, UK
29 Earlsfort Terrace, Dublin 2, Ireland

BLOOMSBURY, BLOOMSBURY ACADEMIC and the Diana logo are trademarks
of Bloomsbury Publishing Plc

First published in the United States of America 2023

Cover design by Louise Dugdale
Cover images © OneLineStock.com

Bloomsbury Publishing Inc does not have any control over, or responsibility for, any
third-party websites referred to or in this book. All internet addresses given in this
book were correct at the time of going to press. The author and publisher regret any
inconvenience caused if addresses have changed or sites have ceased to exist,
but can accept no responsibility for any such changes.

Whilst every effort has been made to locate copyright holders the publishers
would be grateful to hear from any person(s) not here acknowledged.

A catalog record for this book is available from the Library of Congress.

Library of Congress Cataloging-in-Publication Data
Names: Everett, Walter, 1954- author.
Title: Sex and gender in Pop/Rock music : the Blues through the Beatles to
Beyoncé / Walter Everett.
Description: [1st.] | New York: Bloomsbury Academic, 2023. | Includes bibliographical
references and index. | Summary: "Focuses on the relationship between
music, sex, and gender - with emphasis on contemporary pop music, which
has been overlooked in previous related scholarship"– Provided by publisher.
Identifiers: LCCN 2022049840 (print) | LCCN 2022049841 (ebook) | ISBN 9781501345968
(hardback) | ISBN 9781501345951 (paperback) | ISBN 9781501345975 (ebook) |
ISBN 9781501345982 (pdf) | ISBN 9781501345999 (ebook other)
Subjects: LCSH: Popular music–History and criticism. | Popular music–Analysis,
appreciation. | Sex and popular music. | Sex in music. | Sex role in music. |
Gender identity in music.
Classification: LCC ML3470 .E93 2023 (print) | LCC ML3470 (ebook) |
DDC 782.42164–dc23/eng/20221019
LC record available at https://lccn.loc.gov/2022049840
LC ebook record available at https://lccn.loc.gov/2022049841

ISBN: HB: 978-1-5013-4596-8
PB: 978-1-5013-4595-1
ePDF: 978-1-5013-4598-2
eBook: 978-1-5013-4597-5

Typeset by Deanta Global Publishing Services, Chennai, India

To find out more about our authors and books visit www.bloomsbury.com and
sign up for our newsletters.

Contents

Illustrations

Figures

Tables

Preface with Acknowledgments

Food, shelter, and sleep are necessary to maintain an existence, but relationships, sex, and the arts lie at the core of a meaningful life. Sex is naturally a central subject in the arts, particularly in popular music; a book covering shelter in all of its musical manifestations would be hard to imagine! Our purpose is to present a comprehensive introduction to the topics of sex and gender as central to pop/rock music. The theories behind these matters are drawn not only from present-day understandings, but because arguments have changed in both science and practice throughout the historical course of our repertoire, they will be sought from centuries' worth of thought—even in cases where those judgments are now deemed obsolete), as appropriate to the songs under discussion. An almost bewildering array of subtopics confronts us when we approach the characteristics of sex (understood here as physiological and psychological identity), gender (masculine, feminine, trans, and other nonbinary characteristics), sexuality (sexual preference), and erotics, and indeed these have been redefined over the era of recorded music as often as consideration of them has aligned with major societal and cultural shifts in the Western world, shifts that are still very much ongoing.[1]

This book thus wrestles with many clashing and controversial stances. Through most of the period covered here, sex has typically been identified by genitalia at birth but is sometimes ambiguous then and certainly subject to different degrees of alteration through dress, hormonal treatment, and sex confirmation surgery later. Gender has typically followed sex as assigned at birth but is enculturated to varying degrees—perhaps based on some level of genetic propensity—to vary from person to person. Sexual orientation, or object desire, most often fixes on the sex opposite of that assigned at birth, but same-sex attraction is obviously common as well. Pathological considerations (incest, pedophilia, bestiality) are treated in rock music just as are more acceptable forms, although they are most heavily concentrated in the singular work of Frank Zappa. These areas are independently subject to a range of biological, cultural, and social influences and are potentially fluid over the course of a lifetime, to different degrees with

---

[1] This tripartite division of sex, gender, and sexuality follows contemporary scholarship as noted in both Dess, Marecek, and Bell 2018 and Cameron and Kulik 2003, 1.

different individuals, and accepted by different classes/races at different levels at different times. The pop music analyzed here will generally be approached as its contemporaneous practitioners and audiences would have understood its references to matters of sex and gender, with the understanding that today's listeners will have a much broader and sometimes ironic context for interacting with it. Gender, for instance, is tacitly understood to be a binary matter in the voices and ears of nearly all originally involved in the music discussed here, but this does not keep us from a broader grasp today. For the most part, cultural shifts are reflected in music only after some time has passed, but conservative and radical strains have always existed side-by-side. Further, today's preferences for studying the intersection of all of these matters (perhaps particularly involving questions of transgenderism and transsexuality) will not preclude us from first approaching the main topics and their subtopics in isolation.[2] Regarding the subject of controversy itself, this author has endeavored to communicate no moral stances as to artists' biographies, no matter how egregious and—in some cases—criminal they may be.

This book traverses a progression of approaches: following the Introduction, the first three chapters—covering sex, gender, and sexuality in turn—address ideologies by investigating scholarship in a variety of disciplines, drawing from writings in physiology, psychology, sexology, sociology, gender studies, aesthetics, the parsing of poetic texts, linguistics, and music history, criticism, and analysis. Along the way, we will see how hundreds of pop/rock music examples reflect these ideas in their lyrics and in text-music relations. A few thumbnail sketches of particular songs will flesh out some ideas in more detail: phallic attack in Lou Christie's "Lightnin' Strikes," Lacanian imagery in Lorraine Feather's "The Girl with the Lazy Eye," the shame of taboo in Diana Ross and the Supremes, "Love Child," and LGBTQ+ concerns in Conchita Wurst's "Rise Like a Phoenix," Frank Ocean's "Self Control," Rufus Wainwright's "Perfect Man," and Katell Keineg's "Leonor."

Chapter 4 represents a bit of a transition from the theoretical underpinnings of prior units to the deep-dive case study that is Chapter 5. In doing so, Chapter 4 will rely far less on prior scholarship in developing musical approaches

---

[2] The treatment of topics such as transsexuality and transgenderism, but also many other strands of sex-related inquiry, is seen as unhelpfully territorial if researched separately from colonialism, racism, classicism, ableism, feminism, and so on, by Deleuze and Guattari, as cited and elaborated upon in Lykke 2011, 211–14. See also Nagel 2003 and Manalansan 2006, 226–7. A somewhat contrary view is held in Serano 2016, 132. Warnings against anachronistic pitfalls in assigning identities of sex, gender, and sexuality across time periods are provided in Halberstam 2018, 25.

to erotic factors including physical attraction (especially in Roberta Flack's "The First Time Ever I Saw Your Face"), fantasy (Bob Seger's "Night Moves"), romance (the Toys' "A Lover's Concerto"), lascivious ecstasy ("Etta James's "Something's Got a Hold on Me" and the Clovers' "Love Potion No. 9"), and orgasm (the Mothers of Invention's "Brown Shoes Don't Make It," Labelle's "Lady Marmalade," and Jane Siberry's "Mimi on the Beach"). Patti Smith's monumental track, "Land," is then the subject of Chapter 5: the song's eight subsections advance improvised concepts of fantasy that mingle with many matters of sex, gender, and sexuality undertaken in our preceding chapters, and will be engaged in some detail.

Four decades' worth of research into pop/rock music has brought this author no closer to simple definitions of this/these musical style(s). The rock era began sometime in the 1940s, was recognized as rock 'n' roll in the 1950s, and was distilled as rock in the 1960s. But other forms of pop music, including R&B, country, folk, prog, metal, punk, rap, and so on can often be inextricably linked to the rock core; edges marking different means of expression and audiences are substantially blurred, allowing for no easy distinctions. Therefore, we remain primarily interested in popular music of the rock era (that generally registering in *Billboard*'s pop, R&B/soul, C&W, and album charts), but will draw—particularly in the opening chapters—from any works of the recording age, recognizing blues, pop/jazz standards, and musical theater, nearly always from the Anglophone tradition. Music videos, album art, other visual representations; and artists' biographies, interviews, and performing personae will be given attention in only the rarest instances (as they are commonly addressed elsewhere), our focus maintained as much as possible on the music itself.

We will not attempt to interpret the whole of our repertoire through a lens that seeks a neat linear evolution of trends and styles, which in the space we have could only result in unworthy overgeneralizations. We're dealing with a complex tapestry of—again—both conservative and radical attitudes to our topics within competing styles and genres, let alone among coexisting and successive ones. Instead of attempting such a narrative, we provide an online Appendix comprising a detailed chronological throughline of sex, gender, and erotic emotions and behaviors as expressed in more than 3,000 examples culled from the dawn of recorded sound to today, favoring the repertoire of the rock era.

Decades of experience with highly musical university students at all levels have shown they typically have very little background in reading a poetic text, so as preparation for the book proper, we offer an Introduction to the interpretation of expression, metaphor, and irony. Conversely, we hope to reach an audience with little or no experience in the study of musical analysis. If some readers lack a desired foundation in the book's music-analytic techniques that are normally covered in the first year or two of a college curriculum, they are urged to view the videos posted in support of my most recent book, *What Goes On: The Beatles, Their Music, and Their Time*, that cover basics of melody, harmony, rhythm, form, and arrangement.[3] Note that here, scale degrees are designated as ^1, and so on. On very rare occasions (notably, in two instances in Chapter 1), skills attained only in higher-level music study would yield full appreciation.

Finally, a trigger warning is in order. This book does not shy away from the language of its texts, even though social propriety still regards it necessary in many contexts to censor a number of the sex-related words contained therein, as they offend many. More problematic are words offensive to everyone, especially those denigrating classes of people, whether by sex or by race. Today's classrooms in many disciplines do not permit the use of the N-word, in particular, even in the cold analysis of texts that employ it. This text, however, will occasionally quote such words, even though they will pain the reader. Apologies for this decision and its effects.

Acknowledgments. I am indebted to my editor, Leah Babb-Rosenfeld, who provided solid support throughout the creation of this book and especially nimble direction when the project took a major unexpected turn midway through. My partner, Lisa Everett, inspired me in late 2015 to choose Patti Smith as an object of study, a decision that kick-started the entire venture. My colleague Katie Kapurch was key in helping me define the book's trajectory and offered expert and face-saving advice in her thorough readings of the Introduction and Chapters 1 and 5. The Center for Popular Music Studies at Case Western Reserve University, directed by Daniel Goldmark, awarded a Research Fellowship that allowed me to spend a week in July 2016, at the archives of the Rock and Roll Hall of Fame and Museum to study early Smith documents that made Chapter 5 possible. In turn, Chapter 5 is an expansion of a paper presented to the "Women in the Creative Arts" conference in Canberra, Australia, in August 2017. Similarly, several of the book's analytical arguments were tested at the Euromac 10 conference in Moscow, in September 2021;

---

[3] These videos are found at http://youtu.be/3UvJvSJRMrA, http://youtu.be/lv1dHWLg_Rw, http:// youtu.be/XY__57yCviI, http://youtu.be/yWaDafGaLoU, http://youtu.be/fuGQp_6oT8U, http:// youtu.be/kdSv39J22HE, http://youtu.be/hzS5QpY8wkg, http://youtu.be/Fbq43W-Jndw, http:// youtu.be/fCoc0bATJ_Q, and http://youtu.be/36j6CXO8QEM.

I thank the organizers of, and participants in, those events for the opportunities to benefit from feedback on early ideas. Thanks to Ben Ayotte for his expert engraving of Figures 1.1 and 1.2. I am grateful to the University of Michigan for strong research support, including a semester's leave from teaching responsibilities in 2021, and for allowing me to enjoy a thirty-three-year career with a home base of excellent students and colleagues, and an international discipline full of fantastic researchers, while on a path devoted to listening to, and talking about, music, for which life this book is the capstone.

Introduction

Means of Expression and Reception in Poetic Texts

The manner in which sex-related themes are expressed is a marker of how a society sees itself. The breaking of taboos is usually a serious matter that involves the individual participant's superego ("participant" standing in for composer, performer, and listener) and levels of censorship ranging from friendly to litigious on the part of recording teams and corporate ears, radio programmers, FCC guidelines, merchandisers, and the press. When musical output is heavily controlled, as it was through the first half of the twentieth century, sexual ideas emerge only in euphemism and metaphor, humor, and irony, whether intended or not. One interesting aspect about the rock age is that because its music spans an era of tremendous new sexual freedom and openness to new ways of considering gender and sexuality, its expressive nature changes throughout the period. In times when mores change more slowly, "metaphors of poetry become more and more abstract as a result of the law of novelty. [Over time,] metaphors are found further and further away from the object they are supposed to describe" (Høge-Olesen 2019, 125). In the face of relaxing mores, conversely, rock music directs and reflects loosening strictures, as when gradually abandoning such masking devices as the *double entendre* and stating ideas in frank language, Exhibit A being Liz Phair's "Flower" (1994): "I want to be your blowjob queen." Of course, what seemed progressive in the rock era can seem tame today, as Susan J. Douglas notes wryly,

> Eamon's classy 2004 hit record "Fuck It, I Don't Want You Back," with the immortal lyrics "Fuck what I said, it don't mean shit now" and "Fuck you, you hoe." Ditto for Shaggy's "It Wasn't Me" [2000], which urged her to "Picture this, we were both butt-naked banging on the bathroom floor." Or there was 50 Cent bragging metaphorically, "I got the Magic Stick" [2003], which evoked Lil Kim's somewhat less allegorical response, "I got the magic clit." The Beatles' "Why Don't We Do It in the Road" [1968] suddenly seemed like an Osmond Brothers song." (2010, 157)

This introduction will not be the place to track historical arcs of explicit lyrics, but we can investigate here the figures of speech that allow for sexual expression a bit further.

Metaphor and euphemism. Metaphor has always been a property of song.

> Sumerian love songs [c 1500-2000 BC?] are no exception to this tendency. [In one example, the] proximity of her lover has filled Inanna with such passion that, as described by scholar Samuel Noah Kramer, "then and there she composes a song for her vulva in which she compares it to a horn, 'the boat of heaven,' to the new crescent moon, to fallow land, to a high field, to a hillock," and ends by demanding "Who will plow it for me?" How does the royal visitor respond? "Oh Lordly Lady, the king will plow it for you, Dumuzi, the king, will plow it for you." His ability matches his willingness. For as the hymn notes: "At the king's lap stood the rising cedar." (Gioia 2015, 16)

No one reads this literally. Metaphors are ways of suggesting inexactly— ambiguously or even obscurely—one thing in terms of another. In pop music, for instance, references to dance may often represent sex, and border crossings of various sorts may represent transgenderism.[1] The symbols may be employed euphemistically, to avoid taboos; they may also have artistic merit in motivating the listener to work toward an interpretation. Some terms are dead metaphors: designations such as "pussy" and "going all the way" originally masked their intentions but now require no translation. We encounter metaphors (and related speech acts such as simile and, less often, metonymy) for sexual ideas, and such ideas may in turn refer to more general qualities and relationships.

Especially when pop/rock music is approached as art, songs are open to varying interpretations, and these meanings can be idiosyncratic to each listener (perhaps even as a result of mishearing lyrics) or agreed upon in large numbers. After all, art reaches many different audiences, in the past, present, and future. Young, naïve listeners may initially accept all lyrics literally but find new allegorical or less precise symbolic meanings as they mature. The listener need not understand the music as intended by its creators—there are no rules— but parsing applies Occam's razor to achieve the most satisfying and insightful comprehension possible of "hidden meaning."[2] Carrying its own layers of

---

[1] The latter metaphor is discussed in Halberstam 1998, 165. One example might be "Tear Me Down" from the show *Hedwig and the Angry Inch* (2014), telling the story of a male-to-female transsexual, "I was born on the other side of a town ripped in two; I made it over the great divide and now I'm comin' for you."

[2] Much more on these general principles may be found in Basler 1970, Lakoff and Johnson 1980, Lakoff 1987, 409–15, Edwards 1994, Deighnan 1997, Gracyk 2001, 37–53, Chion 2009, 430–3, Moores 2010, and Bradley 2017.

signification, the music accompanying the lyrics may also work empathetically, indifferently, or ironically: tensions in tonal, rhythmic, textural, or formal relations hold metaphoric potential in suggesting sex-related imagery.[3] Table 0.1 presents a representative number of erotic metaphors and similes in pop/rock lyrics dating back to the beginnings of sound recording, reaching back a century to demonstrate the importance of early blues for our understanding of later popular song. Relationships between lyrics and accompanying music will be discussed throughout this book.

Humor and irony. Humor is a celebration of incongruity. For Freud, it is the expression of suppressed thoughts, often lustful ones. Since the bawdy verse within the thirteenth-century songs of *Carmina Burana* and the later tales of Chaucer and Rabelais, sex has been a central topic for humor.[4] Sexual jesting can be particularly incongruous when it is at once disgustingly offensive and ostensibly innocuous, detached from any need for empathy with its target. What is offensive or innocuous will differ from person to person:

> At the furthest, most disturbing end of that continuum, "funny" and "hilarious" become a defense against charges of sexual harassment, misconduct, or assault. Consider the boy from Steubenville, Ohio, who was captured on video joking about the repeated violation of an unconscious girl at a party by a group of his friends. "She is so raped," he said, laughing. "They raped her quicker than Mike Tyson." When someone off camera suggested that rape wasn't funny, he retorted, "Rape isn't funny—it's *hilarious*!" (Orenstein 2020, 32–3)

Musical examples, especially those in the pop-music sphere, are usually not quite so extreme, but cases do come close. Through an over-the-top performance, k. d. lang's perennial concert cover of Joanie Sommers's "Johnny Get Angry" (1962) exposes the original song's potential for veiled violence ("I want a brave man, I want a cave man, Johnny show me that you care, really care for me").[5] Any perceived humor is very dark and removed from irony since the listener can't help but empathize with the singing victim.

---

[3] Pioneering work in this area is found in McClary 1991, Sayrs 1993–94, Reynolds and Press 1995, Cusick 1999a, Gracyk 2001, Macarthur 2002, and Kopkind 2009, 357–9. See also Blecha 2004, 89, on metaphorical implications in early jazz and blues, Hajdu 2016, 108, on the same in jump blues, Green 2009, Stilwell 2010, 71, and de Boise 2015, 134–5, on the same in rock 'n' roll, Weinstein 2000, 35–6, on the same in heavy metal, and Woods 2011 on the same in rap.

[4] The early bawdy song is a topic in Hamm 1983, 8 and 23, Van der Merwe 1989, 80–2 and 189–91, Blecha 2004, Otis 2009, and Gioia 2015.

[5] Lori Burns (1997) presents an insightful take on lang's performance. Jacqueline Warwick's analysis (2007, 64–70) of the Crystals' "He Hit Me (And It Felt like a Kiss)" (1962) is fascinating in a related context.

Table 0.1 Erotic Metaphor and Simile in Popular-Music Recordings

Thing Symbolized	Symbol	Example(s)
Lust	Heat, fire, burning	Georgia Gibbs, "Kiss of Fire" (1952); Martha & the Vandellas, "Heat Wave" (1963); Supremes, "Love Is Like an Itching in My Heart" (1966); Association, "Along Comes Mary" (1966); Doors, "Light My Fire" (1967); Shocking Blue, "Venus" (1969); Elvis Presley, "Burning Love" (1972); Ohio Players, "Fire" (1974); Quincy Jones, "Body Heat" (1974); Pointer Sisters, "Fire" (1978); Blue Öyster Cult, "Burnin' for You" (1981); George Strait, "A Fire I Can't Put Out" (1983); Madonna, "Burning Up" (1983); Bruce Springsteen, "I'm on Fire" (1984); Kenny Rogers, "Morning Desire" (1985); 2 Live Crew, "Me So Horny" (1989); Tina Turner, "Steamy Windows" (1989); Michael Jackson, "Give In to Me" (1991); PJ Harvey, "Rid of Me" (1993); The The, "Dogs of Lust" (1993); Aaliyah, "Hot Like Fire" (1996); Missy Elliott, "Dog in Heat" (2001); LL Cool J, "Control Myself" (2006); Rihanna, "Push Up on Me" (2007); Jonas Brothers, "Burnin' Up" (2008); Kings of Leon, "Sex on Fire" (2008); Adele, "Rolling in the Deep" (2011); Madonna, "Girl Gone Wild" (2012); Coldplay, "True Love" (2014); Adele, "Send My Love (To Your New Lover)" (2015)
"	Magic, witchcraft, devilry	Ivory Joe Hunter, "I Almost Lost My Mind" (1950); Muddy Waters, "I'm Your Hoochie Coochie Man" (1954); Bo Diddley, "I'm a Man" (1955); Ricky Nelson, "Poor Little Fool" (1958); Clovers, "Love Potion Number Nine" (1959); Nina Simone, "I Put a Spell on You" (1965); Cream, "Strange Brew" (1967); Jimi Hendrix Experience, "Voodoo Chile" (1968); Bob Dylan, "Tonight I'll Be Staying Here with You" (1969); Brian Hyland, "Gypsy Woman" (1970); Santana, "Black Magic Woman" (1970); Honey Cone, "Stick-Up" (1971); Don Gibson, "Woman (Sensuous Woman)" (1972); Eagles, "Witchy Woman" (1972); Heart, "Magic Man" (1976); Cliff Richard, "Devil Woman" (1976); Scorpions, "Virgin Killer" (1979); Johnny Gill, "Rub You the Right Way" (1990); Ween, "Voodoo Lady" (1994); Bon Jovi, "One Wild Night" (2000); Holly Near, "Infatuation" (2000); Carrie Underwood, "Cowboy Casanova" (2009)
"	Hunting	Marvelettes, "The Hunter Gets Captured by the Game" (1967); Duran Duran, "Hungry Like the Wolf" (1982); Tom Waits, "Just the Right Bullets" (1993); White Stripes, "Conquest" (2007); Ricky Martin, "Te Busco y Te Alcanzo" (2011); Maroon 5, "Animals" (2014)

"	Illness, fever, need for doctor	Little Willie John, "Fever" (1956); The Young Rascals, "Good Lovin'" (1966); Bill Anderson, "I Get the Fever" (1966); Janis Joplin, "Woman Left Lonely" (1971); Gary Glitter, "Do You Wanna Touch Me?"; The Sylvers, "Boogie Fever" (1975); Tina Charles, "Dr. Love" (1976); Foreigner, "Hot Blooded" (1978); Little Feat, "Rock and Roll Doctor" (1981); Le Roux, "Addicted" (1982); Marvin Gaye, "Sexual Healing" (1982); Thompson Twins, "Doctor! Doctor!" (1984); Warrant, "Machine Gun" (1992); Jennifer Lopez, "Come Over" (2001); Santana, "Why Don't You & I" (2003); Billie Eilish, "My Strange Addiction" (2019)
"	Madness	Michael Sembello, "Maniac" (1983); Rolling Stones, "Sex Drive" (1991); Ricky Martin, "Livin' La Vida Loca" (1999); Enrique Iglesias, "Bailando" (2014)
"	(Interior) beast	Sam the Sham & the Pharaohs, "Lil' Red Riding Hood" (1966); Isaac Hayes, "The Feeling Keeps on Coming" (1973); Ted Nugent, "Stranglehold" (1975); Hall & Oates, "Maneater" (1982); R. Kelly, "Snake" (2003)
"	Machine	Ethel Waters, "My Handy Man" (1928); Steppenwolf, "Born to Be Wild" (1968); Smokey Robinson, "Love Machine" (1975); Daddy Yankee, "Gasolina" (2004)
Gay orientation	Friend of Dorothy	John Lennon, "She's a Friend of Dorothy" (1976)
"	Vampirism	Pet Shop Boys, "In Denial" (1999)
(Erect) penis	Snake	Victoria Spivey, "Black Snake Blues" (1926); John Lee Hooker, "Crawlin' King Snake" (1949); Doors, "The End" (1967); Frank Zappa, "Baby Snakes" (1979); Bow Wow Wow, "Wild in the Country" (1982); PJ Harvey, "Snake" (1993); Nicki Minaj, "Anaconda" (2014)
"	Gun	Bo Carter, "Ram Rod Daddy" (1931); Bing Crosby & the Andrews Sisters, "Pistol Packin' Mama" (1944); Frank Zappa, "Rudy Wants to Buy Yez a Drink" (1970); David Bowie, "Moonage Daydream" (1972); Queen, "Bohemian Rhapsody" (1975); Kiss, "Love Gun" (1977); Bruce Springsteen, "Real Man" (1992); Nine Inch Nails, "Big Man with a Gun" (1994); Jeff Buckley, "I Woke Up in a Strange Place" (2000)
"	Car	Jackie Brentston, "Rocket 88" (1951); The Beatles, "Drive My Car" (1965); Queen, "I'm in Love with My Car" (1975); Scorpions, "Lovedrive" (1979); Prince, "Little Red Corvette" and "Lady Cab Driver" (1982)
"	Rocket	Kiss, "Rocket Ride" (1978); Knack, "Rocket o' Love" (1991)
"	One-eyed cat	Joe Turner, "Snake, Rattle and Roll" (1954)
"	Peace pipe	Loretta Lynn, "Your Squaw Is on the Warpath" (1968)
"	Key	Jimi Hendrix Experience, "Red House" (1969); Melanie, "Brand New Key" (1971); Madonna, "Open Your Heart" (1986); R. Kelly, "Ignition" (2002)
"	(Floppy) disc	Prince, "Batdance" (1989)

(Continued)

Table 0.1 (Continued)

Thing Symbolized	Symbol	Example(s)
"	Food: hot dog	Bessie Smith, "Need a Little Sugar in My Bowl" (1931); David Lee Roth, "Hot Dog and a Shake" (1988)
"	Food: banana	Bo Carter, "Banana in Your Fruit Basket" (1931); Pauline Daniels, "The Banana for My Pie" (1999)
"	Food: lollipop	Bessie Smith, "You've Got to Give Me Some" (1929); Millie Small, "My Boy Lollipop" (1964); Salt-n-Pepa, "Shoop" (1993); Tha Dogg Pound, "Big Pimpin'" (1994)
"	Food: hard candy	George Formby, "With My Little Stick of Blackpool Rock" (1937); Bird & MacDonald, "Candy Wrapper" (1985)
"	Dentist's drill	Dinah Washington, "Long John Blues" (1949)
"	Oil drill	Dorothy Ellis, "Drill Daddy Drill" (1952)
"	Lightning	Lou Christie, "Lightnin' Strikes" (1965)
"	Bee's stinger	Big Mama Thornton, "Bumble Bee" (1966); Carrie Underwood, "Good Girl" (2012)
"	Scorpion's tail	Tori Amos, "Sweet the Sting" (2005)
"	Bone	Wynonie Harris, "Come and Get Your Rib" (1952); Terry Jacks, "Put the Bone In" (1974); Juvenile, "Slow Motion" (2004); John Prine, "Egg & Daughter Nite, Lincoln Nebraska, 1967 (Crazy Bone)" (2018)
"	Trombone	Dinah Washington, "Big Long Slidin' Thing" (1954)
"	Telephone to be plugged in	Meri Wilson, "Telephone Man" (1977); Rufus Wainwright, "Vibrate" (2003)
"	Telephone extension	Nick Lowe, "Switch Board Susan" (1979)
"	Love boat	Bell Biv Devoe, "B. B. D. (I Thought It Was Me)" (1990)
"	"Stiff upper lip"	AC/DC, "Stiff Upper Lip" (2000)
"	Arrow	Sean Paul, "(When You Gonna) Give It Up to Me" (2006)
"	"Disco stick"	Lady Gaga, "LoveGame" (2008)
"	Magic wand	OMI, "Cheerleader" (2015)
"	[Huge size]	Julia Lee, "King Size Papa" (1948); Bull Moose Jackson, "Big Ten-Inch Record" (1952)
Testicles	Two-dollar bill	Hank Williams, "Hey, Good Lookin'" (1951)
Semen	Sugar (for tea)	Ma Rainey, "Bo-weavil Blues" (1923); Neil Patrick Harris, "Sugar Daddy" (2014)
"	Jelly	Tampa Red, "Don't You Lie to Me" (1940)

" Honey	Slim Harpo, "I'm a King Bee" (1957)
" Lemon juice	Led Zeppelin, "The Lemon Song" (1969)
" "A protein surprise"	Frank Zappa, "SEX" (1983)
" Oil	Faster Pussycat, "Little Dove" (1989)
" Rain	Beatles, "Please Please Me" (1963); Rihanna, "Umbrella" (2007)
" Tears	Joni James, "Your Cheatin' Heart" (1953); Rufus Wainwright, "Between My Legs" (2007)
" Seeds	Tyler, The Creator, "Droppin' Seeds" (2017)
Anus "Chocolate starfish"	Limp Bizkit, "Hot Dog" (2000)
Breasts "Big bazookas, big balloons," etc.	Valerie Bader, "Boobies in the Eye of the Beholder" (2008)
Vulva Door	Arthur Collins, "Hannah, Won't You Open That Door?" (1904); Leroy Carr, "Papa Wants a Cookie" (1930); Big Mama Thornton, "Hound Dog" (1953); Gale Storm, "I Hear You Knocking" (1955); Jerry Lee Lewis "It'll Be Me" (1957); Sensations, "Let Me In" (1962); Bob Dylan, "Temporary Like Achilles" (1956); Grand Funk Railroad, "T.N.U.C." (1969); Great White, "On Your Knees" (1984); Rod Stewart, "Love Touch" (1986); Lisa Fischer, "How Can I Ease the Pain" (1991); RuPaul, "House of Love" (1993); Steve Earle, "Hard-Core Troubadour" (1996); Melanie Chisholm, "Never Be the Same Again" (2000); Britney Spears, "Lonely" (2001); Queens of the Stone Age, "Little Sister" (2005)
" Delta	Joe Cocker, "Delta Lady" (1970)
" "Vertical smile"	Insane Clown Posse, "Bitches" (1999)
" Black hole	R. Kelly, "Sex Planet" (2007)
" Muffin	Aerosmith, "Walk This Way" (1976); Lady Gaga, "Poker Face" (2008)
Vagina Treasure	Laura Nyro, "Map to the Treasure" (1970)
" Food: jelly-roll	Bessie Smith, "Nobody in Town Can Bake a Sweet Jelly Roll Like Mine" (1923)
" Food: cabbage	Maggie Jones, "Anybody Here Want to Try My Cabbage" (1924)
" Food: fish (in sea)	Ma Rainey, "Don't Fish in My Sea" (1926); Mary Martin, "My Heart Belongs to Daddy" (1939); Dodie Stevens, "Pink Shoe Laces" (1958)
" Food: candy	Rosemary Clooney, "Come On-a My House" (1951)
" Food: honey	Muddy Waters, "Honey Bee" (1951); Mötley Crüe, "Tonight (We Need a Lover)" (1985); Tom Petty, "Honeybee" (1994)

(Continued)

Table 0.1 (Continued)

Thing Symbolized	Symbol	Example(s)
"	Food: sugar	Doris Day & Frankie Laine, "Sugar Bush" (1952); Archies, "Sugar, Sugar" (1969); Sheena Easton, "Sugar Walls" (1984); Def Leppard, "Pour Some Sugar on Me" (1987); Baby Bash, "Suga Suga (So Fly)" (2003)
"	Food: pie	Aerosmith, "Cheese Cake" (1979); Mötley Crüe, "Slice of Your Pie" (1989); Jewell, "It's Not Deep Enough" (1994)
"	Food: fruit	Peter Gabriel, "Sledgehammer" (1986)
"	Saddle	Bull Moose Jackson, "I Want a Bowlegged Woman" (1948); Lamplighters, "Ride Jockey Ride" (1954); Aerosmith, "Back in the Saddle" (1976)
"	Car	Bruce Springsteen, "Pink Cadillac" (1984); Aretha Franklin, "Freeway of Love" (1985); Pebbles, "Mercedes Boy" (1988); Elastica, "Car Song" (1995); Rihanna, "Shut Up and Drive" (2007)
"	Little red wagon	Miranda Lambert, "Little Red Wagon" (2014)
"	Box (perhaps as piano or accordion)	Toppers, "(I Love to Play Your Piano) Let Me Bang Your Box" (1954); Yoko Ono, "Open Your Box" (1971); Who, "Squeeze Box" (1975); Christina Aguilera, "Your Body" (2012)
"	Garden [note 1973 publication of Nancy Friday's *My Secret Garden*]	John Cougar, "China Girl" (1982); T'Pau, "Secret Garden" (1988); Quincy Jones, "The Secret Garden (Sweet Seduction Suite)" (1990); Heart, "All I Wanna Do Is Make Love to You" (1990); Madonna, "Secret Garden" (1992); Bruce Springsteen, "Secret Garden" (1995); Tori Amos, "Original Sinsuality" (2005); John Mayer, "I Don't Trust Myself (With Loving You)" (2006); R. Kelly, "Pregnant" (2009)
"	Down south	Conway Twitty, "Red Neckin' Love Makin' Night" (1981)
"	Warehouse	Steely Dan, "Pixeleen" (2003)
"	Pocket	Avril Lavigne, "Hot" (2007)
"	Labyrinth	Luis Fonsi & Daddy Yankee, "Despacito" (2017)
Clitoris	Boy in the boat	George Hannah, "The Boy in the Boat" (1930)
"	Button	Lil Johnson, "Press My Button (Ring My Bell)" (1936)
"	Trigger	Beatles, "Happiness Is a Warm Gun" (1968)
"	Bell	Anita Ward, "Ring My Bell" (1979)
Hymen	Beret	Prince, "Raspberry Beret" (1985)
Legs	Wings	Rod Stewart, "Tonight's the Night" (1976)

(Potential for) female arousal	Waves of (ocean) water	Phil Phillips, "Sea of Love" (1959); Phil Ochs, "I've Had Her" (1967); Beatles, "Julia" (1968); Jane Birkin & Serge Gainsbourg, "Je t'Aime" (1969); Harry Chapin, "Dogtown" (1972); Rolling Stones, "Soul Survivor" (1972); Heart, "Soul of the Sea" (1976); Jane Siberry, "Mimi on the Beach" (1984); Belinda Carlisle, "Heaven Is a Place on Earth" (1987) and "I Get Weak" (1988); PJ Harvey, "Water" (1992); Prince, "Crgasm" (1994); Fiona Apple, "Sullen Girl" (1996); Janis Ian, "Ride Me Like a Wave" (1997); k.d. lang, "Love's Great Ocean" (2000); Janet Jackson, "Moist" (2004)
Sexual advances	Game	Mindbenders, "The Game of Love" (1965); Meatloaf, "Paradise by the Dashboard Light" (1977); Britney Spears, "Oops!... I Did It Again" (2000); Katy Perry, "I Kissed a Girl" (2008)
Sexual intercourse	Dance	Frankie Laine, "That's My Desire" (1947); Tommy Dorsey, "The Huckle-Buck" (1949); Hank Ballard, "The Twist" (1959); B2K & P Diddy, "Bump, Bump, Bump" (2002); Janet Jackson, "All Nite (Don't Stop)" (2004)
"	Rocking/rolling	Roy Brown, "Good Rockin' Tonight" (1948); Helen Humes, "I'm Gonna Let Him Ride" (1950); Etta James, "The Wallflower" (1955); Michael Jackson, "Rock with You" (1979)
"	Riding	Fats Noe, "Ride Daddy Ride" (1951)
"	Playing house	Eddy Arrold, "I Wanna Play House with You" (1951); Elvis Presley, "Baby Let's Play House" (1955); Tammy Wynette, "I Don't Wanna Play House" (1967)
"	Sleeping	Everly Brothers, "Wake Up Little Susie" (1957)
"	Playing with toys, playing game	Paul Reed, "A Secretary Is Not a Toy" (1961); Garth Brooks, "Workin' On a Full House" (1991)
"	Faucet needs a plumber	Joni Mitchell, "Marcie" (1968)
"	Steam rolling	James Taylor, "Steamroller Blues" (1970)
"	Getting lucky	George Jones, "I Always Get Lucky with You" (1983)
"	Stabbing the wound	MC Brains, "Oochie Coochie" (1992)
Stamina	All-night-long activity	Ruth Wallis, "Long Playing Daddy" (c. 1953); Bruce Springsteen, "Ramrod" (1980); Eugene Wilde, "Gotta Get You Home Tonight" (1984)
Fellatio	Cigarette smoking	Bo Carter, "Cigarette Blues" (1936)
"	Blowing one's mind	Rolling Stones, "Honky Tonk Women" (1969)
"	Blowing one's whistle	DJ Aligator Project, "The Whistle Song (Blow My Whistle Bitch)" (2002)
Cunnilingus	Sea diving	Bessie Smith, "Empty Bed Blues" (1928)

(Continued)

Table 0.1 (Continued)

Thing Symbolized	Symbol	Example(s)
"	Eating candy	Ohio Express, "Chewy Chewy" and "Yummy Yummy Yummy" (1968)
Anal sex	Servicing trash can	Harlem Hamfats, "The Garbage Man" (1936)
"	Flipping it	Tag Team, Whoomp! (There It Is)" (1993)
"	Back door	Mothers of Invention, "My Guitar Wants to Kill Your Mama" (1970); Iron Maiden, "Bring Your Daughter to the Slaughter" (1990); Scissor Sisters, "Skin This Cat" (2010)
Masturbation	Playing with toy	Chuck Berry, "My Ding-a-Ling" (1972)
"	Crying tears, rain	Everly Brothers, "Crying in the Rain" (1962); Marty Robbins, "Tonight Carmen" (1967); Laura Nyro, "Lonely Women" (1968); Smokey Robinson & the Miracles, "The Tears of a Clown" (1970); Gary Morris, "100% Chance of Rain" (1986); Samantha Fox, "I Surrender (To the Spirit of the Night)" (1987)
Unspecified (perhaps kinky) sex	Freaking	Leon Haywood, "I Want'a Do Something Freaky to You" (1975); Silk, "Freak Me" (1993); Adina Howard, "Freak Like Me" (1995); Coolio, "Too Hot" (1995); Usher, "Nice & Slow" (1998); 2Pac, "How Do U Want It" (1996); Another Level, "Freak Me" (1998); Macy Gray, "Caligula" (1999); Missy Elliott, "Get Ur Freak On" (2001); Macy Gray, "Sexual Revolution" (2001); Christina Aguilera, "Still Dirrty" (2006); Britney Spears, "I Wanna Go" (2011); Lonely Island, "3-Way (The Golden Rule)" (2011); Janelle Monáe, "Q.U.E.E.N." (2013); Jason Derulo, "Kama Sutra" (2014)
Climax, frisson	Shivering	Eartha Kitt, C'est Si Bon (1953); Alma Cogan, "Never Do a Tango with an Eskimo" (1955)
Climax, ejaculation	Blowing one's top	Dominoes, "Sixty Minute Man" (1951); Swallows, "It Ain't the Meat" (1951)
"	Fireworks	Joni Mitchell, "My Old Man" (1971); Starland Vocal Band, "Afternoon Delight" (1976); Krokus, "Long Stick Goes Boom" (1982)
"	Butter flowing	Wynonie Harris, "Keep on Churnin'" (1952)
"	Shooting a gun	AC/DC, "Shoot to Thrill" (1980)
"	Happy ending	Bing Crosby, "Please" (1932); Sharon Brown, "I Specialize in Love" (1982)
"	Busting a nut	N.W.A., "Findum, Fuckum & Flee" (1991); 2Pac, "Me and My Girlfriend" (1996); Lil' Kim, "Not Tonight" (1996); Notorious B.I.G., "Big Booty Hoes" (1999); Wu-Tang Clan, "Let My Niggas Live" (2000); Nicki Minaj, "Slumber Party" (2009); YG, "Do It to Ya" (2014); Lil Yachty, "Dirty Mouth" (2017)
Premature ejaculation	Early appearance of 5 o'clock shadow	Merle Travis, "So Round, So Firm, So Fully Packed" (1947)

Sex-based comedy's origins are in anonymous limericks and, more recently, in American vaudeville and the British music hall, which became the variety show. We thus see the evolution of sex jokes in blue humor such as that of Lenny Bruce, 1970s sitcoms like "All in the Family" (United States), "Mad About the House" and "The Benny Hill Show" (both United Kingdom), "Saturday Night Live," and other late-night TV. Stand-up comics known for delivering bawdy humor include Andrew Dice Clay, Chris Rock, Wanda Sykes, Margaret Cho, Sarah Silverman, and Ali Wong. Cable networks and streaming services have allowed comics and editors to push the limits even more, while the popularity of podcasts— particularly in the pandemic era—made a stage and a live audience less relevant.

In music, such a timeless classic is one bawdy nineteenth-century sea limerick set to a tune, "Friggin' in the Riggin'," which tells of a sailor who "stuffed his ass with broken glass and circumcised the skipper," recorded by both the Sex Pistols (1979) and Loudon Wainwright III (2006, as "Good Ship Venus"). A few years earlier in 1964, the Beatles pleaded in a cover of Carl Perkins's "Matchbox," "if you don't want Ringo's peaches, honey, don't mess around my tree." This sexual innuendo may be traced back to the hokum blues of Ma Rainey's "Don't Fish in My Sea" (1926): "if you don't like my ocean, don't fish in my sea; stay out of my valley and let my mountain be." The topic of sexual stamina followed the blues from Ida Cox's complaints about premature ejaculation in "One Hour Mama" (1939) through Bill Brown's R&B bravado in the Dominoes's "Sixty Minute Man" (1951) (updated by Clarence Carter in 1973), which finds more recent expression in Missy Elliott's "One Minute Man" (2001). In between, Mötley Crüe boasted (presumably for an all-male audience) of getting off without foreplay with the super distorted guitars and strong snare backbeat of "Ten Seconds to Love" (1983). Ruth Wallis's "Long Playing Daddy" (*c.* 1953) was one of her many off-label *double entendre*-packed "party records" sold under the counter. In this song's reference to an outdated mechanical spring-driven gramophone, "I used to have the old-fashioned kind; he used to stop—I had to start him up by giving him a wind," Wallis sang the last four words with a syncopated melody quickly leaping back and forth, ^2 - ^5 - ^2 - ^5 - ^1, to comically simulate a hand job. A similar situation is lampooned in Bull Moose Jackson's "Big Ten-Inch Record" (1952) ("she begs for my big ten-inch *[pregnant pause]* record of the band that plays the blues"), covered by Aerosmith in 1975.

John Lennon's newfound love with Yoko Ono rekindled a youthful intrigue with funny smut. The Beatle was asked to contribute to the crowdsourced book for the show *Oh! Calcutta* (1969), for which he penned an adolescents' circle-jerk sketch in which various wankers would call out names of beauties such as Brigitte Bardot for inspiration until Lennon had an actor break the mood by intoning, "Winston Churchill!" The Beatles' "The Ballad of John and Yoko" (1969) includes Lennon's punning verse, "the newspeople said, 'Say, what'cha doin' in bed?' I said, 'we're only tryin' to get us some peace,'" a conflation of world accord with "piece [of ass]." On their *Wedding Album* (also 1969), "John and Yoko" is a recording of the two calling each others' first names in alternation during twenty-plus minutes of simulated lovemaking, a parody of Stan Freberg's soap-opera send-up, "John and Marsha" (1951).

Many of the euphemisms listed in Table 0.1 appear for humorous effect. Double meaning is rife among them. Terry Jacks's "Put the Bone In" (1974) is ostensibly a woman's dirge begging her butcher for a pork bone as a special treat for her seriously injured dog: "Put the bone in, she asked him, at the store," the dog owner pausing for effect at each comma. Wordplay brought us album titles like Caravan's *Cunning Stunts* (1975). Parodies of known models, such as William Belli's "Love You Like a Big Schlong" (2012)—taking on Selena Gomez's far more innocent "Love You Like a Love Song" (2011)—are often given hard sexual turns. Sometimes hilarious incongruity would play upon musical style earmarks: David Allan Coe satirized country laments with his reaction to the evidence of a cheating spouse in "Cum Stains on the Pillow (Where Your Head Used to Be)" (1978). At other times, incongruity stems mostly from an unexpectedly immature level of public rudeness—an absent superego—as with Frank Zappa's frequent toilet humor or with "Jizz in My Pants" (2009) and "I Just Had Sex" (2011) by Andy Samberg's group, the Lonely Island, joined by Justin Timberlake and Lady Gaga for "3-Way (The Golden Rule)" (2011).

Public displays of sexual funny business can incur censorship. One seemingly innocuous example, Uncle Bonsai's children's-song-like "Penis Envy" (1984), had lyrics that

> were a humorous listing of how the lives of the female members of Bonsai would change if they possessed the valued item, closing with the line, "If I had a penis I'd still be a girl/But I'd make much more money and conquer the world." The song was condemned by some critics for its "revolting lyrics," and in 1989 was cited in obscenity charges filed by the FCC against Florida radio stations WIOD and WZTA. (Gaar 1992, 276)

Perhaps it was the song's then-shocking feminist message, more than the not-so-scandalous use of the word "penis," that resulted in the song's suppression.

One clever means of covering up a taboo word is ghost rhyme, in which the end of a line of verse awkwardly veers away from the expected risqué word.[6] The offense may be scatological, as in Benny Bell's "Shaving Cream" (a radio hit in 1975, but originally released in limited numbers in 1946): "I have a sad story to tell you; it may hurt your feelings a bit. Last night when I walked into my bathroom, I stepped in a big pile of shhhhhaving cream . . ." But sex-related taboo themes often lurk in the unsaid as well:

> Anthrax, "I'm the Man" (1987): "They say rap and metal can never mix / Well, all of them can suck our . . . sexual organ in the lower abdominal area!"

> The Killers, "Mr. Brightside" (2005): "Now they're going to bed and my stomach is sick / And it's all in my head but she's touching his . . . chest now."

> Meghan Trainor, "Dear Future Husband" (2015): "I'll be sleeping on the left side of the bed / Open doors for me and you might get some . . . kisses."

In some cases, nonsense syllables fill the gap:

> Lady Gaga, "LoveGame" (2008): "I can see you standing there from across the block / with a smile on your mouth and your hands on your *huh*!"

Jacqueline Warwick suggests that the vocables in the chorus of the Crystals' "Da Doo Ron Ron" (1963) ("and when he walked me home, da doo ron ron ron") might be "ooh-la-la" sorts of vocalizations for "ecstatic expressions of sexual longing and even fulfillment" (2007, 36–7). Related are the zeugma, in this case a homographic pun in which a single word relates differently to two ideas, and the last-second paragoge, in which sounds are added to the end of a word:

> Blondie, "Look Good in Blue" (1976): "If it's all right with you / I could give you some head . . . and shoulders to lie on."

> Kacey Musgraves, "Follow Your Arrow" (2013): "If you save yourself for marriage you're a bore / if you don't save yourself for marriage you're a whorrrr . . . ible person"

Simple puns run the gamut in Ray Stevens's ode to the mid-1970s fad for public groups of naked sprinters, "The Streak" (1974)—"he likes to turn the other cheek" among them. Two examples are heard in the Australian musical, *Breast Wishes* (2008): "we haven't got time to beat around the bush" in "Let's Not Talk . . . (About

---

[6] Because the technique involves controlling one's anxiety over a taboo, ghost rhyme is found to be an example of anal regression in Adorno 2002, 432. All but three of the examples of ghost rhyme listed previously are taken from Bradley 2017, 123, 125, 160, 169, 281, and 335.

Vaginas)" and "there are sights to behold when there's a nip in the air" in "It's All About Them." Finally, and only humorous in an ironic context, minced oaths are common when profane lyrics are doctored up for social acceptability in alternate mixes for radio play or sale to minors, as when Cee-Lo Green's "Fuck You!" (2010) was also released as "Forget You!" Paul McCartney seems to continue this tradition with his coy "Fuh You" (2018).

Irony may provide humor but not always; some ironic phrasing is harshly judgmental. A popular strain of irony in music performs the sort of halting plot twists of short-story writer O. Henry or the "Twilight Zone" television series. Examples are found in the Ames Brothers' "The Naughty Lady of Shady Lane" (1954) (no, it's not after all about a whore with a heart of gold, but a nine-day-old whose diaper needs changing) and Mary Wells's "Two Lovers" (1964) (no, it's not sung by a philanderer, but one confused by good and bad traits in the same person). In the Monks' "Nice Legs Shame About Her Face" (1979), the tables turn on a misogynist singer who finds his blind date unattractive, when we learn she thinks the same about him. In Nicki Minaj's "Sex in the Lounge" (2012), sustained homophonic synth chords reminiscent of a sacred organ chorale seem incongruous beneath Lil Wayne's secular rap, "sit that pussy on my bottom lip, then after that, you know we gotta switch," until he ends, "if you're scared, go to church—it's open Sunday."[7]

The paradoxical condition may be met any time one imagines a context beyond which the text would constrain awareness, often but not necessarily leading to contradiction. Measuring irony through intertextual reference may focus on lyrics: Conway Twitty sings "I won't talk of starry skies or moonlight on the ground" in "I'd Love to Lay You Down" (1980), but two years later he covered the Pointer Sisters' "Slow Hand," which features the line "moon shadowed ground with no one around and a blanket of stars in our eyes"; the listener aware of both songs has an ironic appreciation beyond the bounds of a single song, despite a lack of incongruity. Unlike the humorous closing twists enumerated earlier, irony may be present right from the song's opening, especially when the musical setting is involved: David Allan Coe, the country singer, seems unaware of "the track's vaguely corny introduction, a vaudeville razzle-dazzle tinged with twang" (Hubbs 2014, 134) when his vocal enters,

---

[7] Tim Riley (2004, 95) finds a related musical irony in the Rolling Stones' "Heart of Stone" (1965), as Stan Hawkins (2016, 58) does in Lou Reed's "Perfect Day" (1972). Musical irony is treated extensively in Everett 2004.

"Hey! Fuck Anita Bryant—who the hell is she?" taking on the anti-gay logroller in "Fuck Aneta Briant" [*sic*] (1978).

Intent is usually irrelevant; irony is present whether or not Frankie Valli is aware of how his squealy falsetto contradicts gender norms in the Four Seasons' "Walk Like a Man" (1963), but the question of his awareness adds an additional layer of possibly humorous interest.[8] Irony can peak precisely because an artist is unaware of self-contradiction; Gilbert O'Sullivan's "A Woman's Place" (1974) contains no trace of irony within, but its theme—boldly stated as "I'm all for a woman who can make it on her own, but I believe a woman's place is in the home"—betrays a miles-wide blind spot. Successful communication of incongruous irony depends on the artist's making clear what's inappropriate. X's "Johny Hit and Run Pauline" (1988) is an ugly tale of rape, its chorus clashing a major VII♯ triad against the major tonic, but with guitar interludes carrying the good-time charm of Chuck Berry licks. If irony is intended here, it is not successful, because fans typically lack the hoped-for disgust, identifying with the rapist: of "Johny," Theodore Gracyk says, "the problem arose when a sizable part of the audience didn't share the band's moral vision and made a different inference at the point where the audience must be trusted to make their own inferences" (2001, 48). Examples of an audience's inability to grasp the performer's intended irony include that for Randy Newman's "Short People" (1977), sometimes misread as offensive to little people, and Bruce Springsteen's "Born in the U. S. A." (1984) as famously misread by George Will as a supposed example of patriotic fervor. In both of these earlier instances, some listeners failed to appreciate how verses provide ironic context for choruses. The X example, however, has far more disturbing results that recall the Steubenville, Ohio, rape witness.

Pastiche, which Frederic Jameson defines as the "wearing of a stylistic mask" (1983, 114), is a common vehicle for musical irony; Ween's tribute to Prince's musical sound is exaggerated, almost to the point of satire, in the lyrics for "She Fucks Me" (1991).[9] Similarly, the slow R&B alternation of I and ♭VII guitar chords in heavy tremolo bespeak a sincerity undermined by the lack of self-awareness in Beck's vocal for "Debra" (1999): "I want to get with you and your sister, I think her name's Debra." Musical figures such as the dandy (e.g., Jimi

---

[8]   Susan McClary (2013, 37) relates this instance to the Bee Gees' reclamation of "the falsettist and even disco itself for heterosexuality" in *Saturday Night Fever* (1977); Jacqueline Warwick (2004, 192) notes a different kind of vocal irony in the Exciters' "He's Got the Power" (1963).

[9]   Prince himself, particularly with his androgynous cross-dressing in many domains, performs gender ironically; see Hawkins 2002, 21–2 and 185.

Hendrix, whose African American lineage itself comments on the nineteenth-century construction of white British masculinity) and the diva (e.g., Judy Garland and the gay camp sensibility she inspired) depend on an unspoken but understood stylistic commentary.[10]

Postmodern irony seemed to have overshadowed all of Western culture in the 1980s and beyond: David Letterman's late-night run, 1982–2015, teeming with conspiratorial cynicism, marks this era.[11] Susan J. Douglas's book *Enlightened Sexism* (2010) shows how messy irony can be when it comes to sexual relations: retrograde presentations of women as sex objects during these decades were interpreted as *empowering* to women because they *chose* to appear this way, as sexual subjects at a time when "full equality has allegedly been achieved" (2010, 9). In this case, near-nudity and sex-kitten behavior are not signs of patriarchal domination; they're feminist and ironic. But, at the same time, if it's titillating to straight men, women are thereby enslaved by a continuing underlying patriarchy. Madonna, Lady Gaga, and many lesser lights become complex topics in this regard.[12] Susan McClary (1991, 155) finds Madonna ironic in using her "little-girl voice" in "Like a Virgin" (1984), but this was already characteristic of Melanie's "Brand New Key" (1971). Such ironic portrayals of children singing sexually knowing songs are seen with Courtney Love performing "Teenage Whore" (1991) in her baby-doll dress and Babes in Toyland's Kat Bjelland singing "Swamp Pussy" (1990) ("looking like a five-foot-something porcelain blonde").[13] More recently, attitudes to sex become ironic metacommentary on themselves. Nicki Minaj (née Onika Tanya Maraj, taking her name from the *ménage à trois*) has a "quirky, cartoon-like, hypersexualized appearance [that] does more than just entertain; it disrupts traditional codes of femininity . . . through the accoutrements of camp, irony, and parody" (Hawkins 2016, 96). Irony can be applied more broadly still; a Chapter 1 discussion on hookup culture will demonstrate that whereas sex itself can be portrayed as uninhibited, romance is in that context often repressed.

The parsing of lyrics in this book will reveal interpretive leaps away from literal readings that some may find imaginative and others, extravagant. To the latter, I offer apologies but defend my decisions as based on the principles given

---

[10] See McRobbie 1994, 86, Hawkins 2009, Taylor 2012, 71, and Hawkins 2016, 14 and 37.

[11] An interesting take on the role of irony in downmarket teen magazines of the 1990s appears in McRobbie 1997, 198.

[12] Such ironic aspects of Madonna's videos are discussed in Leibetseder 2012, 23–6.

[13] O'Brien 2002, 166. For more on Madonna's persona, see O'Brien 2002, 29–36.

earlier. Unfortunately, the musical analytic techniques practiced in the coming pages—sometimes similarly straying above or below the text's surface—are not so easily laid out for the uninitiated. Hopefully, the gist of arguments that follow will be clear to the forgiving reader even in cases where technical mechanisms may not be.

1

The Musical Expression of Identity in Terms of Biological Sex

The Self in Physiology and Psychology

Like Alice discovering the forest of towering, technicolor flowers, we encounter a fascinating array of subtopics when approaching the musical expression of sex and gender, especially when it comes to issues of identity. The image of Alice in her Wonderland is a useful metaphor for thinking about identity, which is shaped by the complex intersections of social categories that include sex, gender, and sexuality. When she falls through the looking glass, Alice becomes variously too tall and too small, the objects around her subject to her changing, curious perspectives. Listeners of pop/rock music are like Alice, often hearing the gendered and sexed representation of identity in terms of their own individual experiences. We find in pop/rock music a touchstone for appreciating and understanding how sex, gender, and sexuality have been defined and redefined, especially over the past century. The many songs we consider in this chapter reflect the myriad ways that writings in physiology, psychology, sexology, sociology, gender studies, aesthetics, the parsing of poetic texts, linguistics, and music history, criticism, theory, and analysis have approached these subjects. As it turns out, pop/rock music has long been both reflecting and participating in the construction of gender, sex, and sexuality. In this chapter, we begin to show how pop/rock music maps the terrain of sex in its broadest sense.

Identity in terms of biological sex, gender, and sexuality is fixed—and made changeable—by both nature and nurture, each in numerous ways that remain contested. Biological factors include inherited characteristics based on genes, their chromosome-encoded switches and regulators, the physiology of erogenous zones and their nerve endings, and hormones and neurotransmitters, all of which make their marks throughout the timeline of individual human sexual development, affecting sex, gender, and sexuality across the lifecourse. Birth sex has been determined historically as a binary division of males and females, but also by degrees of intersex (traditionally known as physical androgyny or—now pejoratively—hermaphroditism); many scientists now recognize birth sex not so much as categorical but as a continuum, despite the dimorphic imperative of "opposites" for sexual reproduction (Kessler and McKenna 1978, 164–6). Each of us forms a self-image in ways deemed healthy and/or unhealthy by medical professionals and psychologists, related to reproduction but also to pleasure, notably with shame, repression, taboo, and sublimation as sex-related psychological issues. Gender is socially constructed (rather than anatomically "hardwired"), leading to nonbinary identities that can unsettle or disrupt associations between male as masculine and female as feminine. Our understanding of sexuality (generally, sexual orientation or preference) is based upon studies of heteronormative and LGBTQ+ identities.[1] This chapter will review physiological and psychological factors in the self as an outline for the musical representation of sexual identity formation, at times intersecting with the topics of gender and sexuality, with political, social, and cultural forces such as patriarchy and sexism, which also have racial and economic ramifications.

Physiological Identity

Conventional understandings of sexual reproduction have depended on dimorphism, a separate existence of males and females, although even this distinction was not understood as to basic anatomical differences before the eighteenth century (Laqueur 1990, 4–11; Hawkes 2004, 101). Human sexual physiology, activity, and response were first studied in comprehensive ways by Alfred C. Kinsey (1948 and 1953), William H. Masters and Virginia E. Johnson (1966), and John Bancroft (1989), and a subsequent explosion of scholarly interest in sex has led to such observations, for instance, as to how discourse and politics shape our understanding of gross physical differences between males and females. Physical characteristics have informed social expectations; whereas females have traditionally been socialized to appear as dutifully acquiescent,

---

[1] The array of identities and communities, abbreviated henceforth as the acronym LGBTQ+, has been extended elsewhere as far as LGBTIQQAA, including "lesbian, gay, bisexual, transgender, intersex, queer, questioning, asexual, and allied" (Stryker 2017, 11).

"men's sexual and reproductive bodies are . . . likened to machines, not as passive instruments, but rather as powerful, high performance machines"—we use words like *drill* or *rod* or *rocket* to connote the expectation that penises are active, ready, and hard. (Rutter and Schwartz 2012, 34, quoting from Crawley, Foley, and Shehan 2008, 9)

Quite the seminal concept!

Biological sex is determined by various internal factors too, of course. Advances in genetics have resulted in a new understanding at the chromosomal level. Instead of recognizing only two pairs of sex chromosomes, generally leading to XX (for female) and XY (male) combinations, more nuanced studies consider how the expression of sex-related genes may be modified by DNA proteins that operate both on a fixed schedule and by environmental alterations (Kelly 2012, 136–41, and Dess, Marecek, and Bell 2018, 86, 251). Genetic instructions in turn regulate the release of hormones including testosterone, estrogen, and progesterone produced in the testes, ovaries, and adrenal glands; principally in utero, infancy, and at puberty; in different ratios to shape male, female, and intersex anatomies. Additionally, largely due to experiences, neuropeptides (notably oxytocin) and neurotransmitters (such as dopamine, serotonin, and opioids) are released to the brain's synapses to model sexual feelings and behaviors such as desire, aggression, and pleasure (Barmak 2016, 66–8).

All of this must seem pretty formalistic and unrelated to music. But consider Kurt Cobain, Ke$ha, and Four Bitchin' Babes.

In Nirvana's "In Bloom" (1990), the liftoff phase midway through the first verse (0:37–0:48) sets the line "spring is here again—reproductive glands," ramping up to the song's chorus in a flowering burst of sex hormones.[2] Similarly, Nirvana's 1993 album *In Utero* includes Cobain's song "Milk It," which contains the line "we can share our endorphins," a dispassionate suggestion of a mutual activity that would stimulate the brain's opiate receptors. Narcotics are often posed as metaphors for naturally produced neurotransmitters: Ke$ha's "Your Love Is My Drug" (2010) focuses on a concept predicted by Roxy Music's 1975 single "Love Is the Drug." The bridge of Ke$ha's song features a melody (at 2:00–2:16) as hypnotically dull as an opiate nod, alternating three pitches over its first twenty-eight monosyllabic words with no rhythmic relief: "[^3] I [^1] don't [^7] care [^1] what [^3] peo- [^1]

---

[2] Heetderks 2020, 2–3, defines three zones of the verse-chorus form: the initiation, liftoff (possibly a prechorus) and arrival (marking the chorus). I use the term "liftoff" broadly here, as "In Bloom" does not introduce a change of harmony at this point but increases textural and melodic tension in seeking the release of the chorus.

-ple [^7] say, [^1] the [^3] rush [^1] is [^7] worth [^1] the [^3] price [^1] I [^7] pay; [^1] I [^3] get [^1] so [^7] high [^1] when [^3] you're [^1] with [^7] me [^1] but [^3] crash [^1] and [^1] crave [^1] you [^5] when [^4] you [^3] leave." On a more playful note, Four Bitchin' Babes produced the comedic album—often in four-part harmony—*Hormonal Imbalance: A Mood-Swinging Musical Revue* (2006), celebrating women having come a long way in "Hot Flash" and using breast sizes as "a set of metaphors to symbolize everyone's fear of human inadequacy," a line intoned in the spoken-from-the-heart bridge of "The Boob Fairy." The album's highlight might be "Viagra in the Waters," a pseudo-tragic minor-mode country tune with fiddle, concertina, and banjo that relates the tale of a truck carrying 30,000 pounds of Pfizer's penile-artery enzyme inhibitor Viagra accidentally released into a town's water supply; the result "was instant rigor mortis" for roughly half the population.

Jorge Drexler's "El Plan Maestro" (2022) returns us to the Mesoproterozoic Era of a billion years ago, when the first merging of DNA molecules from two different single-celled organisms began the evolution of sexual reproduction and therefore of love. The off-Broadway musical about a transgender woman, *Hedwig and the Angry Inch* (2014) provides another relevant example. The musical features the song "The Origin of Love," which mythologizes a time of three sexes—one of two males in a single body, a second of two such joined females, and a third of a male and female so fused, until the gods divided each pair with a lightning bolt, resulting in humans desiring to shove themselves back together again.[3] Despite the musical's claims, sexing began in prehistory, and since the eighteenth century (when the womb was first recognized as more than simply an inverted penis), "western culture [has been] deeply committed to the idea that there are only two sexes" (Fausto-Sterling 2002, 468), based solely on the presence or absence of a penis at birth (or in *in utero* sonograms).[4] Because it became culturally accepted that procreation required two "opposite" sexes, nineteenth-century medical research promoted surgical intervention in cases of intersexuality, pronounced where genitalia (or—less overtly—internal reproductive system and chromosomal makeup) were ambiguous. Recognizing

[3]   The term "trans," here equivalent to "transgender woman," illustrates the ways that notions of biological sex and gender are closely interwoven; to maintain an understanding of a separation between the domains, the same status could also be reported as male-to-female (MTF) transsexual. Politics decides, and the heat of the difference is measured in the trans community's contestation of issues as presented in *Hedwig*.

[4]   Economics, politics, and family structure are discussed as motivating factors for the division into two sexes in Laqueur 1990, 12–13, 152, and 154, Padgug 1999, 21, Weeks 2011, 69, Ellwood-Clayton 2012, 133, and Leibetseder 2012, 154 and 157.

cultural change, Malta "became the first country in the world to outlaw" genital "correction" surgery on newborns in 2015; other nations have followed.[5]

Anxieties about determining biological sex, or the celebration of its ambiguities, have permeated Western society and therefore popular music: a few songs seem to relate to ambiguity in the determination of sex. In her early 1930s number "Till the Cows Come Home," Lucille Bogan seems to boast of having well-functioning male and female genitalia when she sings "you can fuck my cock or suck my cock" and then "if you suck my pussy baby, I'll suck your dick." In a lesbian context in the 1990s, Lynn Breedlove of Tribe 8 performed onstage bare-chested with "a dildo hanging out of her black leather pants" (McDonnell 1997, 463). Bogan's off-label record was banned from regular distribution for more than just its superficially obscene words—the apparently intersex condition would have been taken as threateningly bizarre at the time—but Tribe 8 would have appealed to a more receptive audience. Some might particularly appreciate a trans combination of male and female signifiers; in the spoken introduction to "Tranny Chaser" (1996), Tribe 8 say, "Lynnee, you're the only one I really love, you have a soft heart inside a hard dick." They go on to sing, "I'm a tranny chaser, manly made-up faces . . . skirt as big as a postage stamp, package tantalizing just below the hem," and—as if to make things perfectly clear—"gimme chicks with dicks!"

Bogan and Tribe 8 (taking the latter's images as symbolic) present somewhat anomalous cases of musical interest in intersexuality. Otherwise, musical expressions of related ambiguities treat matters of socialized *gender* as opposed to biology. The Who's "I'm a Boy" (1966) has bass, guitar, and drums banging away ever louder to portray a frustrated resistance to a mother who insists on dressing the young singer as a girl. David Bowie opens "Rebel Rebel" (1974) with matriarchal hostility to an undesirable gender expression: "you've got your mother in a whirl; she's not sure if you're a boy or a girl." It is indeterminate whether the word "boy" refers to sex (is it addressed to a particular person or is it just the confounding placement of a colloquial interjection?) in the line, "Boy, you been a naughty girl" in the Beatles' "I Am the Walrus" (1967). But ambiguity is puzzling for reasons other than rhetoric in Prince's lyric, "If I gave you diamonds and pearls, would you be a happy boy or girl?" ("Diamonds

---

[5] Lester 2017, 62. Fausto-Sterling has proposed "at least five sexes—and perhaps even more" (2002, 468–72). Intersexuality and associated postnatal surgery, increasingly studied after the 1980s, is discussed in the sources listed in n. 4 and in Bancroft 1989, 158, Weeks 2010, 46–7, Kelly 2012, 128, Barmak 2016, 34–5, Hegarty 2018, 63–4, and Hines 2018, 254–62.

and Pearls" [1991]). Still, except for Bogan's eccentric song, such boy/girl ambiguities seem more to do with the pressure of social either/or choices of gender identification than with intersex mergings and certainly reflect a cultural preoccupation with correct binary labeling throughout these decades.

A current understanding of queer politics would group together considerations of liminal sex, gender, and sexuality inclusively as trans issues, but for most of the rock era, sex change through surgery was understood as separate from cross-dressing, fluid orientation, and other trans expression. The medical condition gender identity disorder long pathologized those whose sense of self contradicted their birth sex. The term "transsexual" is now less often used than it once was to refer to those who have submitted to credentialed gatekeepers and undergone expensive and grueling hormone replacement therapy, electrolysis, and/or male-to-female or female-to-male sex-confirmation (top and/or bottom) surgery in order to address their dissonance with their bodies or dissatisfaction over how they are treated because of them.[6] Among the best-known women who transitioned through operations are musicians Rae Bourbon (who underwent surgery in 1956), Angela Lynn Douglas (1969), Canary Conn (1972), Wendy Carlos (1972), and Beth Elliott (1976?); athletes Renée Richards (1975) and Caitlyn Jenner (2017) have perhaps received the most press. Author Thomas Beatie, declared female at birth, had sex-confirmation surgery in 2002 and became pregnant as a man five years later.

In popular music, a trans fantasy is sometimes expressed as either a desire to be treated differently or as an actual goal. Lesley Gore's "Sometimes I Wish I Were a Boy" (1964) is a rare older example; among more recent ones are Prince's "If I Was Your Girlfriend" (1987), Julie Andrews's "If I Were a Man" (1995), Barenaked Ladies' "I'll Be That Girl" (1998), Antony and the Johnsons' "For Today I Am a Boy" (2005), the Dresden Dolls' "Sex Changes" (2006), Beyoncé's "If I Were a Boy" (made popular in 2008 but especially as performed with

---

[6] The adjectives "trans," "trans*," "genderqueer," and "nonbinary" are sometimes used to refer collectively to a number of transformational conditions that had been in the past defined separately. Those who sometimes adopt the grooming and clothing "opposite" those of their birth sex were long referred to as transvestites, those who live full-time against their birth sex as transgender, and those who permanently change their body to conform to their gendered identity as transsexual. (None of these situations is necessarily related to sexual preference.) There are of course no firm borders, and those in unclassified or of simultaneously multiple trans identities often identify as queer. Hormonal and/or surgical transsexuality is discussed in Gagnon 1977, 336, Shapiro 1991, Stone 1991, Abbate 1993, 256, Connell 1995, Elliott 1996, Halberstam 1998, 144 and 166, Althof 2000, 247, Diamond 2008, 193–4, Halberstam 2012, 31, 35, 76, and 144, Leibetseder 2012, 150–60, Rutter and Schwartz 2012, 42 and 121, Seidman 2015, 223, Bornstein 2016, Hawkins 2016, 110, Serano 2016, Stryker 2017, Gowarty 2018, 80, Halberstam 2018, and Mozer 2021.

Michael Jackson-like crotch grabs at the 2010 Grammy Awards ceremony), Nicki Minaj's "Did It On 'Em" (2010), William Belli's "The Vagina Song" (2012), and Lil Dicky's "Freaky Friday" (2018). In the chorus of Counting Crows' "I Wish I Was a Girl" (1999), the harmony cycles three times from IV through V to vi and back through V to IV to demonstrate a meandering intensity to the singer's wish that he could be of the opposite sex. Transsexuality is treated in Suzanne Vega's "As Girls Go" (1992); Katastrophe's "Something Different" (2004), "Man Enough" (2005), and "The Life" (2007); "Man Enough to Be a Woman" (2006) and "Surrender Your Gender" (2017) by Jayne County (né Wayne Rogers), and MEN's "Who Am I to Feel So Free" (2011). An MTF procedure gone wrong is the premise of *Hedwig*; in "Angry Inch," the lead character complains, "My sex-change operation got botched . . . now all I got is a Barbie-doll crotch—I got an angry inch!"; the chorus is sung and played in bitter parallel-fifth power chords.

Psychological Identity

Self-image. Interrelated matters of sex, gender, and sexuality cohere into a primary lens through which people see themselves and others, especially when they are growing up. This lens is formed by historical, institutional, and social relationships and perceptions (particularly patriarchal ones), and unconscious ideas, as much as—if not more than—by physical properties and processes. Throughout its history, various styles of pop/rock music have reflected the sex-related agencies and subjectivities of adolescents, those in a transitional period when they are most attentive to—and anxious about—these qualities in their emerging selves. As the Who suggest in "Baba O'Riley" (1971), adolescence is a time of in-between alienation, a "teenage wasteland"—or the "teenage blues" of Elton John's "I Think I'm Gonna Kill Myself" (1972) or the "weirdo" self-label in Radiohead's "Creep" (1993). Such angst is related directly to sex assigned at birth in Porno for Pyros' "Cursed Female" (1993), where an irregular metric accent of 3+3+2 beats offsets an already displaced set of angry power chords: "[I5] Cursed to be born, [bII5] beautiful, [I5] poor and female; [bII5] there's none that [I5] suffer more." Songs related to adolescents also express a desire for autonomy, as Green Day protest in "American Idiot" (2004): "Maybe I'm the faggot America; I'm not part of a redneck agenda," using a shocking epithet to express intense repulsion against an institutional status quo.

Whether or not they intend to do so, artists and their music help shape teens' understanding of their sex-related attitudes, channeling their feelings and thoughts in styles with which many young people are apt to identify, while reflecting broader cultural shifts. In the 1970s, "disco fed on homosocial optimism and hope; punk, nihilistic cynicism and despair" (Hajdu 2016, 182). In later decades, slacker Gen-X'ers and young Millennials consumed grunge and expressed dissatisfaction in flannel. Later Millennials' burgeoning social media outlets pushed a false positivity of smiling selfies and feel-good partying (Rebecca Black's "Friday" [2011]) even though their depression raged (Twenty-One Pilots, "Stressed Out" [2015]) alongside mounting durations of socially isolating screen time. For the digitally native Gen Z'ers, however, Billie Eilish ("Bad Guy" [2019]) and Lizzo ("Truth Hurts" [2017]) kicked the door down on facades, singing openly about the falsity of cultivated images while being unapologetic about their own nonnormative gender performances and body images.

Psychological approaches to adolescence are often concerned with how teens are vulnerable to culturally induced low self-esteem. The quintessential songster of teen angst and psychodrama is Morrissey, whose "November Spawned a Monster" (1990) laments in a minor key, "Poor twisted child, so ugly, so ugly." Historically, girls and young women have been even more acculturated to self-criticism: "Women are more critical of their appearance than men are of theirs, and most women in Western cultures are dissatisfied with their bodies, which affects their sense of self and sexual identity" (Ellwood-Clayton 2012, 3). In 1975, Janis Ian sang in "At Seventeen," "I learned the truth at seventeen that love was meant for beauty queens." Three years later, in "Identity," Poly Styrene of X-Ray Spex shouted over a repeated lamento bass pattern "do you see yourself in the magazine? When you see yourself does it make you scream?" Eating disorders such as Karen Carpenter's tragically passive fear of weight gain and the fat-shaming of Heart's Ann Wilson by her management are evidence of an industry obsessed with image and so-called bodily improvement, all part of a patriarchal regime whose institutions have for millennia kept women feeling inadequate from a young age to justify their subordination.

The constant demand for self-improvement is a persistent theme in postfeminist media culture, which privileges *white* femininity in its construction of the good neoliberal subject who is always aspiring but never attaining a goal (Gill 2007). In "Unpretty" (1999), TLC voice a powerful critique related to both gender and race, singing "you can fix your nose if he says so." The makeover paradigm, which encourages women to be good consumers, serves the agenda of capital: beauty and therefore power are available to purchase through a never-ending stream of over-the-counter cosmetics and creams. This is an ironic confirmation of the Greek Pandora's ancient predicament: hope was left in the jar when she let out all the other evils, which raises the question: is hope an evil, too? When the empty promises of labels don't come true, Botox injections and more extreme measures are called in, from liposuction to surgical "enhancements" such as cosmetic breast implants, gluteal augmentation, and even labial trimming. "We make her paint her face and dance," as John Lennon sang in "Woman is the Nigger of the World" (1972). Paul McCartney anticipated part of Lennon's judgment when he sang, in the Beatles' "Eleanor Rigby" (1966), that a lonely unmarried woman lives in a fantasy, "wearing the face that she keeps in a jar by the door—who is it for?" Clearly, she never goes out without a cosmetic mask worn for some man's approval, never to be received.

Like TLC, other women artists have sung their resistance to social demands for a particular kind of perfection. Journalist Tim Riley finds rhythmic self-assurance in the chorus of the Ronettes' "Be My Baby" (1963), "suddenly trumpeting a woman's desire just as confidently as any man ever had" (2004, 48). This grit would later respond to political motivation. Like TLC, other women artists have projected such determination in singing their resistance to social demands for a particular kind of perfection. Following Madonna, whose assertiveness is perhaps best visualized in her iconic Jean Paul Gaultier cone bra, the subversive Riot Grrrl movement of bands and fanzines in the 1990s empowered women, appropriating misogynist terms like "slut" and "bitch" for themselves. Courtney Love's band "Hole's music deals with themes of rape, eating disorders, mental health, nonconformity, beauty pageants, suicides, and sex work."[7] In a more optimistic vein, Alanis Morissette learns from setbacks in 1995, in both "You Learn" and—boasting a healthy happiness in the simple, satisfied, double-plagal support for the "everything's gonna be fine, fine, fine" hook—in "Hand in My Pocket." Even the Spice Girls, exemplars of postfeminist media culture's contradictory representations of conventional femininity and feminist themes, can be credited for their "Girl Power" mantra, which is taken as

> a female's right to display her sexuality, to be autonomous and free from
> dependence on a man, and instead to find empowerment in girl-friendships

---

[7] Jasmine 2018a, 272. See also Bayton 1998, 75, and Leibetseder 2012, 27–9, on Riot Grrrls. Groundbreaking discussion of the Shirelles' and other "girl-group" music is found in Warwick 2007, and Warwick and Adrian 2016.

and group solidarity. The Spice Girls were freely expressive, physical, exhibited emotional control and confidence in their sexual image and were dismissive of authority. They therefore appeared to offer a positive representation of female autonomy. (Dibben 1999, 343)

In "Video" (2001), India.arie is direct in her advocacy for a positive self-image while flaunting social norms: "Sometimes I shave my legs and sometimes I don't . . . it really just depends on whatever feels good in my soul. I ain't built like a supermodel but I learned to love myself unconditionally." Although boys' self-image may suffer in adolescence and young adulthood, the record is replete with sex-based issues for young women.

Psychoanalytic identity formation. Twentieth-century psychoanalysts, chief among them Sigmund Freud, Carl Jung, and Jacques Lacan, instrumentally theorized how sexual identity develops through early familial and societal relationships. Many of their theories have been contested, problematized, and—in some cases—totally debunked, but the socializing influence of their ideas did not suddenly disappear, continuing to inform the understanding and expression of power, especially a patriarchal dominance that reflects family dynamics (i.e., paternalistic power). By the 1920s, Freud came to believe that children are born "polymorphously perverse," positing that "all babies and small children are *sex-monsters*, focused on satisfying all their sensual urges, without shame and without regard for the feelings of others."[8] In this sense, Freud used "sex" as a catch-all for any sort of sensual gratification, beginning with infants' oral, anal, and phallic discoveries and not necessarily tied to the stimulation of sex organs. For Freud, those early experiences inform later, post-Oedipal excitations, whereby gratification is found in the genital pleasures of puberty and range from hearing "a gentle word on the wind that lifts her perfume through the air" (the Beach Boys, "Good Vibrations" [1966]) to the thrill of revenge. An instinct Freud called the libido governs both the drive for pleasure and the opposing death wish (Ellwood-Clayton 2012, 101–4). Freud viewed the psyche as tripartite: (1) the unbridled, lustful pursuit of gratification in the unconscious *id* would come to be regulated by (2) the also unconscious *superego* (composed of values instilled by familial and societal upbringing) while these principles—the competing

---

[8]   deBerg 2003, 9; see also Lacan and the *école freudienne* 1982, 203–4, and Ellwood-Clayton 2012, 101–4. Theories of poetry and song as regressions to the fulfillments of first motherly bonds are presented in Kramer 1984, 130, and Goodwin 1994, 66.

wishes of self and others—are balanced by (3) the *ego*, which mediates rationally between gratifying fantasy and success-supporting reality.[9]

All phases of Freudian identity formation are treated in popular song; we'll provide just three examples here. E. Ann Kaplan relates the eternal pansexual love offered in the video for Cyndi Lauper's "Time After Time" (1983) to a pre-Oedipal mother-daughter bonding (1987, 59, 127–8), but the same characterization could reasonably be made for the song's audio aside from its associated visuals. John Lennon worked through his separate abandonments by father and mother in analysis that involved scream therapy, culminating in the *Plastic Ono Band* album (1970), whose lead track, "Mother," grieves these losses and offers to the world his lessons learned.[10] The Who's rock opera, *Tommy* (1969), is based on the title character's debilitating trauma from being "struck deaf, dumb, and blind by witnessing his mother in bed with a lover after his father, presumed dead, fails to return from war."[11]

In Freud's setting, special attention is given to the Oedipal stage (roughly three to six years of age), when he believed sex roles are first determined. Cultural rules teach once-pangendered preschoolers that incestuous desires for mother and father are wrong, that *he* has and *she* lacks a penis, and that they must break primordial bonds with the mother if necessary to identify with the same-sex parent to prepare for an eventual search for a mate. For Freud, awareness of the phallus or its lack leads males to fear castration, and (most controversially) drives females—despite their phallic clitoris—to gradually substitute a desire for their own penis with the temporary acceptance of one from another. Such a male's fear is undisguised when Lloyd Banks raps, "I never trust a bitch, I blame Lorena Bobbitt," in "Playboy" (2004). Also in Freud's phallic stage, all children contain both "masculine" and "feminine" properties and inclinations, but the working out of the Oedipus complex usually leads to the suppression of "inappropriate" gender characteristics.[12]

---

[9] deBerg 2003, 50. See also Marcuse 1956, 29–32.

[10] Lennon is widely thought to have replaced his absent mother with Yoko Ono; see discussions of substantiating imagery in Everett 1986, 376–85, and 1999, 170–2 and 182, re the Beatles' "Julia" and three other *White Album* (1968) songs.

[11] Riley 2004, 104. For much more on war-related psychological trauma in the Beatles' *Magical Mystery Tour* (1967), the Kinks' *Arthur* (1969), and Pink Floyd's *The Wall* (1979) in addition to *Tommy*, see Cox 2018.

[12] Various aspects of the Oedipus complex are discussed in Freud 1953–74, vols. 3, pp. 214–15, and 7, pp. 216–17, Benjamin 1978, 39, Segal 1990, 71, Connell 1995, 9, Cameron and Kulik 2003, 109–11, Weeks 2010, 58 and 68–70, and Carlson 2012, 59. Psychoanalyst Marie Bonaparte's theory of the clitoral phallus is covered in Rabaté 2014, 127–8.

Again, this phallocentric model is widely contested for many reasons, which will be taken up in due course.

The Oedipal struggle underlies the Doors' epic closer, "The End" (1967), to their eponymous first album. The nearly twelve-minute track proceeds through phallic images as singer-songwriter Jim Morrison "ride[s] the snake," then reveals his desires in spoken and screamed lines as the climax approaches: "Father? Yes, son. I want to kill you. Mother? I want to . . . fuck, fuck, fuck," rhythmically intoning the repeated verb as his backing guitar/ organ/drums trio speeds up to their improvisational ejaculatory crest.[13] Phil Rose notices a similar process in his study of Pink Floyd's *The Wall*, both album (1979) and film, wherein an unsuccessful resolution of the Oedipal conflict lies beneath the castration anxiety of lead personage, Pink, who "remains in a state of infantile object dependency due to the disturbances that he experiences in his early attachments, primarily because of his unsatisfactory mothering and the loss of his father" (Rose 2015, 91). Castration is also the threat underlying Liz Phair's "Dance of the Seven Veils" (1994), in which the singer plays Salome to her "Johnny" the Baptist, and Regina Spektor's emasculated "Samson" (2002).

The Doors and Pink Floyd offer overtly Oedipal tales, but rock music can also carry this theme in a much more subtle fashion. Queen's "Bohemian Rhapsody" (1975), for instance, can be read as an Oedipal story. The opening lyric, presented over a romantically lachrymose hand-crossing pianistic setting, recounts a shooting in phallically sexual imagery: "Mama, just killed a man. Put a gun against his head, pulled my trigger, now he's dead." Freddie Mercury, who had been living with a woman for seven years but had just begun his first gay relationship at the time of writing the song, might be understood as singing of gay fellatio, thereby killing any identification with his unnamed and now-dead father. Of a later portion of this song, Sheila Whiteley writes of how the "heavy timbres of the lower voices, underpinned by the phallic backbeat of the drums and tonic pedal, traditionally connote the masculine ('We will not let you go'), while the shrill, higher voices in first inversion chords imply the feminine 'Other' ('Let me go'). They signal entrapment and the plea for release" (2007, 24–5). A Freudian view might read this as the Oedipal struggle playing itself out, a son pulling away from the father's heterosexual rule.

---

[13] Doors keyboardist Ray Manzarek suggests a Dionysian basis for the orgasm, relating Morrison to a priapic Pan, in Manzarek 1999, 199–200.

Phallic themes. A scene in the Beatles' first film, *A Hard Day's Night* (1964), features this dialogue:

George: What's the matter with you, then?
Ringo: It's [Paul's] grandfather. I can tell he doesn't like me. It's 'cause I'm little.
George: Ah, you've got an inferiority complex, you have.
Ringo: Yeah, I know, that's why I play the drums—it's me active compensatory factor.

According to this scripted scene, what Ringo lacks and must make up for—apparently because of his modest size—is confidence in his natural phallic power. The phallus notoriously symbolizes the erect penis as a sword-like vital body penetrator metaphorically moving like a train in a tunnel, a bolt of lightning in the sky, or drumsticks on the skins. But the quality of phallicism is generalized by Slavoj Žižek as "the detail that 'does not fit,' that 'sticks out' from the idyllic surface scene and denatures it, renders it uncanny" (1991, 90), such as high heels or the shine of leather, common fetish objects for that reason.[14] This understanding is closely related to other theories of uncanny difference: Stan Hawkins defines (musical) queering, which for him "always connotes a sense of difference by rejecting the contours of normativity" (2016, 13). Before Hawkins, bell hooks (1994, 131), Steve Waksman (1999, 4), and Matthew Bannister (2006, 33–4) critiqued the neo-colonialist perception of the African American "difference" from Euro-Americans involving a racially "primitive" influence on rock, creating sexual powers feared by whites in the drums and guitars of rock 'n' roll.

The phallic appendage most familiar to rock scholars is the electric guitar, vehicle of virtuosic soloing and distorted perfect-fifth power chords (or, for that matter, the harsh tritones of The Jimi Hendrix Experience's "Purple Haze" [1966]) in "cock rock." As theorized especially by Simon Frith and Angela McRobbie (1990 [1978]), Robert Walser (1993), Steve Waksman (1996 and 1999), Deena Weinstein (2000), and Susan Fast (2001 and 2005), the instruments of so-called rock gods suggest male sexual power play. Recall Hendrix's humping in "Wild Thing" at the 1967 Monterey Pop Festival, Jimmy Page's potent emergence out of the amorphous instrumental passage in Led Zeppelin's "Whole Lotta Love," or the climax of their "You Shook Me" (both 1969). As Frank Zappa explains, "One way to ensure that you look like the greatest thing going when you play

---

[14] See also Butler 1993, 62, regarding the transferability of the phallus.

your big solo is to make sure that you end your solo by going *up the scale*, then grab that last note and repeat it as fast as you can. The statement is the same on any instrument: '*Oh, I'm squirting now!*'" (Courrier 2002, 458). In fact, one of Prince's "guitars 'ejaculated' water onto the audience when played" (Kearney 2017, 169).[15] Not only a big African drumbeat (thanks, Ringo!), but rock vocals as well also carry phallic power. Whiteley conjures up a throbbing erection in Mick Jagger's vocal for the Rolling Stones' "(I Can't Get No) Satisfaction" (1965): "There is a strong sense of arousal in the ascending sequence on 'and I try' which is brought to a climax on the 'I can't get no . . .'" (1992, 88–9).

The gender-specific binary opposite of cock rock might be *la musique féminine*. This term is an adaptation of Hélène Cixous's *l'écriture féminine*, which privileges a woman's "nonlinear, cyclical discourse" (Kearney 2017, 218) of passive and sometimes circular, non-goal-oriented metaphors such as ocean waves that repeat in place, perhaps representative of the nonlinear, multiple orgasm. Women, long nearly excluded from electric hard-rock performance, had been allowed in previous decades to perform softer roles. Unthreatening teenybop— classified by critics as pop, as opposed to rock music—has been cock rock's foil; where the latter is heard as aggressive, loud, hot, expansive, and often based on the bluesy minor-pentatonic mode, the former would be passive, soft, warm, diminutive, and contained in the undarkened major mode.[16] Generalizing along these lines, it is often said that the Stones (macho rock) exemplify sex where the Beatles (epicene pop) sing of love.

While there is obvious value in recognizing the distinctive qualities of feminine writing, especially as it relates to the production and reception of girls and women, we reject essentialist, monolithic considerations that bind discourse to a particular sex or gender. Historically and culturally situated definitions of "masculinities" and "femininities" vary, have transformed over time, and are otherwise unstable. We see this especially in popular music: punk and reggae styles, for instance, were anti-phallic forms fostered by the "virile" as much as by the "fair." In the 1970s and 1980s, gender could be assigned to masculine guitar/effeminate vocal pairs: the Stones' Glimmer Twins, Keith Richard and Mick Jagger (see Bannister 2006, 107–8), the Who's Townsend and Daltrey, Led

---

[15] See also Wise 100, 392, on Elvis Presley's guitar, Kearney 2017, 141–2, on Pete Townsend's, Auslander 2006, 95–103, on Marc Bolan's, Greene 2016, 123, on Frank Zappa's, and Hawkins 2002, 165–6, on Prince's.

[16] Such distinctions are drawn or questioned in Frith 1981, 240, Hebdige 1988, 213, Bordo 1990, 135, Frith and McRobbie 1990 [1978], 375, Shepherd 1991, 167–8, Bayton 1993, 185, Reynolds and Press 1995, 233, O'Meara 2004, 302, Lankford 2010, 39–40, and Smith 2017, 418.

Zeppelin's Page and Plant (Waksman 1996, 15–26), and Aerosmith's Joe Perry and Steven Tyler (Kearney 2017, 122). But the 1980s and 1990s set Michael Jackson's (castration-fearing?) crotch-grabbing against his hard-driving guitarist Jennifer Batten. Batten's career disrupts the stereotype of the male guitar god; since the later twentieth century, many women have proven their hard-playing credentials on the electric guitar and bass, among them Nancy Wilson (Heart), Bonnie Raitt, Lita Ford, Joan Jett, Tina Weymouth, Suzi Quatro, Tal Wilkenfeld, Brittany Howard, and Samantha Fish.[17]

Rock music can be obviously phallic: note Jackie Brentston's Oldsmobile in "Rocket '88," Steppenwolf's motorcycle in "Born to Be Wild" (1968), Paul McCartney's "polygon" in Wings' "Hi, Hi, Hi" (1972), and Dweezil Zappa's fingerboard-tapping intro to Extreme's "He-Man Woman Hater" (1990). Despite their light qualities in comparison to rock, pop songs can also uphold phallic superiority, as in Lou Christie's number-one pop hit of 1965, "Lightnin' Strikes." In a case of eye-rolling mansplaining, the speaker of "Lightnin' Strikes" is a wolf in sheep's clothing, opening, "Listen to me baby, you gotta understand; you're old enough to know the makin's of a man." He continues to seduce through bubblegum fantasy interludes ("there's a chapel in the pines waiting for us around the bend") and presses his case in agitated, threatening prechoruses ("I can't stop, I can't stop myself!"), culminating in raucous, phallic choruses, "Lightning is striking again!" This duplicitous confession tells of a compulsive philanderer who claims to always hold the addressee in his heart, but who just can't help himself every time he comes across a girl who is "put together fine."

The twisted logic of "Lightnin' Strikes" claims that sexual conquest is just nature taking over; phallic fraud and conquest are presented to teenagers as the way of the natural world. The speaker wants his steady girl to wait for him each time he disappears and to live by his rules of "forgive and forget." The lightning in the song's choruses has poetic precedent: the notion of "conception" dates from William Harvey's seventeenth-century belief that sperm ignites an "idea" in the womb: "impregnation for Harvey becomes metaphorically the igniting of women, setting them aflame as if struck by lightning" (Laqueur 1990, 142, 146). "Lightnin' Strikes" was released at a time when pop expressed graphic sex only through metaphor—in this case, the electric fire of lightning for desire, phallus, and attack. The speaker of Christie's song almost seems to be

---

[17] Jackson and Batten are juxtaposed in Fast 2012, 285. See also Whiteley 2005, 39, on the phallic qualities of Jackson's childhood fixation.

saying what metaphor theorists observe about these emblems: "I could feel the *electricity* between us. There were *sparks*. . . . The *atmosphere* around them was *charged*" (Lakoff and Johnson 1980, 49). The song thus presents misogynist lust in coded language: "desire is often talked of as if unwelcome, malicious, dangerous. . . . Fire and electricity are other natural forces which are important metaphors for desire" (Deighnan 1997, 25–6).

Christie's accompanying music cleverly conveys his conscious and unconscious messages: the intro (from 0:05) presents forceful baritone saxes and electric bass in open fifths, suggesting (as understood in retrospect) the singer's primitively propulsive id. This is covered by the piano and lead guitar's repeated double-plagal cadences, pretending smooth natural resolutions. This combination riff, the power-chord wolf's id beneath the double-plagal sheep's ego, continues through verses. Texture falls away for the charming major-mode interludes ("Every boy wants a girl . . ."), which back off to the ♭VI key area with an ingratiating, mildly rocking mid-register piano, a deferentially sequencing, nursery-rhyme-like tune, and (in the second half of the passage) tubular bells that evoke the deceitful promise of a church wedding. Tumescent prechoruses ramp up, with snare hits on every beat and predatory bass pacing the floor, continually marching down from each downbeat root to its fifth; a phallic trombone ushers in minor-mode choruses (now tonicizing ii) where the full erection is put to work amid dire vocals. The singer perceives each victim as complicit—her lips are "beggin' to be kissed," she's "readin' [his] mind"—and the listener only hears the predator's perspective. Music thus portrays both a lustful phallicism and the cultural sexism that supports it.

Adaptations of Freud in Jung and Lacan. C. G. Jung, Freud's most famous student, rejected his mentor's obsession with sex and developed his own complicated system of thought for the interpretation of dreams. Put simply, Jung's path to individuation is marked by two layers: one by the individual's unconscious thoughts and memories (akin to Freud's), but also another by a collective unconscious, "a shared human spiritual heritage, a storehouse of latent memories inherited from our ancestral past" (Ellwood-Clayton 2012, 105). Jung's concept of collective unconscious (related in its way to Harold Bloom's intertextual readings invoking the influence of precursor poets) is a treasure trove of mythical and dreamed archetypal symbols supposedly common to all cultures. As a musical example, the career of Kate Bush "has explored and celebrated female archetypes and iconography, scouring mythology, history, literature, Arthurian legend and Jungian psychology for provisional identities, and using femininity as a cipher of masks and poses" (Whiteley 2005, 70). The Eastern philosophical underpinnings (coupled with a dose of LSD) of the Beatles' "Within You Without You" (1967) and the Plastic Ono Band's chant of "Give Peace a Chance" (1969) seem spiritually related to Jung's work, which is not coincidental given Jung's interest in and reliance on the Hinduism that informed the Beatles.

Despite his split with Freud, Jung upheld a gendered approach to psychoanalysis, which can veer toward essentialism in its female/feminine and male/masculine applications. Jung was a firm believer in all persons containing a lifelong yin/yang polarity of male (*animus*) and female (*anima*) attributes. This Jungian battle is invoked in two 1993 songs by PJ (Polly Jean) Harvey: in "Man-Size," she

> plays the part of a leather-booted macho man whose tyrannical bluster seems largely a battle to "get girl out of my head." Following the logic of "the best form of defence is attack," the character ends up torching this feminine alter-ego or anima-spirit. [In a second song,] "50 Ft. Queenie" is the ultimate phallic woman, a well-endowed Amazon who proclaims herself "king of the world." Queenie's a titanic, tyrannical figure in the tradition of Jimi Hendrix's "Voodoo Chile" [1968] or the swaggering Staggerlees of the blues. . . . Men, in Harvey's world, are both ludicrous and larger than life; they're bullies with an undeniable power and freedom, a "birthright" that Polly wouldn't mind usurping. (Reynolds and Press 1995, 243)

These and other notions of gender will be teased out in due course. For now, we move from Jung to Lacan.

Rereading Freud in the mid-twentieth century, Jacques Lacan posited that our desires can never be met; we strive to express ourselves in speech despite never having adequate words, as the euphemistic symbolic proxy for a *jouissance* that has been lacking since infancy. At six to eighteen months, the child reaches the mirror stage, developing their own subjectivity as split from the mother, wherein the ego recognizes in the self a contained body image filled with desires both unsatisfiable and idealized as fantasies in both role models and passive love objects. This phase, according to Lacanian thinking, prepares the child for recognition of the phallus (and its different implications for boys who possess and girls who lack them), a sexed relationship with others, and the learning of a symbolic vocabulary to seek what is forever lost.[18] For Lacan, the infant's mirror-stage learning also informs adolescent development.

---

[18] Basic ideas in Lacanian psychology are presented in Lacan 1977, Lacan and the *école freudienne* 1982, Butler 1993, Harvey and Shalom 1997, and Rabaté 2014. Debra Winger's character in the film *Black Widow* (1987) is seen to yield a mirror-stage understanding of gendering in Traub 1991, 316–17.

Lorraine Feather's "The Girl with the Lazy Eye" (2010) is a study in Lacan's mirror-stage sexual subjectivity formation in a young girl. Here, an awkward and bullied middle-schooler (who at such an age depends upon peers for her self-image) exhibits many traits reflecting the caterpillar she studies while lying belly-down in the grass: the nameless protagonist wears "bunchy socks"; "she shuffles"; "her thoughts . . . wander sideways." At times, she doodles skin-shedding visions of abandoned containers in ruins such as the Roman Coliseum and a ghost ship. The girl's schoolmates steal her pencil box, stunting her artistic creativity and—because the box can be interpreted as the symbol of a vessel for phallic objects—abducting her awakening sexual agency in a kind of castration of her creative powers.

In this song, a dynamic central catharsis exemplifies the Lacanian psychology of sexuality. The early-adolescent girl—portrayed alongside the caterpillar that serves as a mirror of her own ego formation—desires to metamorphose into a fully sexual woman. Figure 1.1 represents an interpretation of the song's pitch structure, its A section on the first system and B section and coda on the second. This reading suggests how the girl's struggles, in a fantasy of fluttery escape through her transformation into a butterfly, are painted in many of the song's tonal peregrinations in harmony and voice leading. Note particularly the A section's many initially repressed inner-voice ideations that are projected above the fundamental $\hat{3}$-line, and the B section's wandering structural arpeggiated fully diminished seventh rendered in outer-voice parallel tenths.

In "Lazy Eye," the frequent chromatically colorful ascending arpeggiations unlock a butterfly's inner-voice tones from a caterpillar's symbolic inner world and highlight them in imaginative fancies on the consciously performed surface, as with G♯4 rising to G♯5 at 0:25, or E♯4 moving to D♯5 at 0:39. These gestures fill out a middleground-level tonic arpeggiation rising from primary tone D♯5 at 0:18 through F♯5 at 0:46 and up to the B section's B5 at 3:27. A struggle over a stolen pencil box—an eternal loss of something considered vital for this always-doodling artist—is set in the second verse, with the castration occurring at 1:14, exactly at the poignant immediate juxtaposition of a far-removed G major tonicized against a false representation of the home B major, actually demoted to plagal subdominant of its dominant. Upon metamorphosis, however, the girl puts these issues behind her and "goes flying away" with the narrator's prediction of success: "someday you'll love," the sexual equivalent of an ultimate achievement of prosperity.

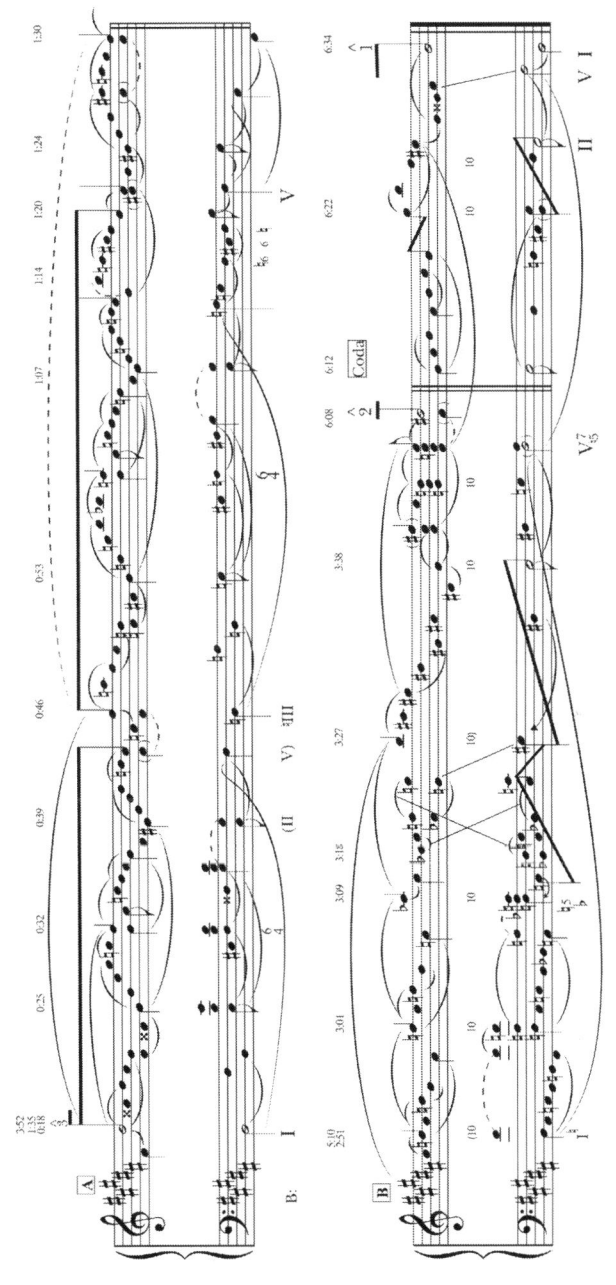

Figure 1.1 Voice-leading sketch of Lorraine Feather, "The Girl with the Lazy Eye" (2010).

Taboo, Shame, and Repression

Given the sexual nature of popular music and its omnipresence in the culture, it may be odd that many Americans have an ironic aversion to comprehensive sex education, which teaches non-abstinence-only birth control and protection methods for hetero and LGBTQ+ youth in public schools. Indeed, sex-related societal taboos, the superego's resulting shame and repression, and attractions to forbidden fruits proliferate in much of the history of Western culture. Lacan and his school lectured that although taboos alienated people from their own sexuality, this loss—which they believed is first felt in infancy—would heighten desire (1982, 5–6). The arts both portray and rebel against such strictures, and music has played a particular role in helping to promote a healthier and more sex-positive perspective.[19] Some claim that rock music "offered liberation from old taboos," others that it "released primitive instincts" (Middleton 1990, 259). This evocation of the "primitive" is particularly problematic in a context wherein racist stereotypes fueled the panic with which influential whites received Black rock 'n' roll. Throughout the rock era, society's sexual values have changed enormously; stars such as Julia Lee, Dinah Washington, Little Richard, Elvis Presley, Jim Morrison, Loretta Lynn, David Bowie, Madonna, Boy George, and Lady Gaga defied prohibitions, bringing hard-won acceptance to behaviors and attitudes previously considered outré, sometimes by using the word "taboo" itself. The story of Boy George, in fact, is retold in the Broadway musical, *Taboo* (2002). In the early years of rock, it had not been many decades since respectable women were not seen in the streets; pop music has allowed us all to dance there. The title concept of Macy Gray's 2001 album *The Id* breaks through in "Sexual Revolution": "you've got to express what is taboo in you and share your freak with the rest of us 'cause it's a beautiful thing." Gray delivers her lyrics in a monotone but sets them against a sexually knowing, bluesy alternation of I$\flat$7 and IV7.

Repression and sublimation. One of Freud's most foundational and now ubiquitous concepts, repression, explains the consequences of sexual thoughts, memories, and desires routinely chased by the superego into the unconscious. As Korn screams over dissonant intervals played on distorted guitars, "Deep inside, it can hide!" ("Deep Inside," 2003). A decade later, Ani DiFranco's

---

[19] Consider Klimt's drawings of masturbating women (see Kandel 2012, 90–3), or Alma Schindler-Mahler's song of a woman's sexual desire and orgasm, "Ansturm," as discussed by Sally Macarthur (2002, 69–76), as examples of daring early twentieth-century taboo smashers. Film in the 1960s and cable television (see "Skinemax") at the current century's turn burst through all sorts of prudery.

"Studying Stones" (2005) is an essay on radical repression and its relation to the death drive. The singer contemplates stones, "trying to learn to be less alive," working to feign lifelessness. She has achieved degrees of numbness as old as her first memories of parents; she does not allow a tossed-stone ripple of emotion to show on her face now that all the forbidden fruit has rotted. Along with the evanescent harmonics from DiFranco's guitar, strings exemplify what DiFranco's speaker has buried in their dying pizzicati and diminuendos. DiFranco worries, "any more pent-up emotion, I think I'm gonna explode," as if agreeing with the argument that "free sexual expression was a safety valve that spared society the violence that repressed sexuality produced" (Dean 1996, 75). Lucy O'Brien's *She Bop II* (2002) tells of how DiFranco along with women like Grace Slick, Janis Joplin, Madonna, Courtney Love, Liz Phair, and many others have thrown off repressive shackles in their lives and music. As Madonna whispers in "Human Nature" (1994), "express yourself, don't repress yourself."

Just how much must be repressed ranges widely: "In practice, most writers on our sexual past have assumed that sex is an irresistible natural energy barely held in check by a thin crust of civilization. . . . Liberatory theorists such as Wilhelm Reich and Herbert Marcuse tended to see sex as a beneficent force which was repressed by a corrupt civilization."[20] Most active in the 1950s and 1960s, Marcuse called for a revolution to reinvigorate humanity's pleasure drive, believing that the institutional forces behind "surplus" repression should relax social discipline and that civilization should feel freer sexually, now that much necessary work has been automated (Marcuse 1956). In many ways, his call has been accompanied by just such a relaxation of a repressive regime, a change always celebrated in rock music through its toppling of middle-class propriety. Following the mildly unsettling swooning of Frank Sinatra's fans in the 1940s and the shocking adulation of Elvis the Pelvis in the 1950s came the hysterical explosion of Beatlemania in 1964: "to abandon control—to scream, faint, dash about in mobs—was, in form if not in conscious intent, to protest the sexual repressiveness, the rigid double standard of female teen culture. It was the first and most dramatic uprising of *women's* sexual revolution" (Ehrenreich, Hess, and Jacobs 2009 [1986], 217).

A few years after Beatlemaniacs unleashed their scream, Frank Zappa's music advocated scornfully for the necessity for a greater, faster end of repression. In "Harry, You're a Beast" (1968), the speaker offers a scathing critique of American

---

[20] Weeks 2010, 19. In Chapter 5, Reich will be seen to hold particular import for Patti Smith.

attitudes toward sex: "You're phony on top, you're phony underneath. You lay in bed and grit your teeth—that's you, American womanhood." The song's more universal implications are read by Doyle Greene as "a virulent attack on women as the epitome of rampant consumerism, mass culture phoniness, and apparently the most egregious thing for Zappa, sexual repression" (2016, 115). Many Zappa compositions—in many styles—pierce social mores with misogyny; of "Latex Solar Beef" (1971), Kelly Fisher Lowe says "it constitutes the theme of repressed sexuality in a heavy metal setting" (2006, 92). His album *Joe's Garage* (1979) featured an omniscient narrator who calls himself The Central Scrutinizer ("it is my responsibility to enforce all the laws that haven't been passed yet"), a thought-policing role recognized by Ben Watson as "a parody of the super-ego" (1994, 369). The sex-controlling persona came to life six years later in the form of Tipper Gore in the 1985 PMRC hearings of the US Senate Commerce Committee, wherein Zappa locked horns with her over rock lyrics that offended Gore enough to seek an ultimately produced obscenity ratings system for record releases.

Donna Freitas notes that while a promiscuous hookup culture is usually considered to be a lifestyle of great freedom, it can be seen as "a culture of repression. If the Victorian era represents the repression of sexual desire, then the era of the hookup is about the repression of romantic feeling, love, and sexual desire, too, in favor of greater access to sex—sex for the sake of sex" (2013, 182). Like Don Giovanni with his list, Usher brags of his number of conquests in "Pro Lover" (2010): "I'm better when I touch and go; I'm tryin' to add yo name to my hall of fame"; Miranda Lambert advertises pretty much the same in "Fastest Girl in Town," as do Pink in "Slut Like You" and Christina Aguilera in "Your Body" (all 2012). We count 242 named objectified women in Insane Clown Posse's hour-long "Freaky Tales" (also 2012), each quatrain carrying a different sexual boast. Twenty-first-century sex may be free, but clearly all related repression has not been resolved.

If one may combine psychological and cultural-studies theories, it could be said that because the impetus for and consequences of repression are socially governed, standards have varied between racial groups as well as by gender and by historical contexts:

> Early in the twentieth century, black males and females sought to create an alternative sexuality rooted in eros and sensual pleasure distinct from the repressed sexuality of white racists and the puritanism that had been embraced

as a protective shield to ward off racist/sexist stereotypes about black sexuality. Black males, deemed hypersexual in a negative way in the eyes of whites, were in the subculture of blackness deemed sexually healthy. . . . Since whiteness had repressed black sexuality, in the subculture space of blackness, sexual desire was expressed with degrees of abandon unheard of in white society.[21]

In the first half of the century, the African American music clubs of Harlem "attracted many middle-class, heterosexual whites who sought an escape from the puritanical culture they perceived in conventional white society. Harlem gave these fugitives from white society a chance to indulge in an exotic, primitivist fantasy about black culture and the sexuality of African Americans" (Dean 1996, 49). In a parallel and similarly exploitive way, white youths commodified Black culture just as their elders repressed sex to "create" rock 'n' roll in the 1950s, a movement branded as dangerously decadent in its "primitive" permissiveness.[22]

Beginning with the Oedipal struggle, sexual drives deemed taboo are sublimated, unconsciously redirected into either dreams, fantasies, slips of the tongue, jokes, or culturally acceptable works including the making and appreciation of music. Illustrating sublimation, Žižek speaks for heterosexual men: "Rather than making a direct assault upon a woman, we try to seduce and conquer her by writing amorous letters and poetry."[23] Sublimation of drives stemming from the bond between fetus and mother is theorized by Reynolds and Press in their study of rock music: "Psychedelia's oceanic feelings of 'intimate immensity' are a sublimated longing for 'womb-space,' for a time when the infant and mother together made up the entire universe" (1995, 286). A brief but fitting early example of this is Cream's "Tales of Brave Ulysses" (1967): as in Homer's verse, the mythic hero is "tortured by the sirens sweetly singing, for the sparkling waves are calling [him] to kiss their white-laced lips." To convey this sense, Eric Clapton's guitar (pickup and tone setting chosen, and amplifier tuned, to what he calls his "woman tone") are run through a psychedelic wah pedal, forming rolling breakers of sonic partials, while a repeated cascading bass

---

[21] hooks 2004, 70–1. Other important statements on race and repression are found in hooks 1994, 127, and Bannister 2006, 27.

[22] Sexual repression, race, and rock 'n' roll are considered together as a trope in Street 1986, 15, Frith 1996, 127–31, Waksman 1999, 4, Gendron 2004, 298–9, Bannister 2006, 33–4, and deBoise 2015, 132–5. The moral panic surrounding the foundation of rock music, as expressed in a terrorizing *Melody Maker* essay, is covered in Hebdige 1988, 55. Hawkins 2002, 187–8, discusses how Prince satirizes this trope.

[23] 1991, 83. Information on sublimation and the arts is found in Marcuse 1956, 3, 12, 40, 81–3, 140–4, and 185, Basler 1970, 15–16, Roszak 1970, 107, Epstein 1994, 17, Lambert 1997, 207, Williams and Stein 2002, 27, de Berg 2003, 11–2, 66, and 84, Carlson 2012, viii and 1, Rabaté 2014, 225 and 233, and Høge-Olesen 2019, 6.

line, ^8 - ^b7 - ^6 - ^b6, drowns the listener in what might be amniotic fluid. A larger perspective is provided by John Lennon: in his 1970 psychoanalysis sessions, he may have learned that the artist presents worked-out symptoms of Oedipal traumas, because in "I Found Out" (1970), he sings, "I heard somethin' 'bout my Ma and my Pa—they didn't want me so they made me a star."

Shame and nudity. In Western thought, innocent children leave Eden for a life of sexual shame; lust, with its absence of control, has been subject to suspicion since prehistory, even in non-Judeo-Christian traditions. Today's young men and women remain subject to double standards concerning their sex lives. Nudity, still governed and stigmatized, has gradually returned to Western culture after hundreds of years of repression: mainstream men's magazines showed women's bare backs in the 1940s, sides of breasts in the 1950s, nipples and then pubic hair in the 1960s. In the 1970s, photos of men's erections broke the last such taboo (Gagnon 1977, 356) and Nevada's communal clothing-optional event, Burning Man, continues in the current century of internet-enabled freedoms in nakedness.

The 1960s counterculture in particular allowed for undressed displays. Nudity was embraced with 1968's Broadway musical, *Hair*, 1969's off-Broadway *Oh! Calcutta*, and in British and Australian TV and mainstream European magazines in the 1970s. John Lennon and Yoko Ono shockingly displayed full-frontal nude shots on the cover of their *Two Virgins* (1968) album (compare her stage work "Cut Piece" and film, *Fly*), which their home record label, EMI, would not carry. The Jimi Hendrix Experience's *Electric Ladyland* (also 1968) and Blind Faith (1969) were given alternate covers to replace nude photos (the latter allegedly modeled by an eleven-year-old girl), but the sleeves of Santana's *Abraxas* and Miles Davis's *Bitches Brew* (both 1970), with their *paintings* of nudes, were allowed for sale. Women's nipples and pubic hair would make it to mainstream rock-album artwork only in the liberated 1970s (Roxy Music) and beyond (XTC).

Early on, as a pop-song topic, the naked (or nearly naked) body was appropriate only in humorous novelty songs like Brian Hyland's "Itsy Bitsy Teenie Weenie Yellow Polkadot Bikini" and Andy Stewart's "Donald Where's Your Troosers" (both 1960), Peter and Gordon's "Lady Godiva" (1966), and Ray Stevens' "The Streak" (1974). But in later years, the vulnerability of the naked body could yield poignancy, as in Elton John's "Candle in the Wind" (1987), wherein Marilyn Monroe's body was exploited at her death: "All the papers had to say was that Marilyn was found in the nude." Undress was celebrated in Meatloaf's sacramental ode to "Paradise by the Dashboard Light" (1977), revelation coming in its stark modulation from a fast, excited boogie, "glowin' like the metal on the edge of a knife," to a half-time, haloed gospel choir for a magnified moment in the titular chorus.

Still, even with such countercultural strides, backsliding reversals occurred in the following decades, the result of a 1980s Reagan-driven conservative backlash. The 1990s, for example, brought heavy criticism to Demi Moore for posing naked for a *Vanity Fair* cover and to Sally Mann for publishing nude photos of her three young children. In the 1990s, "girls still [felt] shame about their adult bodies, particularly breast development and menstruation. . . . Girls come to associate sexuality with danger, shame, and dirt" (Martin 1996, 2, 20). With their emphasis on sisterhood and homosocial friendship, the Spice Girls in particular responded at the end of the century to such sex- and body-negative messages that conditioned girls into psychic ills. Inner truth is revealed through nudity by the Spice Girls in "Naked" (1997), a song reflective of third-wave feminism's push for body positivity and stance against sexual judgment. In this song, the woman gets to assume the position of the undressed *and* the gazer, the latter a privilege usually reserved for men: "Don't be afraid to stare, she is only naked; [She will] undress you with her eyes, uncover the truth from the lies," lines set with three different piercing major-major seventh chords. During this decade and the one that followed, other songs used nudity to address gay desire. In Pet Shop Boys' "Dreaming of the Queen" (1993), Fred E. Maus (2001, 388) reads the gay singer's dreamed accepted public nakedness as a symbolic form of emerging from the closet. "Nakedness is just another window to the soul" is the key line in "Gratuitous Nudity," a song from the 1999 musical, *Naked Boys Singing!*

Sex-related nudity is a frequent occurrence in twenty-first-century club music, as related in Christina Aguilera's "Dirrty" (2002), Ke$ha's "Take It Off" (2010), and many other songs. A commonplace and sexually innocent nudity once considered an unrealized or fabled ideal by the Mothers of Invention ("there will come a time when you can even Take Your Clothes Off When You Dance" [1968]) is realized by Prince & the New Power Generation in "And God Created Woman" (2007): "and we were naked and did not care." Despite such idealism, and (semi-)nudity having become so prevalent in rock and pop videos, America was still not prepared to tolerate without shame Janet Jackson's televised "wardrobe malfunction" in 2004. Social discomfort in displaying and observing nudity results in two conditions covered together next.

Exhibitionism and voyeurism. Exhibitionism and voyeurism are judged to be the two most common forms of paraphilia, sexual behaviors "far outside" statistical norms (and once grouped together as perversions) (Wincze 2000, 453). The acts have manifestations that are considered healthy or unhealthy, as they may be either benign or harmful in practice.

> Of all the practices on the sexual menu, only vaginal intercourse has nearly universal appeal. . . . A distant second in appeal was watching a partner undress. . . . And men liked watching a partner undress more than women did. Yet 30 percent of women age eighteen to forty-four found it very appealing and another 51 percent said it was somewhat appealing, so young women as well as young men seemed to like watching their partner undress. (Michael et al. 1994, 145)

Contrary to some cultural myths about gendered differences related to looking and desire, clinical studies measuring sexual response (via penile tumescence and vaginal lubrication) suggest that women are as—or nearly as—aroused as men by visual sexual stimuli.[24] The increase of broadcast bandwidth afforded by the ethernet beginning in 1997 has expanded access to pornography, and amateur webcams have allowed for DIY participation; right alongside, sexual content has been amplified in the rock video, including portrayals of voyeurism and exhibitionism.[25] In 2006, ex-Mouseketeer Britney Spears insisted that she was not that innocent by flashing her vulva for the paparazzi, joining a short line of female stars showing their stuff in the course of everyday life.

Pop and rock songs have extolled the pleasures of looking, going back as far as 1936 when British music-hall veteran George Formby shared his views in "When I'm Cleaning Windows" (1936) ("ladies' nighties I have spied; I've often seen what goes inside"). Artists are still singing about window-scrutinized nudity, as contemplated in Dave Matthews Band's "Crash Into Me" (1996), B*witched's "C'est la Vie" (1998), and "Window to Window" (from the 1999 show, *Naked Boys Singing!*). Early rock examples include Joe Turner's "Shake, Rattle and Roll" (1954) ("well, you wear those dresses, the sun comes shinin' through"). Since then, dozens of songs have treated exhibitionists like Widow Jones in Jeannie C. Riley's "The

---

[24] See Gagnon 1977, 126; Leibetseder 2012, 86–7; Rutter and Schwartz 2012, 67; and Bergner 2013, 28 and 76–7.
[25] Following a decade of films such as *American Beauty* and *Eyes Wide Shut*, Laura Mulvey 2009 covers the male gaze in cinema and other visual arts. Lori Burns writes extensively on the erotic gaze in rock videos; see Burns and Lafrance 2002, 77–8, for instance, on Tori Amos's "Crucify" (1992). Madonna's videos are cited in regard to exhibitionism and many other sexual topics (see, e.g., Kaplan 1987, 157, Paglia 1993, O'Brien 2002, and Gioia 2015, 248), as have those of Lady Gaga (Lieb 2013, and Iddon and Marshall 2014). Other important treatment of the rock video, including its relation to voyeurism, is given in Longhurst 1995 and Dibben 1999.

Harper Valley P.T.A." (1968) and voyeurs like the singer herself in Debbie Harry's "Picture This" (1978).

The ability to show or view a nude body (or part of it) while in public becomes more arousing when the activity involves sex acts. Sex in public places is considered or performed in Janet Jackson's "Any Time, Any Place" (1993), T-Spoon's "Sex on the Beach" (1997), Scissor Sisters' "Lovers in the Backseat" (2004), Usher's "Love in This Club" (2008), Katy Perry's "California Gurls" (2010), and R. Kelly's "Crazy Sex" (2013). One setting is identical in the Strokes' "Meet Me in the Bathroom" (2003), Anal Traffic's "Two Pumps and a Squirt" (2005), and Jay-Z and Kanye West's "Niggas in Paris" (2011). Quaint permission for a view is sought by Romeo Santos in "Propuesta Indecente" (2013), "Permiteme apreciar tu desnudez," and we suppose the same polite sentiment is behind Peaches' rapped request in "Two Guys (For Every Girl)" (2006), "I wanna see you work it guy on guy, I wanna see you boys get down with each other." PJ Harvey aggressively asks her lover to take a good look at her attributes in "Sheela-Na-Gig" (1992), but he rejects her as a vulgar exhibitionist: "please take those dirty pillows away from me."[26] Frank Zappa goes full raunch in "Dinah-Moe Humm" (1973), in which a woman bets the singer $40 that he can't make her come. After bringing to bear many failed techniques, he wins the wager by screwing Dinah-Moe's sister in full sight; "Dinah-Moe watched from the edge of the bed with her lips just a-twitchin' and her face gone red."

Two popular activities involve both exhibitionists and voyeurs: stripping and sexting. The former's association with music is not surprising given the often public nature of its performance, whose roots are in vaudeville and the fan dance of the 1930s. The striptease is memorialized as far back as the Andrews Sisters' "Strip Polka" (1942), which oozes lasciviousness from the introductory wah trumpet glissando, through dirty growly multiphonics sung on the word "hot," to the stop-time emphasis in the line, "So she stops! And always just in time." Eartha Kitt's "I Want to Be Evil" (1953) ends with a metric modulation to a slow tempo for a stripper's finish at "whatever I've got, I'm eager to lose," and David Rose's "The Stripper" (1962) opens with a phallic sliding trombone, features lots of bumps and grinds from drums and brass, and works out tassel-twirling trumpet trills (as at 0:42).[27] The Beatles, who featured a stripper in their

---

[26] "Sheela-Na-Gig" is discussed elsewhere: see especially O'Dair 1997, 544, and Lankford 2010, 25–6.

[27] There is nothing new in 1962 about the slide trombone as phallic symbol. Dinah Washington sang sassily about the "Big Long Slidin' Thing" in 1954. In 1907, Ada Jones sang, "Get wise to my sighs and the light in my eyes; 'I'm in Love with the Slide Trombone.'" Ted Gioia finds this lyric in a sixteenth-century collection: "Although our trombones are bent, we can quickly straighten them

Magical Mystery Tour TV film (1967), incorporated salacious half-step slides of chord roots (G - F♯7 - F) in "Sexy Sadie" (1968). Stripping is invoked in songs as diverse as Iggy Pop's "Lust for Life" (1977), 2 Live Crew's "Strip Club" (1990), Eminem's "Shake That" (2005), Flo Rida's "Right Round" (2009), and Migos's "All Ass" (2017), and is shown in many rock videos. One humorous such promo is for Robbie Williams' "Rock DJ" (2000), in which the singer does not stop in time, stripping down through the flesh to his skeleton so he can literally dance around in his bones.

The sharing of nudes by smartphone texts and tweets, sexting, led to a twenty-first-century moral panic when criminally abused by teens who were often unprepared for its consequences. Sexting also led to political downfalls for those who really should have known better, such as Anthony Weiner, former congressman from New York: his first round of furtive sexting brought down his career in 2011; a further 2017 incident involved a minor and landed Weiner in prison. These examples underscore a titillating Freudian aspect of sexting as a taboo related to exhibition, namely being caught and punished. Similarly, sexting brings about online embarrassment in Katy Perry's "Last Friday Night (T.G.I.F.)" (2010), treatment for sex addiction in Ludacris's "Sexting" (2010), and parental fears in Nas's "Daughters" (2012). Still not all sexting-related music is shameful: Lil Yachty boasts of sexting with a groupie in "Dirty Mouth" (2017), and then there is simply friendly sharing going on in The 1975's "The Man Who Married a Robot" (2018).

Shame in sex. In the West, acceptance of sex among unmarried partners has only recently reached "an all-time high" (Julian 2018); out-of-wedlock sex has long carried a strong stigma, especially for American women. The so-called walk of shame is predicted in the Everly Brothers' "Wake Up Little Susie" (1957): "what're we going to tell our friends when they say 'ooh la la?!'" and in the sin-pronouncing "morning's echo" of Merrilee Rush's "Angel of the Morning" (1968). These concerns are still available and voiced by women, as in Pink's "Walk of Shame" (2012) ("where'd I get the wristband? Tell me there's no tramp stamp"), and Meghan Trainor's "Walkashame" (2015), whose speaker evades notice ("I beat the sunrise again").

Owing to a legacy of Puritan values, unmarried women and girls in their teens who get pregnant have long faced (and still do) a loss of status, in the United

---

and make them of great length or short; when we *lanzi* wish to play, we push it in and pull it out and play the whole range" (2015, 143).

States and the United Kingdom (Harris 2004). In these countries, sex education has lagged behind that of Scandinavia and the northern continent, which have tolerated out-of-wedlock cohabitation and births increasingly since the 1960s. Before oral contraception became available to most in the mid-1960s, homes for unwed mothers shielded or hid those who forswore illegal abortions and adoption. Marilyn Adler Papayanis (2010, 652) points out how Joni Mitchell's "Little Green" (1971), a single mother's tender ode to an adopted-out newborn, contrasts sharply against the pain of guilt over social stigma in Diana Ross & the Supremes' "Love Child" (1968) and Cher's "Gypsies, Tramps & Thieves" (1971). The verses of "Love Child" feature a tense tonic pedal and the internal rhyme of "I shared the guilt my *mother knew*, so afraid that *others knew* I had no name" that emphasizes the scornful last four words, also overlaid by Louvain Demps's siren-like shriek, "ah," on a high fifth scale degree. But tension is present throughout the song, captured in the opening accented diminished and six-four triads (see Figure 1.2), cymbal roll, and the violin's cascading sixty-fourth notes to a portentious open fifth on A minor's tonic (0:03). The soft smoothness of a repeated major mode double-plagal progression, G major—D major—A major (0:05–0:08) is undercut by tense repeated eighths on a tonic bass pedal and the extension of a single 6/4 bar with tambourine, guitar, glockenspiel, and piano then supporting an additive three-part vocalization over a chromatic bass descent (depicting a run-down "tenement slum") to the siren-shriek (0:18–0:19). Adding to the strain, Ross's vocal is tacet through the entire first verse (still labeled "Intro" in Figure 1.2), not entering until the prechorus (0:19).[28] David Temperley (2018, 210) talks of choruses and verses typically being harmonically "opposite"; here, the chromatic descent of the major-mode verse is opposed by the chorus's diatonic, minor-mode "lamento bass" (Everett 2009, 241–2; Ross 2010, 22–54) and parallel perfect intervals that portray the harsh relentlessness of poverty and the tragedy of being misunderstood, following the frank structural-downbeat 9-8 suspension (0:29). Inner-voice material depicts the singer's inner guilt (E4, at 0:56–1:04, and A3-E4, 1:55–1:57), her own love (D4-B3, 1:04–1:06), and self-doubts (E4, 1:50), but the outer, upper voice projects others' reflection of rejection (F4-B4, 0:24–1:29), their scorn (G4-B4, 1:20–1:23), and their naming her shame (G♯4-B4, 2:05–2:07); all is connected with great harmonic tension.

---

[28] As the prechorus begins, tonic harmony supporting the vocal ^3 is part of an intensifying pre-dominant prolongation as discussed by Drew Nobile (2020, 100), and perhaps also an example of Mark Spicer's "weakened" tonic (2017, ¶ 1). For more on the prechorus in general, see Summach 2011 and Heetderks 2020.

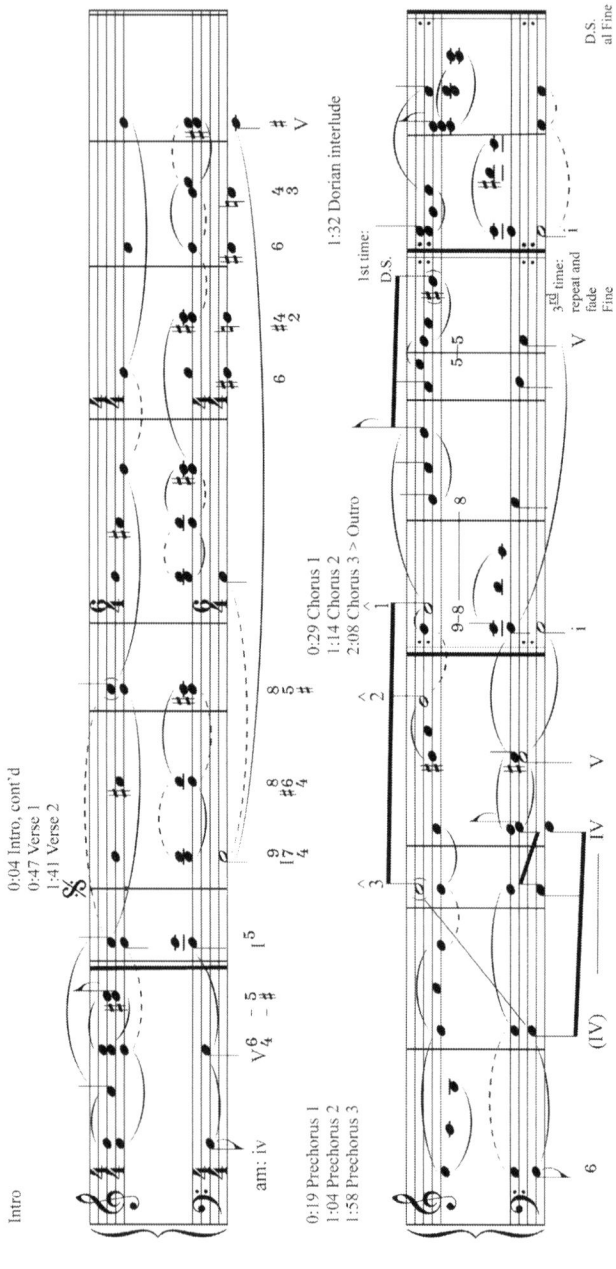

Figure 1.2 Voice-leading sketch of Diana Ross and the Supremes, "Love Child" (1968).

Similar disgrace is conveyed in First Choice's "Smarty Pants" (1973). "Little Green," on the other hand, opens with a major-major seventh chord that portrays both the infant's vulnerability and the earth-mother hippie-mom's disinterest in social censure. The speaker has to beg her father for support in the face of an illegitimate pregnancy in Madonna's "Papa Don't Preach" (1986). In Cheryl Pepsii Riley's "Thanks for My Child" (1988), the melody is smooth and calm when referring to the speaker's love for her child even if it becomes angular with chromatic applied dominants when referring to the father who "ran away free," taking off in a high-flying melisma at song's end.

Despite occasional signs of acceptance when American teen pregnancies rose to their peak in 1990 (Rutter and Schwartz 2012, 139), in 1992, US vice president Dan Quayle felt compelled to stigmatize them. He actually blamed the Los Angeles riots (a response to the brutal police beating of Rodney King) on a decline in morals exhibited by the pregnancy of a *fictional* single career woman (by her ex-husband) portrayed on the television sitcom "Murphy Brown." A couple of decades later, a love child born to 2008 presidential candidate John Edwards forced him to drop out of a strong run. Consequences of teen motherhood are even harsher for women of color, particularly below the poverty line; this is apparently the background of a tragic suicide by a fourteen-year-old in Outkast's "Toilet Tisha" (2000). The last verse of Ludacris's "Runaway Love" (2006) tells of an eleven-year-old single mother who "lives poor, so no money for abortion." Kid Rock's rapped "Black Chick White Guy" (1999) is a twelve-minute tale of a ninth-grade girl who announces "I'm pregnant" with a dramatic stop-time moment and fermata; she goes on to have three children, all with different men. In "Sweet Sixteen" (also 1999), Destiny's Child provides a polyphonic superego angel-on-the-shoulder for a young single mother by quoting lyrics from both "59th Street Bridge Song" ("Slow down, you move too fast") and "Theme from Mahogany" ("Do you know where you're goin' to?"). A seventeen-year-old also matures too quickly in "All Grown Up," from *Bare: A Pop Opera* (2000), singing "Feel it, how it grows inside me, swirling ball of anguished cries; haunted, daunted, so unwanted, feel its anger in me rise" over the repeated lamento bass figure, $\hat{8}$ - $\hat{b7}$ - $\hat{b6}$ - $\hat{5}$. None of these songs address the feelings, shame or otherwise, of a girl's sexual partner, the future baby's father, but John Prine does so in "Unwed Fathers" (1984), taking on men who "can't be bothered" with their progeny.

Shotgun weddings brought many young American couples to marriage, especially for first births in the pre-pill era of the 1950s and 1960s. The topic may have been too delicate to sing about for a full decade after that, perhaps first turning up overtly in the Honey Cone's soul song requiring such a wedding, "Stick-Up" (1971), and then in Jim Ed Brown & Helen Cornelius's country number in which a woman fights off a man's temptations, "I Don't Want to Have to Marry You" (1976). A tragic dorian coloring suggests no wedding is in store for Michael Jackson's "Billie Jean" (1982), as the singer claims no responsibility for a pregnancy. In "Loser" (1993), Beck raps that "Someone keeps sayin' I'm insane to complain about a shotgun wedding." The Dixie Chicks relate a forced wedding to economic and social status in "White Trash Wedding" (2002): "say I do and kiss me quick because baby's on its way." Although "Get Me to the Church on Time" (*My Fair Lady*, 1956) can't be read as a song about an unplanned pregnancy, the newly middle-class singer there intends to make an honest woman out of his longtime live-in lover.

In spite of these cautionary tales of pregnancy and forced marriage, overall, women's shame about sex falls away by degrees in the twentieth century's last three decades. Donna Summer sings about her desire in "Love to Love You Baby" (1975). The disco anthem includes Summer's whispering moans and vocal fry for repeated orgasms fantasized over a shimmering wah-shaped rhythm guitar, persistent four-on-the-floor bass drum, and bass and lead guitar doubling a bluesy minor-pentatonic melody. Madonna sings directly to her lover in "Burning Up" (1983), in which she pleads, "don't put me off 'cause I'm on fire and I can't quench my desire." The song's frustrated instrumental bridge, set off by the admission, "I have no shame—I'm on fire!," 2:03–2:04) ends on a dissonant anticipatory V7 chord with ♯9th (2:36–2:40), preparing for the return of a minor-pentatonic vocal. One Riot Grrrl example of frank sexuality from the 1990s would be Liz Phair's "Flower" (1994), in which the singer declares at various points, in two vocal parts, "Every time I see your face I get all wet between my legs . . . I want to fuck you like a dog. . . . I want to be your blow job queen. . . . I just want your fresh young jimmy jamming, slamming, ramming in me. . . . I'll fuck you till your dick is blue." Phair's two vocal parts, suggesting conscious and unconscious layers, are ironically innocent in a childlike major-mode sing-song quality, an arpeggiating jump-rope chant above a long-remaining chordal seventh that finally, dutifully, resolves down by step.[29] The guileless style is called *Kinderwhore*,

---

[29] "Flower" is discussed extensively; see Reynolds and Press 1995, 255, Lankford 2010, 56–9, Arnold 2014, 45 and 96, Kearney 2017, 225, and Centauer 2018, 63–9.

also exemplified by Courtney Love. One can't imagine a woman's song from 1956 containing anything remotely like such a profession of desires.

The forms of psychological self discussed earlier lead in the following chapter to the notion of gender, a cultural expression of sex contained in personhood as defined by masculine and feminine impressions. As true of biological birth sex, understandings of gender will be seen to change radically across the history of recorded popular music.

2

Gendered Identity

Modernist roles constituting neatly assigned men's and women's behavioral characteristics have been deeply questioned in the postmodern age, leading to new understandings as to how gender is constructed and how it may be expressed in many more than the conventional two opposing ways. Because most of recorded popular music has historically reflected a traditional binary view of gender (itself a support for the long-standing Western binary view of birth sex), our chapter on gendered identity opens with a summary of traditional men's and women's traits in pop music. But as rock music is transgressive at its core, it became a natural vehicle for resisting and problematizing established attitudes about what it means to be a boy or a girl, a man or a woman, and these developments will be covered once the earlier conventions are clear. First, though, a little theory about the nature of gender.

Cisgenderism, Essentialism, and Broader Thinking

Our working understanding of gender follows from Jeffery Weeks: he writes that gender

> refers to symbolic, social and historical rather than biological or essential differences—and similarities—between men and women. Rather than seeing biological men and women as the fount and origin of gender, gender is now widely seen as a social structure and set of relationships within which masculinities and femininities are produced. As such it has become a key term in feminist analysis, and in wider sexual politics. (2011, 68)

Gender is often coextensive with sex, leading to biological males and females who accept their assigned anatomical configuration as their gender, in which case we say they are cisgendered—a status *seen* (or, in the case of misogynists and homophobes, *taken*) by many as privileged. In the essentialist view, core questions of reproductive biology (e.g., does one produce eggs or sperm?) fully determine invariant gender and sexuality; as noted by Mary Celeste Kearney (2017, 226), it's no accident that in "Born to Run" (1975), Bruce Springsteen sings of girls who "comb their hair in rear-view mirrors" and boys who "try to look so hard." However, feminists, ethnomethodologists, and other researchers have come to understand since the 1970s—and moreso since the 1990s in light of the third feminist wave and intersectional understandings of race/ethnicity, economic class, dis/ability, age, nationality, and sexuality as they reciprocate with gender—that coercive social forces play a large role in the creation of gender roles and identity that are overlaid upon the landscape provided by the physical body.[1] Therefore, the play of gendered personality traits within any one individual can run the gamut, and proportions of "masculine" and "feminine" behaviors can vary significantly across a wide nonbinary spectrum in the identity of any given person, or in their expression or their role-playing preferences. It was only during the Enlightenment period, in the eighteenth century, that two stable (separate and unchanging) genders became recognized, setting the stage for "the political, economic, and cultural" ranks of men and women as solidified by social Darwinists.[2] Patriarchal capitalism dictated, for instance, that women "perform domestic tasks for free" (Halberstam 2012, 14). In 1963, Jack Jones sang flippant misogynist lines such as "don't send [your husband] off with your hair still in curlers—you may not see him again" in Burt Bacharach and Hal David's song, "Wives and Lovers"; in 2015, Cécile McLorin Salvant would cover this song from a wittily ironic perspective.

But as the nature of men's dominance was interrogated throughout the twentieth century, it came to be understood just how socially established, and not innate, simplistic gender distinctions and the sexism that followed notions of "opposing sexes" were.[3] We learn very young that masculinity is unmarked as a

[1]	Of course, by arguing that "biology is not destiny, and that gender is made and not inborn" (Bell 2018, 198), Freud separated gender expression from birth sex in "polymorphously perverse" infants, through his understanding of the social forces at work in his Oedipus complex. See also de Beauvoir 1989, Cameron and Kulik 2003, and Carlson 2012. Donna Haraway explains that, like the self/other and many other often-illusory Western dualisms, the gender binary tends to the "domination of women, people of color, nature, workers, animals" (2003, 35).

[2]	The quoted phrasing comes from Laqueur 1990, 6. To Laqueur's three caste systems, I would add the legal category as well. The history of gender is covered in such sources as McRobbie 1994, Connell 1995, Kleinberg 1999, Hawkes 2004, Moores 2010, Weeks 2010, Dyhouse 2017, Hegarty 2018, and Magnusson and Maracek 2018.

[3]	For more on the social constitution of gender, from parenting throughout the lifecourse, see Gagnon 1977; Bancroft 1989; Flax 1990; Martin 1996; Halberstam 1998; Leibetseder 2012; Rutter and Schwartz 2012; Freitas 2013; Seidman 2015; Hawkins 2016; and Biernat and Sesko, Hines, Leaper, and

standard, and that we should "see someone as female only when [we] cannot see them as male" (Kessler and McKenna 1978, 158).[4] Pressure from media would usually lead to self-stereotyping, often to depression and anxiety. Children and adolescents, often punished or taunted by parents, teachers, and peers if not rigidly conforming through the cultural, interpersonal and psyche-permeating display of their binary gender enactments in "clothing, body modification, speech, posture, movement, language, attitude" (de Lauretis 1987, 31), "manners, decorum, protocol, and deportment" (Bornstein 2016, 32), "interests, activities, dress, skills, and sexual partner choice" (Kessler and McKenna 1978, 11–2), have received great support from gender-queering scholars who have subverted "the logic of the sex/gender paradigm" with the notion of genderfuck (Taylor 2012, 99). Of course, adults are also subject to gender harassment, as portrayed in Tribe 8's "Wrong Bathroom" (1996): "'Is that a he or a she? Is that a him or a her?' . . . I'm gonna have a bladder burst while you ponder gender!"[5] Such persecution can be fully internal, as in Frank Zappa's "Bobby Brown" (1979): "Am I a boy or a lady, I don't know which!" (1:25–1:30), sung in three octaves as if representing three gender possibilities: man, woman and (post-castration) nonbinary person, all at once. Also to be considered is the theory of intersectionality noted earlier; this is especially true in the common confusion of gender and sexual preference: in "Stronger than Me" (2003), Amy Winehouse complains that her sensitive man is just a "lady-boy" and asks, "are you gay?" The same bullying attitude is espoused by Katy Perry in "Ur So Gay" (2008): "you don't eat meat and drive electrical cars; . . . you need SPF 45 just to stay alive."

The ties between gender and sexual preference are strong, especially given the cultural norms of compulsory heterosexuality:

> One response to the blurring of gender identities was a new emphasis on the norm of heterosexuality as a way to reassert gender difference and the normality

---

Rodger in Dess, Marecek, and Bell 2018. Some recent findings, particularly by neuropsychologists sometimes dismissed as patriarchally biased, show that aspects of gender may indeed be hard-wired; see Moores 2010, Kelly 2012, deBoise 2015, Seidman 2015, Donaghue 2018, and Leaper 2018. The role of culture in determining gender is borne out in R. W. Connell's observation that rape is extremely rare, homosexual behavior can be a "majority practice," and mothers are not the primary caretakers in various societies (1995, 47). Transgender peoples in various non-Western cultures are handled variously in Epstein and Straub 1991.

[4]   Sociologists Friedman and Maxwell find that "children at a fairly young age (around five or six) have a good understanding of how they identify, in terms of race, gender, and sexuality" (2021, 126).

[5]   In "Androgyny" (2001), Garbage tries to ease such pain: "Boys in the girls' room, girls in the men's room, you free your mind in your androgyny." A very unusual tonicization of the leading tone, D♯ in the key of E, is heard in the bridge, where "it doesn't matter where you are," years in advance of North Carolina's oppressive 2016 bathroom law.

of dichotomous gender roles. By emphasizing the naturalness and rightness of heterosexuality, people could view the differences between men and women as natural and good. (Seidman 2015, 48)

As called out by social theorist Judith Butler (1999, 24), such an approach continued to exert a morally regulatory linking of sex, gender, and sexuality. Gayle Rubin argued that "sex is fundamentally about erotic desires, fantasies, acts, identities, and politics—none of which are reducible to gender dynamics."[6] In "I Wanna Be Your Lover" (1979), Prince suggests a rich repertoire of sex acts, including even the simulation of incest, that could be performed by a genderically diverse lover: "I wanna be your lover, I wanna be the only one that makes you come [slight pause] running. . . . I wanna be your brothers, I wanna be your mother and your sister too."

Institutional Gender Conventions

Gender stereotypes arose in the nineteenth-century West as a means of establishing a tough, dominating "breadwinning" man's agency and group solidarity in the face of Industrial-Age economic battle, and a receding woman's domesticity—and to enforce compulsory heterosexuality as well as traditional predator/prey, penetrative/receptive attitudes. Men and their bourgeois businesses are rational; women are more often than men "in touch with their emotions"—owing, asserts Julia Serano, to levels of estrogen and testosterone, as experienced especially by transsexuals undergoing hormone therapy (2016, 323). As if fearing a reversion to a pre-Oedipal lack of gender identity, men tend to overcompensate by striving and conquering; even their desk jobs in modern economies are based on "powerful" computers. Nadine Hubbs provides an excellent overview of the underlying dichotomy:

A good deal of theory and criticism has already deconstructed the myriad ways our cultural discourses are rooted in notions of dialectical gender. If I rehearse some of the well-worn facts of these genders—that the masculine is constructed in terms of primacy, strength, action, and independence, and the feminine as its opposite and Other, secondary and different, weak, inactive, and dependent—

---

6   Seidman 2015, 23, quotes from Rubin's essay, "Thinking Sex" (1984). Re gender versus sexuality, see also Halberstam 1998 and Leiblum and Rosen 2000. "Compulsory heterosexuality" is a term coined in Rich 1980.

my litany is intended as descriptive (of long-standing, powerful, and constructed cultural products), and surely not prescriptive (according to essentialist or any other assumptions). (1996, 270)

To their litany, we could add rational, goal-oriented, aggressive, assertive, competitive, territorial, adventurous, self-confident, rugged, ambitious, inventive, promiscuous, and technophiliac as masculine traits, and emotional, nurturing, affectionate, quiet, meek, risk-averse, sensitive, helpless, fragile, deferential, technophobic, "gentle, aware of others' feelings, neat, tactful, and [expressive of] tender feelings" (Biernat and Sesko 2018, 172–3) as feminine ones. Men of the ruling class are responsible for armed assault, empire building, and war (each involving a combination of violence and cold rationality, as per Connell 1995, 185–98). In the extremes of romance fiction, "women desire the men who intimidate them" (Talbot 1997, 119). Misogyny underlies most such partitions; "certain pursuits and interests that are considered feminine, such as gossiping or decorating, are often characterized as 'frivolous,' while [men's sports] generally escape such trivialization" (Serano 2016, 326–7). The roughest team sports are deadly serious; according to BMI in 2010, Queen's threatening "We Will Rock You" (1977), which aggressively taunts an addressee who would be "a big man," was the most-often played song at NFL American football games. These interpretations, however, ignore class distinctions (macho blue-collar versus civilized white-collar workers; gang or prison violence as compensation for dismissed or sidelined virility) and racial bias (because "Black women are seen as assertive, confident, and aggressive" [Biernat and Sesko 2018, 176]), and render obscure the gender roles of gays; within Western culture, variances exist between countries as well (Kelly 2012, 23–4). And a paradox exists in the fact that "few men actually match the . . . toughness and independence acted by [John] Wayne, [Humphrey] Bogart, or [Clint] Eastwood. . . . Are we to say the majority of men are unmasculine?"[7] Manly music may be ironic: soldiers exhibit all sorts of masculine qualities in SSgt. Barry Sadler's ironically timid music (despite its Boléro-like growth, unprepossessing with major mode and

---

[7]   Connell 1995, 70. She goes on (p. 79) to state that "the majority of men . . . benefit from the patriarchal dividend [that subordinates] women," regardless of their own individual degree of masculinity. (For instance, it's not just the highly aggressive men who earn more, on average, than women in comparable positions, the wage gap still 17.7 percent in 2020 [Goldberg 2021, 5].) One might view this hegemony dividend rooted in complicity as parallel to the nature of institutional racism. As an example of "gendered" variances between countries, consider how the global "strength" of the British monarchy came into widespread question, as if its manly qualities had waned to its detriment, when the power of the empire was (again) reconsidered upon the death of Queen Elizabeth II in September 2022, and the accession of a weak, ill-suited (and tree-hugging) Charles III.

quiet, conciliatory sequences) for "The Ballad of the Green Berets" (1966), but Edwin Starr's antimilitarist "War" (1970), which emphasizes a mother's tears, is conversely aggressive (in its punchy [025] trichords and sparring teams of vocal and instrumental forces).

Despite the patriarchal norm, Dorothy Dinnerstein points out that women have power over cowering men in intimate relations: "Men try to handle this danger with the many kinds of sex-segregating institutions that they seem always and everywhere to create. Secret societies, hunting trips, pool parlors, wars—all of these provide men with sanctuary from the impact of women" (2002, 15). This selective autonomy and the power it both enables and avoids (being pussy-whipped or—worse—being seen as pussy-whipped) are central to the rock aesthetic; "a classic example from the sixties is the Who's song 'A Legal Matter' [1965], in which the hero feels his willpower enfeebled by the 'household fog' of furnishings, baby clothes, marriage, and the like" (Stein 1999, 219). Masculine aversion to domestic traps is the attitude in Squeeze's "Up the Junction" (1979); the Extreme song, "He-Man Woman Hater" (1990), takes such an anxiety to a murderous level. Dion's "The Wanderer" (1961) exhibits a macho, all-powerful independence in its cavalier celebration of a domesticity-dodging absentia: "I'm the type of guy who'll never settle down; [pretty girls are] all the same; I hug 'em and I squeeze 'em, they don't even know my name." In the intro, the bass defies the long-held tonic chord by hopping from ^1 to a neighboring ^2 on every beat (a similar avoidance of "staying home" is portrayed in the piano's shuffling boogie pattern above it); in the bridge ("well, I roam from town to town . . ."), warbling backing vocals mirror this departure with quick simultaneous chromatic *lower* neighbors of all members of the V triad. Thus Ricky Nelson: "in every port I own the heart of at least one lovely girl" ("Travelin' Man" [1961]), and "Wham-bam, thank you ma'am" (David Bowie, "Suffragette City" [1972]). In "All the Girls in the World Beware" (1974), which begins with an aggressive minor-pentatonic organ, Grand Funk boasts even of a manly disdain for housebound hygiene: "I got tartar on my teeth, but I don't care; I got dark brown stains in my underwear." Really.

Language differences separate binary genders by reflecting stereotypes in coded discourse. Conventionally, adjectives of approval such as "great, terrific, cool [or] neat" are neutral and therefore masculine whereas "adorable, charming, sweet, lovely, [and] divine" are used by women only (Lakoff 2004, 44–5). Such descriptors are judged feminine because they are primarily gentle and powerless (Cameron and Kulik 2003, 56–7). Grammar is also policed—if carelessly informal, it's typically masculine and if formally correct, feminine: with Grand Funk, it's a primitive "I got tartar," whereas female singers are more likely to express "I have" (see Karen's opening words in the Carpenters' "I Have You" [1976] and Camila Cabello's "I Have Questions" [2017]). Music can help define gender for listeners (especially adolescents working at individuation) who identify with expressed feelings and behavior that suit—and help form—their self-images, their perceptions of others, and their social networks, whether following or defying conventions. A performer may express gendered imagery variously as part of their biographical persona or as character or narrator within a song.[8] In a larger arena, record executives, artist managers, rock journalists, and popular-music scholars have perpetuated binary essentialisms, mostly male-dominant ones, for many decades.[9]

Masculinity in music. "Hegemonic masculinity" is a term coined in 1982 by Raewyn Connell for the force by which not only do the thoroughly masculine dominate over women, but they also hold power over other men with effeminate traces. A macho man can't be sensitive, use discerning vocabulary, cry, or be gay. Many feel driven to exercise and display punishing forms of manliness. The man's man drinks, gambles, and philanders, all justified by the frontier-spirit heroism of a Gable, Wayne, or Eastwood.[10] The he-man action figure is both predator and protector of women. The more manly, the less he can control his behavior—male aggression to the point of rape is excused as the expected result of an excess of testosterone, because males have "twenty to thirty times as much" as do females; the fact is, however, that "low levels of testosterone have been linked with aggression, and higher levels have been associated with calmness, happiness, and friendliness."[11] So, biological reasons for the behavior seem not well understood. The behavior is quite evident however, and frequently so in music. Consider Michael Jackson's abrasive "Beat It" (1982), in which the singer assumes a macho posture in spitting out tough talk to a gang-challenged boy who would be a man. "Funky and strong" are the popping snare, the verse's

---

[8] Some of the many important writers on this topic include Kristina Busse; Eric Clarke, Nicola Dibben, and Stephanie Pitts; Simon Frith; Theodore Gracyk; Judith/J. Jack Halberstam; Stan Hawkins; Dick Hebdige; Sally Macarthur; Caroline O'Meara; Tim Riley; Arlene Stein; Jodie Taylor; Sheila Whiteley; and Sarah Williams.

[9] See Frith 1981 and 1990, Frith and McRobbie 1990, Gaar 1992, Sayrs 1993–94, Solie 1993, Longhurst 1995, 121–3, Auslander 2000, 4–5, and Bennett 2001.

[10] The nature of hegemonic masculinity is treated in Foucault 1978, Dean 1996, 63–4, and Halberstam 1998, 274, and as related to music in Shepherd 1991, Bannister 2006, xii, xxiv–xxv, and 13, Halberstam 2012, 9, King 2013, 45–8 and 57, and deBoise 2015, 178–80.

[11] Both quotes are from Rutter and Schwartz 2012, 9–10. Kelly 2012, 144, reports that this sex steroid modulates neurotransmission in the brain in ways both "conducive or constraining to partnering."

aeolian ♭VI - ♭VII - i cadence, and especially Eddie Van Halen's harmonic-flashing distorted metal guitar guest solo that climbs mightily to gritty heights. A man cannot handle having been managed by a woman: "you're way on top now since you left me; when the sun comes up I'll be on top; . . . you're gonna cry" ("96 Tears" [1966] by ? and the Mysterians).

Nowhere is macho musical conduct more evident than in heavy metal and industrial rock, men's music for men, diametrically opposed to the puerile pop of teenybop bubblegum. Here, born in the hard side of Led Zeppelin, the hyper-powerful electric guitar is played in such near-constant masturbatory exercise, it exemplifies "cock rock"—a term in universal use upon creation in 1978 by Simon Frith and Angela McRobbie.[12] The style is epitomized in the crudely loud and pounding Mötley Crüe, Twisted Sister, and Iron Maiden, their tight Spandex showcasing "the muscle that gets pumped up by lust rather than by a workout at the gym" (Weinstein 2000, 221), and their legendarily treating groupies like warm sex dolls. The brute power chord—sounding only the authoritative root and fifth but omitting the conditional third, staggering in its distorted, nihilistic charge—is the technique's core currency; see Quiet Riot's "Cum On Feel the Noize" (1983). Related hard-rock styles are also given to masterful command of the fingerboard in fiercely extemporized solo shredding (Van Halen's tapped-out Frankenstrat in "Eruption" [1978]) and harsh duets (Pulp's "I'm a Man" [1998], 3:04–3:44, which features overdriven distortion in one guitar and overblown tremolo in the other). Male vocals are gruff shouts, made tense with tightened vocal cords, "produced overwhelmingly in the throat and mouth, with a minimum of recourse to the resonating chambers of the chest and head" (Shepherd 1991, 167); see Nine Inch Nails' "Big Man with a Gun" (1994).

It has been said of synthesizers that "technology and machines align most frequently with masculinity, with male-dominated disciplines of math and engineering [that carry] patriarchal power and control" (Peraino 2015, 294), but surely the content of their output is more important than their timbres or elements of construction in suggesting gendered roles. Even Roxy Music's ferocious "Editions of You" (1973) features a VCS3 synthesizer along with alto sax and Farfisa organ in order to portray the slinky crooning of the (female) Lorelei, and Donna Summer's synth-heavy "I Feel Love" (1977) would be characterized as sensually feminine. Michael Jackson's *Thriller* (1982) is replete

---

[12] See their 1990 reprint and also Walser 1993 and 2004, Waksman 1996 and 1999, Weinstein 2000, Whiteley 2000, Fast 2005, and Leonard 2007.

with multiple synthesizers, but its two most macho tracks, "Beat It" and "Billie Jean," are driven far more by electric guitars and bass. The relentless synths in Eurythmics' "Love Is a Stranger" (1983) bring to life Annie Lennox's female obsession. The staccato synth articulations in Lisa Lisa & Cult Jam's "I Wonder If I Take You Home" (1985) bring out a woman's emotional distance, the staccato sixteenths in Whitney Houston's "So Emotional" (1987) suggest an unanticipated woman's frisson at the end of the chorus: "ain't it shocking what love can do," and the staccato sixteenths in synthesized strings in Ana Gabriel's "Ay Amor" (1987) portray the tension of the female singer's lust. Rihanna's "Push Up on Me" (2007) synthesizes an insistent backbeat snare to suggest the heat of her desire, and her "Te Amo" (2009) creates a similar heat in a synthesized conga beat. I detect nothing particularly masculine in these and countless other synthesizer examples from women musicians, although the instrument's typically mechanistic quality (also true of the organ—the instrument about which Stravinsky complained, "the monster never breathes") may indeed support the androgynous nature of Lennox's drag.

Voices, largely as determined by biological sex, confer gender identity: in most cultures, low voices are traditionally identified as male (and authoritative), high as female (and less potent).[13] The comic irony of the anti-sissy "A Boy Named Sue" (1969) is multiplied by the rich depth of Johnny Cash's basso profundo. On the other hand, Robert Plant's, Steven Tyler's, and Rob Halford's very high full-voice tenors are never described as feminine, perhaps because of their strained-throat, distorted timbres. Many would say, then, that it's the use of the voice, as much as its inborn register, that relates to conventional gender roles. The harsh "macho" deliveries, rather than range, of John Lennon, Johnny Rotten, and Eddie Vedder (and Laurie Anderson's vocoder-altered tone) are often cited as gender signifiers.[14] Falsetto is more problematic; it is debated as to whether this pure, high male range (as in the doo-wop countertenor, in Frankie Valli, Justin Hawkins, or the Bee Gees) necessarily indicates a feminine, drag persona (the usual interpretation of Tiny Tim's twee "Tip-toe Thru' the Tulips with Me"

[13] Such stereotypes are considered in Graddol and Swann 1989, Green 1997, 30, Cusick 1999a, Warwick 2009, Hawkins 2016, Askerø 2017, and Kearney 2017, 193–4.

[14] Timbre, gender, and these particular voices are related to each other in Shepherd 1991, 170, Frith 1996, 193–4, Cusick 1999b, 34–6, Weatherall 2002, 52, Whiteley 2005, 131, Fast 2006, 367, Middleton 2007, 105, Fast 2010, 215, McClary 2013, 39–40, and Hawkins 2017, 1.

[1968]) or merely affords emotional drama (as in the retransitional climaxes that end the bridges of the Four Seasons' "Sherry" [1962]).[15]

Intersections with class and race. Graddol and Swann (1989), Jonathon Epstein (1998), Matthew Bannister (2006), and Nadine Hubbs (2014) have shown how class and gender intertwine. The working-class man (perhaps with dreams of transcending his position in hard or menial labor and his "deplorable" lack of social power, or perhaps resigned to his fate) and those in urban poverty would gravitate to more aggressive forms of rock than to bourgeois and (progressively "feminine") upper-class art rock and psychedelia, all worked out in the Brits' mods-vs.-rockers polemic of the 1960s. Such is the distance between leather jackets and Johnny Kidd & the Pirates' tumbling-strain-and-stop-time-whammy-bar lewd "Shakin' All Over" (1960) on one hand, and Carnaby Street and the Small Faces' precious "Itchycoo Park" (1967) on the other. In "Poor Side of Town" (1966), Johnny Rivers notes how "that rich guy" exercises dismissive misogyny from a position of class privilege. A decade later, the British skinhead subculture embraced the DIY, deliberately grungy, offhand aggression of punk as with the Sex Pistols, whose misogynistic "Bodies" (1977) besieges with loud sneers a girl who's had an abortion as "an animal; she was a bloody disgrace."

White heterosexual masculinity is often unmarked (as "normal") and assumed unless race and orientation are characterized otherwise. With roots in patriarchy and colonialism, received ideas about race and gender intersect just as do class and gender: to this day, the pernicious white-supremacist trope of the "vulnerable white woman threatened by the predatory black man" (Ware 1997, 138) is basic to arguments for various forms of segregation, such as through the American justice/penal system. The stereotype that men are mind-oriented and women body-centered is countered by fearful conventions about hypermasculine Black men. In modern times, puritanically repressed American whites have seen Blacks—culturally more open to a healthy appreciation of sexual pleasure—as hypersexual, Latinos as "hot blooded," and Asian men as hypomasculine (while Asian women are submissive; see John Cougar's "China Girl" [1982]): all are exotic Others.[16] Just to be clear about whites and Blacks, "research finds that

---

[15] For various views on the expressive meaning of falsetto, see Frith 1996, 194, Miller 2003, Riley 2004, 24, Whiteley 2007, 31, Hawkins 2009, 121–2 and 143, and McClary 2013, 37. Whether or not the operatic castrato voice or the countertenor, in and of themselves, should be assigned as feminine is debated in McClary 2013, 34, and Gioia 2015, 160.

[16] See more on the intersectionality of race (and other factors) and gender in Bordo 1990, hooks 1994 and 2004, Halberstam 1998, Hawkins 2002, Haraway 2003, Nagel 2003, Perry 2004, Bannister 2006, Peoples 2007, Warwick 2007, Lutz, Vivar, and Supik 2011, D'Emilio and Freedman 2012, Trier-Bieniek 2015, Williams and Tyree 2015, Djupvik 2017, Lester 2017, and Orenstein 2020. Cougar's

'the sexual behaviors of the two groups did not significantly differ.' Similarly, other researchers warn us against seeing Asian-Americans' reluctance to discuss sexuality in more public ways as asexuality" (Martin 1996, 16–17).

The sexualized role of Blacks in the formation of rock 'n' roll (we've mentioned the Dominoes' "Sixty Minute Man" [1951]) was behind the moral panic that led white leaders to ban the offensive music as dangerous to a civil society. The threat of Muddy Waters's carnal bravado in "I'm Your Hoochie Cooche Man" (1954) reappeared decades later in hip-hop records with the aggressively hypersexual, misogynistic, and homophobic posing that is endemic to male MCs' gritty rapping.[17] In one of hip-hop's first rap recordings, Sugarhill Gang's "Rapper's Delight" (1979), Big Bank Hank brags of stealing Lois Lane from Superman thus: "He's a fairy, I do suppose, flyin' through the air in pantyhose. . . . He can't satisfy you with his little worm, but I can bust you out with my supersperm!" (The idea here of booty shaking, "I'll put TNT in your behind!," forms the penetrative foundation for later odes to anal sex.)[18] In Janis Ian's "Society's Child" (1967), the white singer acquiesces to her mother's racist fear of her daughter's Black boyfriend; one can hear the family's social propriety in the refined harpsichord and the uncontrolled anger and pain experienced by the jilted Black "boy" in the Hammond B-3 organ's closing minor-pentatonic solo licks.

Feminine stereotypes

The feminist Catherine MacKinnon once wrote: "man fucks woman. Subject, verb, object" [1982: 541]. This observation encapsulates a pervasive and persistent piece of common sense about gender and sexuality: that only men can be active sexual subjects, while the role of women is to be passive objects of male desire. (Cameron and Kulik 2003, 29)

In this analysis, much can be understood about the coercive patriarchal picture of domesticated femininity that is so deeply entrenched in our culture (in medical, legal, clothing, cosmetics, advertising, religious, educational, etc. fields) that it seems natural to many. This is structural sexism. As we hear in "It Takes a Woman" from *Hello, Dolly!* (1964), "it takes a woman all powdered and pink to joyously clean out the drain in the sink." Judith Butler showed that

---

"China Girl" is discussed in Hisama 1993, 91–3. Leonard Cohen's "Suzanne" (1968) is seen as an exotic Other in Crafton 2018, 72. Orenstein 2020, 141, shows how the stereotype of huge Black penises is satirized in Lil Dicky's "Freaky Friday" (2018).

[17] Hypermasculinity in hip-hop culture is covered in Bradby 1993, Kimmel 2008, Woods 2011, and Lafrance, Burns, and Woods 2017.

[18] "Rapper's Delight" is given detailed analysis in Kajikawa 2015 and Orejuela 2015.

socially created, "performatively produced" dominant men's and submissive women's roles can, in fact, be made unstable and subject to change—especially in the middle class—by "troubling" them.[19] Thus Butler (1999, 29) understands Aretha Franklin's chorus in the Gerry Goffin/Carole King-penned "A Natural Woman (You Make Me Feel Like)" (1967) to reveal that only a man can excite the singer to that sensation, far better than, say, masturbation. Another song on the same album, "Ain't No Way" (written by Aretha's sister Carolyn), is more overtly misogynist; Aretha sings, "I know that a woman's duty is to help and love the man." Such examples—and Aretha's "Respect" (also 1967), now taken as a feminist anthem—illustrate how endemic structural sexism was. And is: in 2015, Selena Gomez's #1 Mainstream Rock hit, "Good for You," purrs in a soft, submissive voice, "Gonna wear that dress you like, skin-tight . . . 'cause I just wanna look good for you; . . . let me show how proud I am to be yours." One poignant rock song to lay bare how woman is kept silenced is Laura Nyro's "The Right to Vote" (1984). In its chorus, she alternates high and low vocal registers to express submission: "they say a [high:] woman's place is [low:] to wait and serve, [high:] under the veil, [low:] submissive and dear."

Peggy Lee brags of an ability to wash socks as a woman's attribute just as important as being able to bring a man to climax in "I'm a Woman" (1962; written by Jerry Lieber and Mike Stoller as an answer to Bo Diddley's "I'm a Man" [1955]). Gillian Gaar (1992, 107) characterizes Bobbi Martin's dutiful "For the Love of Him" (1970) as a "doormat" song. Such submission—often at the root of a masochistic woman's "torch song," in which she might express undying love for a cruelly abusive man, or in demonstrations such as Tammy Wynette's obsequious "Stand By Your Man" (1968)—is given as a reason that depression is twice as pervasive in women as in men.[20] Even at the height of the sexual revolution, hippies kept their earth women (see the Beatles' "Dear Prudence" [1968]) in their place as fertility objects; in a related way, Susan Fast (2009, 184–5) finds a suggestion of birth pains in Clare Torry's wordless vocal contribution to Pink Floyd's "Great Gig in the Sky" (1973). Another common trope in popular song is the mystical woman as fortune teller or evil witch; the Clovers' "Love

[19] See Butler 1999, Carlson 2012, 141–2, D'Emilio and Freedman 2012, 312, and Thiel-Stern 2014, 3. Bancroft 1989, 272, wonders if the more obviously phallic male uses his erection as the basis of this subjugation; for Whiteley (2000, 52) the man's point of view thus creates "the phallic woman." The history of the West's submission of women in the nineteenth and twentieth centuries is told in Dean 1996, 2 and 40, Halberstam 1998, 268, Kleinberg 1999, 142, Hewitt 2000, 4–5, Durham 2002, Diamond 2008, 21, Powell 2010, 65, Dabhoiwala 2012, 143, and Thiel-Stern 2014, 89.

[20] See Burns 1999–2000, 303–5, and Middleton 2007, 116, on the torch song, and Twenge 2017, 108, and Heywood and Garcia 2018, 306, on depression in this context.

Potion Number Nine" (1959), Cliff Richard's "Devil Woman" (1976, featuring sustained backwards guitar for an otherworldly, "masked" sound), and Holly Near's "Infatuation" (2000) are typifying examples.

The active male gaze generally controls how passive women see themselves.[21] It also governs how they perform:

> In "A Good Man is Hard to Find" [1927], for example, Bessie Smith frequently begins a vocal phrase with a growl of "sexual" aggressiveness appropriated from the traditional "macho" timbre, then moves to her standard, hard, "woman-as-sex-object"' timbre for the majority of the phrase, and then lets the phrase fall away with a hint of the softer "woman-as-nurturer" timbre. Such changes in voice tone imply a dialogue with the unseen male as voyeur, initial aggressiveness and closure moving to the openness of personal encounter. (Shepherd 1991, 172)

Linda in *Flower Drum Song* ("I Enjoy Being a Girl," 1958) and Kim in *Bye Bye Birdie* ("How Lovely to Be a Woman," 1960) demonstrate Broadway's mid-century understanding of how girls know they are attractive—it's signaled by wolf-whistling boys. For Frank Zappa and the Mothers of Invention, the woman's desire to accommodate at any length is the mark of "Plastic People" (1967): "she paints her face with plastic goo and wrecks her hair with some shampoo." Among many others, later artists such as Kate Bush, Sia, Bow Wow Wow, and even PJ Harvey are discussed as fulfilling erotic fantasies for the male listener.[22]

We've previously discussed language differences between the genders, as researched by Graddol and Swann, and by Robin Lakoff. "Your scarf, it was apricot" (Carly Simon's "You're So Vain" [1972]) hardly seems a line that could have been uttered by a male, for both the precision of color and the elegance of the syntax. Women tend to hedge declaratives with tag questions, such as when a description is followed by "you get the picture?" in the Shangri-Las' "The Leader of the Pack" (1964). Similarly, a woman's rising intonation when *not* expressing a literal question undercuts any attempt at assertiveness; such shallow "uptalk" pervades Moon Zappa's featherbrained speech in her father Frank's "Valley Girl" (1982). Baby talk, which mothers use with infants, was used as a sign of submission in film by Marilyn Monroe and Jayne Mansfield (Stilwell 2010, 72). Musically, whispery baby talk, uptalk, and a male-imitating "downtalk" are

---

[21] Woman as (perhaps unknowingly) objectified by the male gaze is the topic of Lacan 1982, 29 and 48–9, Powell 2010, 174, and Dyhouse 2017, 10. The phenomenon particularly governs music videos; see Dibben 1999, 336, Burns 1999–2000, 306 and 316, and Lieb 2013, 149–50.

[22] See, respectively, O'Brien 2002, 214, Hansen 2017, 97–8, Watson 1994, 50, and Dibben 1999, 337–8.

combined by Meri Wilson in her innuendo-filled "Telephone Man" (1977) and "Peter the Meter Reader" (1981).

Following the leads of Hélène Cixous and Luce Irigaray (both of whom wrote of *l'écriture féminine*, whereby specifically feminine writing could issue supposedly only from a woman's libido) and Janet Wolff (who wrote of *la peinture féminine*), music scholars including Marcia Citron and Susan McClary have debated as to whether there exists what might be called *la musique féminine*, a music that could only have been written by a woman.[23] Björk speaks of her womanly inspiration: "When I write tunes, they're more about the foreplay than the intercourse, because as a true female, I guess that's what I'm more interested in!" (Evans 1994, 84). As a specific example, the rolling waves that characterize a woman's serial orgasms (as opposed to the male's typically single climax) give rise to the cyclic imagery in Debbie Harry's "French Kissin" (1986), in which the lead singer's line "lips are in motion" is answered by backing singers softly singing "ocean to ocean to ocean, ocean to ocean to ocean" underneath Harry's "oh-oh-oh" melisma sustained while slowly alternating ^3 and ^4. As also described by Lucy O'Brien, Susan McClary has hailed Laurie Anderson's "non-linear and typically 'feminine'" "O Superman (for Massenet)" (1982) as a subversion of "phallo-centric, triumphalist structures of Western classical music" (2002, 153–4). Perhaps, though, men can pretend to a role *féminine*. As if donning a feminine mask, Barry White gradually builds to repeated tensions that then drop back in waves (also suggested on the foreground in very liquid wahs in rhythm and lead guitars) in his seductive "I'm Gonna Love You Just a Little More Baby," and Marvin Gaye adds a magnetic Donna Summer-like vocal fry to his timbre when he asks "I'm asking you, baby, to get it on with me" in "Let's Get It On" (both 1973). When Gaye sings "the waves are rising" and ascends nonaggressively through an inverted dominant chord, IV - V - vi - V6 - I, in "Sexual Healing" (1982), he seems to be ministering to a woman's fantasies more than expressing his own "masculine" ones. The key relation of sex and waves will be discussed more thoroughly in Chapter 4.

Despite the legendary talents of Orpheus and all of his male followers through the millennia, it has long been a cultural position that because of its close ties to emotion, music itself is a feminine art. Particularly through the first half of

---

[23] See Abbate 1993, 229, Citron 1993, 159, Solie 1993, 4, Sayrs 1993–1994, 50–1, Beizer 1994, 152–3 and 164, Reynolds and Press 1995, 284, Gracyk 2001, 195 and 199, Lorraine 2001, 12, Macarthur 2002, 11–12, 14, 18, 70, and 113, O'Brien 2002, 176, Whiteley 2005, 2, 70, 72, and 81, and 2009, 210, McClary 2006, 206, deBoise 2014, 231–2, Pecknold 2016, 80, and Kearney 2017, 29 and 218.

the twentieth century, male musicians were often seen as sissies, and "musician" was code for "homosexual."[24] Liz Phair speaks of the rituals of mothers' singing to infants and young girls chanting rhymes, adding, "I don't think boys do this" (Centawer 2018, 62). Despite these practices, a patriarchal train of thought had it that women could sing and play piano (for more than a century, a home parlor divertissement) or strum a folk acoustic guitar, but not write songs, play most other instruments—particularly electric guitar (Sister Rosetta Tharpe notwithstanding), electronica (Pauline Oliveros aside), or drums (Moe Tucker leading the way in contradiction)—with any skill before mid-1970s punk and new wave, or for that matter produce records, whereas men have always done all of this with authority.[25]

Because aggression has been considered masculine, and romantic passivity feminine, "authentic," artistic, and raw rock music had long been the exclusive province of men while women were confined to less-valued commercial, conventional pop styles. (Anomalies like Joan Baez and Janis Joplin would be seen as radical.)[26] An interesting example in this discussion is Helen Reddy's "I Am Woman" (1972), accepted by many as a proud and sincere, early feminist anthem but castigated by others as slick, exploitative pop. As Taylor and Laing characterize an analysis by Frith and McRobbie, "not even the progressive message of her song can rescue the voice from its consumerist lack of authenticity (its stylistic features belong to a popular music without folk roots); [for them,] Reddy's voice is 'cute, show-biz self-consciousness' [and] that of an idealised consumer" (1979, 46–7). What Taylor and Laing say about Reddy's vocal effect is true, and the sweet head tone (as opposed to deep-chested) performance's untested, narrow dynamic range—particularly in the lightly sung would-be-climactic words "strong," "invincible," and "woman" (!)—adds to this problem. But the song also fails for its sing-songy rhythms and its blithe tonal language: instead of a hard use of minor-pentatonic grit, with not a single blue note, all

---

[24] Maus 2006, 207. An 1840s incident based on the same supposition is recounted in Scott 1994, 93. See also Cook 2005, 82, and Cavicchi 2011, 179.

[25] See facets of such ideas in Gaar 1992, 92, Bayton 1993, 185–6, Evans 1994, 14, Green 1997, 53, Frith, Straw, and Street 2001, 231, Gracyk 2001, 172, Hoke 2001, 414, Grajeda 2002, 238, O'Brien 2002, 206, Mahon 2004, 206–7, Riley 2004, 124, Auslander 2006, 102, Biddle and Jarman-Ivens 2007, 12, Reddington 2007, 107, McCracken 2015, Kearney 2017, 119, and Sciortino 2018, 36. In Latinx culture, the accordion is assigned as a man's instrument (Berrios-Miranda, Dudley, and Habell-Pallán 2018, 43)—perhaps because of its tumescent swells?

[26] Such pop/rock sex-role stereotypes are discussed in Frith and Goodwin 1990, 370, Frith and McRobbie 1990, Middleton 1990, 260, Weinstein 1994, 17, Coates 1998, 81, Schippers 2002, 25, Warwick 2007, 6 and 36–7, Arnold 2014, 44–5, de Boise 2015, 72, Coulter 2017, 267, and Kearney 2017, 93 and 118.

pitches politely conform to the major mode in a graceful, sequence-bound melody; an easy-listening verse/chorus modulation; a clearly notated (prescribed and therefore domesticated) brass arrangement; and a radio-format fade-out to inconsequential nothingness. Almost all aspects of the production say watered-down pop. Interestingly, though, the single blatty trombone underneath the second verse (1:06–1:28) seems to represent well both the casual bending and breaking the singer has suffered at men's hands, and the firm determination by which such experiences lead her forward in "wisdom born of pain."

Race intersects with feminine qualities in different ways than it does with masculine. Whitney Peoples finds that rap music is "highly marketable in America because of already existing ideologies of racism that long ago named the black male as supreme aggressor and physical and sexual threat. Similarly, [these ideologies] designated black women as hypersexual and morally obtuse" (2007, 24). Dionne P. Stephens and Layli D. Phillips (2003) identify eight "sexual scripts" for African American women in hip-hop, with roots in such pre-Second World War racist stereotypes as the exotic and oversexed Jezebel, the asexual nurturing Mammy, the contemptuous and emasculating Matriarch, and the lazily breeding Welfare Mother. Their eight scripts are characterized succinctly thus by Williams and Tyree (2015, 55), with musical examples given by Stephens and Phillips except where bracketed:

The Diva: "a woman [with attitude] who had material items, which she attained herself"; expects to be worshipped—e.g., Destiny's Child, "Independent Women, Part 1" (2001)

The Gold Digger: "looking for men based on what financial and material goods they could provide"—e.g., L L Cool J, "Jingling Baby" (1990)

The Freak: "calling attention to their [uninhibited, often kinky] sexuality"—e.g., Lil' Kim, "How Many Licks" (2000)

The Dyke: "artist expresses desire for or mention of sexual interactions with other women"—e.g., 2 Live Crew, "Bulldagger Stole My Bitch" (1996)

The Gangster Bitch: "women were performing illegal acts, particularly . . . in partnership with men"—e.g., Apache, "Gangsta Bitch" (1992)

The Sister Savior: "depicted in situations where they expressed moral or religious reasons for not being sexually active"—[e.g., Erica Mason, "Beautiful" (2015)]

The Earth Mother: "women who did not have straightened hair and instead wore hairstyles considered to be Afrocentric, such as dreadlocks, short-shaved hairstyles, braids, or Afros"—e.g., Lauryn Hill, "Doo Wop (That Thing)" (1998)

The Baby Mama: "mothers of children born out of wedlock were depicted arguing with the child's father in front of the child in such a way that the child seemed to be used in the argument"—e.g., Luniz, "My Baby Mamma" (1997).

Nontraditional Gender Roles

Having considered traditional gender roles, we turn to the knotty ways in which recent Western culture and therefore popular music have turned these on their heads. It's long been known that all people carry both masculine and feminine traits as potential aspects of their personalities, as a repertoire of learned yin/yang behaviors. As noted previously, Carl Jung wrote about the syzygy of opposing anima and animus psychic energies, the union of "contrasexual archetypes" integral (when not repressed) to a healthy consciousness. Very much in tune with this idea, Alanis Morissette asked of her desired mate, "Are you both masculine and feminine?" in "21 Things I Want in a Lover" (2002). Writ large, Western cultural periods may be defined by degrees of repression of the contrasexual other: the classical Enlightenment period tended to order gender representations strictly (effeminacy in men was socially unacceptable in most classes) whereas the following Romantic period of the nineteenth century allowed for the gothic representation of a wide, "dark" variety of gendered balances (to the point of projecting a monstrous *Doppelgänger*). The modern era, with its celebration of scientific exactitude and categorization, saw a retrenchment to strictly, patriarchically defined gendered dress and behavior, partially thrown aside in the freer postmodern climate (wherein Lada Gaga, for instance, self-identifies as the monster).[27] Early twentieth-century women bursting through submissive expectations by claiming suffrage and entering competitive colleges and public nightlife, men taking on more white-collar cubicle jobs that required civility, and the eventual endings of compulsory military conscription in the United Kingdom and United States all led to the collapse of many stereotypical gender roles.[28]

Thus, institutional assignments of gender traits and the stigmata that come with deviance from them change across time within cultures—especially as social

---

[27] The union of opposing gendered souls in a single being is discussed in Lacan 1982, 6–7, Žižek 1991, 47, and Hawkes 2004, 32. This theme in Romantic literature is the topic of Moores 2010.
[28] These changes are explored in Williams 2007, 147–9, King 2013, 55, and Seidman 2015, 48 and 111–2.

requirements evolve—as well as across different ones. Judith Halberstam notes that masculinity sides with essentialism "to define itself as nonperformative," "as 'natural,' 'original,' and absolute."[29] But as investigated in feminist and queer theory, gender codes are unstable and hierarchical, with hegemonic prestige and power conferred in patriarchically ordered arrangements.[30] Judith Butler (1999) recognized that masculine power constructs the feminine to be of lesser value, lacking agency, and that such behaviors are not only culturally established, regulated, and unconsciously learned through childhood and adolescence but performed (and parodied in drag) as scripts—as opposed to biological drives—under the domineering male gaze. Julia Serano problematizes the notion that gender is largely or entirely performed in social scripts: "Sure, I can perform gender: I can curtsy, or throw like a girl, or bat my eyelashes. But *performance* doesn't explain why certain behaviors and ways of being come to me more naturally than others" (2010, 85); "further, since some attributes that are considered feminine (e.g., being more in tune with one's emotions) or masculine (e.g., being preoccupied with sex) are clearly affected by our hormones, attempts by some gender theorists to frame femininity and masculinity as being entirely artificial or performative seem misplaced" (2016, 75). Victor Lockhart has said, "As America limps toward recognizing the rights of transgendered people, there is a growing movement to bring visibility to those who embrace no gender at all. Known as Nonbinary or genderqueer, these individuals aren't specific about the nature of their gender because they choose to live beyond its confines or preferences to remain gender fluid" (quoted in Perez 2021, 181–2).

If gender traits are learned, they can be resisted. Early in this chapter, we listed a few rock songs in which singers expressed a desire to "switch" gender roles; such play is also expressed by Lady Gaga in "G.U.Y." (2013), in which she suggests a link between gender and sex acts: she speaks, "Feast as this audio guides you through new and exciting positions," then sings, "I wanna be the girl under you; I wanna be your g.u.y." In "In or Out" (1997), Ani DiFranco adds non-chord tones to triads in subverting norms accompanying the lyric, "He says, 'Call me, Miss DiFranco, if there's anything I can do'; I say, 'It's Mr. Di [stop time] Franco to you.'" By the 1970s, men came to accept having emotions and other vulnerabilities that were no longer seen as the sole property of the feminine and even learned to get in touch with their feelings. The Schwarzenegger type

---

[29] Halberstam 2007, 375; see also Plummer 2002.
[30] General thoughts on cultural and political aspects of gender expression can be read in Cook 2005, 81–2, Diamond 2008, 48–9, Weeks 2011, 69–70, and Halberstam 2012, 71 and 75–6.

was no longer the sole male role model; once a misogynist, a reformed and domesticated John Lennon was portrayed as a progressive househusband from the 1975 birth of his son Sean to his death in 1980. Regressives saw this trend as a crisis of masculinity; in his book *Iron John* (1991), poet Robert Bly denounced the "soft male" emerging from too close a social relationship between men and women.[31] The 1980s "Sensitive New-Age Guy," perhaps a "tree hugger" with "raised consciousness," was "portrayed as a hapless and unappealing loser" (Donaghue 2018, 143). Anxiety showed in hypervirile cowboy poses such as that of the brush-clearing George W. Bush (a character type spoofed early on in Andy Warhol's 1968 film *Lonesome Cowboys* and later in Devo's 1980 "Whip It" video). The ambiguity of her piano's thirdless tonic chords and deceptive V - ♭VI cadences bring a touch of confused anxiety to Tori Amos's "Real Men" (2001): "What's a man now, what's a man mean? Is he rough or is he rugged, cultural and clean?" Confusion becomes panic when gender crossing is linked, as commonly done, to the once vilified practice of gay sex, but late-century social pressures (including environmentalism as well as fast-growing empathic support for gay rights and nonbinary recognitions) began to require men to be less macho and rapacious, breaking past patriarchal binary portraits. The 1990s "metrosexual" was an affluent, gay-aware, and confidently glamorous straight man who might have a yen for decor. Some sociologists such as Raewyn Connell (1995) wrote of "multiple masculinities" whereby men were able to demonstrate a range of gender-defining features—sometimes linked to intersectional components such as class, race, age, and sexuality. Others denied there need be any gender-related link between biological sex and personality traits at all. In the new century, "masculinity was declared to be 'broken' and 'toxic.'"[32] The late century social transition produced tragic figures: Kurt Cobain, who struggled, unto a 1994 suicide, against his father's macho modeling, once said "I definitely feel closer to the female side of the human being than I do the male—or the American idea of what a male is supposed to be" (Muto 1995, 71). In "I'm Not

[31] See also Epstein and Straub 1991, and Kimmel 2008. The trauma of the Oedipus complex leads R. W. Connell to see adult masculinity as fragile, as it is "founded on the tragic encounter between desire and culture," and to see a refusal of "the phallic position" of power as having drastic consequences (1995, 12 and 20). The "soft male" allegation is of course a charge of sexual impotence; "in Lacanian terms [the creation of the sensitive male] means attacking the Phallus, the point of intersection between patriarchal dominance of culture and the bodily experience of masculinity" (Connell 1995, 232).

[32] Orenstein 2020, 2. The metrosexual is discussed in Hawkins 2002, 133–4, and 2009, 106, King 2013, 52, Seidman 2015, 83 and 85, and Friend 2017, 366. Re multiple masculinities, see, for example, Berger, Wallis, and Watson 1996, Halberstam 1998, 14, Schippers 2002, 29–30, de Boise 2015, 11 and 186, Kearney 2017, 29, and Scholnick and Miller 2018, 334.

a Man" (2014), Morrissey decries typically reckless macho men's moves in an initially grotesque chord progression that then becomes philosophical, sad and self-aware: "[Db] Don Juan, picaresque, [C7] wife-beater vest; [Cb] cold hand, ice man, [Bb7] warring cave man—[Gb] well if [Gbm] this is what it [Db] takes to des-[Bbm]-cribe, [Gb-Gbm] I'm [Ab7] not a man."

Despite society's commonly slow acceptance of unstable gender identities, a parade of artists, musicians among them, led the vanguard in disturbing the status quo. Beginning with the seductive late-1920s crooners like Rudy Vallee, Bing Crosby, and Frank Sinatra, who expressed with intimate subtleties a vulnerable new male tenderness to eroticized female listeners through the first electrically amplified phonographs, recorded popular music entered the rock 'n' roll era with Johnnie Ray, who—when jilted—cried about crying with outsized unmanly emotions in large vocal leaps, lots of sighing appoggiaturas, drawn-out consonants that postponed and weakened the placement of vowels, and heightened pitch in the last verse of "Cry" (1951).[33] In "Woman" (1980), John Lennon graces the tonic harmony with a tender, vulnerable major seventh in the chorus, gently rises and falls with apprehensive contrition through stepwise I - ii - iii - ii - I triads in the verses that can't manage to progress, and breaks off in half cadences on expressive 4-3 dissonances to concede his crippling "thoughtlessness"—and on which he also reveals "the little child inside the man," literally fracturing that last persona as if reverting to a damaged, pre-Oedipal creature who has yet to form its gender.

Kanye West's inward-looking 2008 album *808s and Heartbreak* broke behavioral stereotypes for both men and for Blacks. As a middle-class lifelong poet having grown up in bourgeois surroundings, West meditates in this work not on women and money but on life's dreams and values in the face of his struggle with the damaging effects of fame; it resists the stereotypical misogyny of hip-hop "by privileging a different kind of black masculinity; that is, one focussed less on 'domination, aggressiveness, competitiveness, stoicism and control' and more

---

[33] Crooners and the genderist slander they endured are front and center in McCracken 2015, Hajdu 2016, 67–8, and Dyhouse 2017, 1. Of course there are many earlier examples of male sensitivity in song, as in the nineteenth-century *Lied* and chanson directed at an absent lover. "In any man who utters the other's absence *something feminine* is declared; this man who waits and who suffers from his waiting is miraculously feminized," as Roland Barthes writes (1978, 14). And a man's ability to speak the woman's soul has perhaps no stronger forerunner than James Joyce in Molly Bloom's soliloquy at the end of *Ulysses* (1920–22). Eve Kosovsky Sedgwick locates Captain Vere in Melville's posthumously completed *Billy Budd* in between the 1950s–1960s "tears" songs and a nineteenth-century woman's sentimentality; she says Vere exemplifies "a struggle of masculine identity with emotions or physical stigmata stereotyped as feminine" (2008, 146).

on 'love, affection, pain, and grief'" (Lafrance, Burns, and Woods 2017, 296). The track "Welcome to Heartbreak" opens with a dark aeolian phrase on cello that is then taken up by a synthesized bass; a keyboard then reworks the cello idea over an electronic snare backbeat and strong-beat bass drum synthesized on a Roland TR-808 drum machine (a throwback to the early 1980s), this mechanistic foil replaced by a vocal made gloomy with echo. West sings with a heavy dose of autotune, which "weirding of his voice helped him to achieve musical and emotive effects that his natural voice could never achieve on its own" (Bradley 2017, 213). With or without such effects, singing in and of itself is unusual for males in hip-hop, as women typically take on such roles; guest artist Kid Cudi sings gently about the vision of real life that West perceives only in a dizzy state ("my head keeps spinnin'"). In the sparse third verse, percussion falls away as a low synth wash reinforces the loneliness of West's lament; the outro and distorted final chorus "communicate a desperate and sorrowful sentiment of being trapped in this lifestyle."[34] West deems emotional connection to be more important than the material goods he's spent a career amassing.

Ted Gioia writes of the embarrassment men feel in admitting to listening to "wimpy" love songs (2015, 45–6). Frank Zappa had a cynical aversion to romance:

> I think one of the causes of bad mental health in the United States is that people have been raised on "love lyrics." You're a young kid and you hear all those "love lyrics," right? Your parents aren't telling you the truth about love, and you can't really learn about it in school. You're getting the bulk of your "behavior norms" mapped out for you in the lyrics to some dumb fucking love song. It's a subconscious training that creates a desire for an imaginary situation which will *never exist for you*. People who buy into that mythology go through life feeling that they got cheated out of something. (Zappa 1989, 89)

Table 2.1 presents a representative sample of rock-era recordings (in R&B, rock, pop, soul, psychedelic, folk-rock, glam, disco, metal, indie, emo, and hip-hop styles) that in some way exhibit "feminine" qualities in men who either sing or are sung about. Chapter 4 will look more closely at the ways men as well as women address romance in pop songs.

Women's roles were problematized in these decades right alongside men's. Before we address deeper subversions such as cross-dressing and transgendering,

---

[34] Burns, Woods, and Lafrance 2016, 165; this essay includes a wonderful discussion of the accompanying video's expressive techniques.

Table 2.1 Musical Examples of Feminine Qualities in Men

Chart Year	Artist	Song Title	Comments
1956	Little Willie John	Fever	Singer expresses lust as malady brought on by a woman
1959	Bo Diddley	Crackin' Up	"I do your laundry and your cooking too . . ."
1960	Miracles	Shop Around	Smokey Robinson sings of a mother's advice
1961	Elvis Presley	Can't Help Falling in Love	Singer powerless against inevitabilities of bridge's falling fifths (C♯7 - f♯m - B7 - em - A) and of cadential 6/4s
1962	Joanie Sommers	Johnny Get Angry	Her man is not macho enough; crude opening parallel fifths from I5 to vi5 are played meekly, soft and low in the electric guitar
1963	Beatles	Please Please Me	Sexual demands ("come on, come on!") expressed politely
1965	Miracles	The Tracks of My Tears	Taboo of the crying man
1965	Beatles	Help!	Shrieks for help; change to minor iii and vi triads for "I'm not so self-assured," "I feel so insecure"
1965	Beatles	You've Got to Hide Your Love Away	Subtle vocal dynamics express frustration in loss; stylized sobbing in melisma on "state I'm i - i - in"; concluding flutes more sensitive than Dylan's harmonica
1966	Simon and Garfunkel	For Emily, Whenever I May Find Her	Soft acoustic guitars; "I kissed your honey hair with my grateful tears" sung over major seventh chord on ♭VII
1967	Scott McKenzie	San Francisco (Be Sure to Wear Flowers in Your Hair)	"Gentle people with flowers in their hair" sung over tentative, non-goal-oriented iii and vi chords
1969	Elvis Presley	Don't Cry Daddy	Taboo of the crying man
1970	Neil Young	Only Love Can Break Your Heart	Vulnerability in unison double-tracked falsetto, major-seventh tonic chord in verse and minor mediant (for broken heart) in chorus
1970	Jackson 5	I'll Be There	Male sensitivity; bridge "I'll be there to comfort you" submits in gentle falling fourths from deep in the deferential flat side: ♭III - ♭VII - IV - I

1970	Led Zeppelin	Tangerine	Soft acoustic guitars at slow tempo; emptiness expressed in sustained eleventh sung at non-resolving cadential "between"
1971	Jimi Hendrix	Drifting	"Drifting on a sea of forgotten teardrops" over aimless chords in accent-less, meandering changing meters
1971	James Taylor	You've Got a Friend	Empathetic opening tonicizes troubled vi chord; chorus features sensitive major seventh on tonic
1971	Led Zeppelin	Battle of Evermore	"Plant's male traveller submits to the so-called Queen of Light," surrounded by mandolins and acoustic guitar" (Smith 2017, 411; see also Auslander 2006, 102)
1972	Roxy Music	2HB	Bryan Ferry exhibits the "Sapphonic voice" (Wood 2006, 32) in his ode to Humphrey Bogart
1973	Marvin Gaye	Let's Get It On	"We're all sensitive people with so much to give" in high register embellished by falsetto
1976	Rod Stewart	Tonight's the Night	Verse alternates tonic with seductive major seventh in IV chord
1977	Bee Gees	More Than a Woman	Sensitive major seventh chord appears on C (overall tonic), E (center of verses) and D (V of prechoruses)
1978	Village People	Macho Man	"I've got to be a macho man" comes off as parody
1980	John Lennon	Woman	Contrition expressed tenderly with vulnerable major-seventh tonic chords, V4-3 suspensions on "thoughtlessness," "the little child inside the man"
1983	The Smiths	This Charming Man	Title sung with emotive melismas on "charm" and "man"
1986	Depeche Mode	A Question of Lust	Longing with major seventh sung against tonic, sensitive but noncommittal iii chord
1987	Def Leppard	Hysteria	Sensitive singing and unresolved Vsus4 chord, despite distorted guitars and loud electronic drums
1987	The Smiths	I Started Something I Couldn't Finish	Impotently thwarted aeolian: "I started [bVI7] something and [bVII7] now I'm [VII#7] not too [I] sure"

(Continued)

Table 2.1 (Continued)

Chart Year	Artist	Song Title	Comments
1987	Paul Young	Why Does a Man Have to Be Strong	Opposes "masculine" voice ("I'm not lyin' when I say that . . .") with falsetto for "feminine" attitude (". . . you can hurt me too")
1987	R.E.M.	It's the End of the World as We Know It	Vulnerable major seventh on IV chord and resignation in minor mediant
1988	Richard Thompson	Don't Tempt Me	Opening parallel fifths and hard vocal minor-pentatonic scale satirize macho stance
1989	The Cure	Love Song	Cadences on impotent minor v chord
1991	Right Said Fred	I'm Too Sexy	Entirely in vulnerable vocal fry
1993	Björk	Venus as a Boy	Soft wave-like Rhodes arpeggiations
1993	Pet Shop Boys	Can You Forgive Her?	Tragic aeolian: "She made [i] fun of you, and [v6] even in bed said she was [iv6] gonna go and get herself a [v6] real man instead"
1995	Jeff Buckley	Mojo Pin	"High, gentle voice enters imperceptibly from within intricate, delicate guitar movement" (Goldin-Perschbacher 2007, 217), vulnerable tonic major seventh chord
1998	Pulp	I'm a Man	Verses feature vulnerable vocal fry
2001	Saves the Day	At Your Funeral	First verse sung over soft unaccompanied guitar played one string at a time
2001	Tori Amos	Real Men	"Is he rough or is he rugged, cultural and clean?" Ambiguity in piano's thirdless tonic chords and thirdless "real man" $\flat$VI5 - $\flat$VII5 - I cadences
2002	Beck	Lonesome Tears	Lugubrious tempo; sustained, mournful low strings
2002	Euan Morton	Stranger in This World	I "can't be a man; I'm too fragile" in I - $\flat$VII - $\flat$VI - minor v6 lament; about Boy George
2005	Sufjan Stevens	John Wayne Gacy, Jr.	Long high mournful "ooh" melisma on slow trill, as on the word "dead"
2008	Kanye West	Welcome to Heartbreak	Male singing (West and Kid Cudi) unusual in hip-hop; low synth wash reinforces loneliness
2011	Ricky Martin	Te Busco y Te Alcanzo	"Me pierdo en tu llanto. . . . Soy flecha perdida"; loss expressed by sensitive solo cello
2019	Khalid	Talk	Vulnerable autotune for apologetic sensitivity

we can outline a few ways in which women transgressed gender norms. Many early blues singers were tough women who would push their men around, like Marion Harris ("St. Louis Blues" [1920]) and Ma Rainey ("Don't Fish in My Sea" [1926]). Rock 'n' roll allowed rebellious female listeners to develop fantasies of power: Motown empowered women to take charge (the Supremes' "Stop! In the Name of Love" [1965]).[35] Table 2.2 lists a number of rock-era recordings in which women defy gender expectations, as either performers or characters. Strong and daring examples increase in number following feminism's second wave in the 1960s–1970s ("women's liberation"), especially in movements such as 1970s' punk and the 1990s' riot grrrls and kinderwhores that came with feminism's third wave, with large numbers of women finally able to record their own compositions for the first time. Whereas "masculine" women in broader society (e.g., Janet Reno) were often openly ridiculed, strong women found great support as rock musicians.[36] Ironically, an "enlightened sexism" that ensued pretends that the work of feminism is complete in the twenty-first century, and women can now claim their attractiveness to men as being under their own control; such is suggested in Marianne Faithfull's general "sounds of damage or disability" (Apolloni 150), Madonna's pride in her looks, the Spice Girls' Barbie style, and Pink's reclaiming promiscuity as a virtue in "Slut Like You" (2012).[37] As a direct outgrowth of the 1980s "sex wars," in which Catherine MacKinnon and Andrea Dworkin argued that pornography objectified women but Gayle Rubin and Eve Sedgwick held that it was not in and of itself antifeminist—many now believe it can be a sex-positive, liberating force—Madonna provides a particularly trenchant example of a woman reclaiming ownership of her sexual materialization. "Where once sexualized representations of women in the media presented them as the passive, mute objects of an assumed male gaze, today women are presented as active, desiring sexual subjects who choose to present themselves in a seemingly objectified manner because it suits their liberated interests to do so" (Gill 2009, 100). Madonna and Lady Gaga, Miley Cyrus, Nicki Minaj and others who followed her are anything but inactive and "mute," the sure sign that they are not girlie-objects, victims of sexual and economic commodification: they are empowered, critiquing subjects. Sleater-Kinney

---

[35] See Warwick 2007, 55, re the Motown choreographer's choices of aggressive body language, such as the Supremes' straight-arm, palm-out gesture that exclaims "Stop!"

[36] For thoughts on women's "masculinity," see McClary 1991, 17–19, Bradby 1993, Halberstam 1998, Clawson 1999, Stein 1999, Rutter and Schwartz 2012, and Kurtis 2018.

[37] Enlightened sexism and its traces (particularly regarding Madonna) are covered in Paglia 1993, Longhurst 1995, 125, Douglas 2010, Householder 2015, and Friend 2017, 83–4.

Table 2.2 Musical Examples of Women Defying Gender Expectations

Chart Year	Artist	Song Title	Comments
1964	Honeycombs	Have I the Right?	Four men on front line backed by aggressive woman drummer
1968	Marvelettes	Destination: Anywhere	"The Marvelettes adopted the stance of an aloof, brooding, and, above all, *masculine* archetype" (Warwick 2007, 201)
1969	Tina Turner	Bold Soul Sister	"Screeches, grunts and squeals" like James Brown (Fast 2010, 225)
1971	Yoko Ono	Open Your Box	Angry ululating vocal for feminist appeal
1975	Suzi Quatro	Your Mamma Won't Like Me	Aggressive minor-pentatonic melody; thrusting horns; Quatro plays phallic electric bass
1978	X-Ray Spex	Identity	Rant against obsession over beauty with aeolian power-chord lament progression, I5 - bVII5 - bVI5 - V5
1979	Raincoats	Fairytale in the Supermarket	Escape from misogyny in aggressively loud, harsh punk instrumentation, sneering vocal
1979	Slits	Love and Romance	Ridicules Rod Stewart's male-centered approach to lovemaking, piano often atonal
1981	Joan Jett and the Blackhearts	Bad Reputation	Defiant feminist anthem: "A girl can do what she wants to and that's what I'm gonna do"
1981	Pretenders	Bad Boys Get Spanked	Chrissie Hynde sorts out an asshole punk over raucous drums and guitars
1985	Pat Benatar	Invincible	Powerful aeolian do-or-die stand
1990	Babes in Toyland	Swamp Pussy	Kat Bjelland shouts over her distorted guitar
1991	Bikini Kill	Suck My Left One	Hanna's voice points "to the hypocrisy of a culture in which young women are expected to remain pure" (Apolloni 2016, 159)
1992	Tori Amos	Me and a Gun	"The feminine voice of courage and power" (Whiteley 2005, 85); aeolian dirge on rape
1993	Breeders	Do You Love Me Now?	Aggressive distorted guitars with deep tremolo on minor-pentatonic (025)s
1993	PJ Harvey	Dry	"A stinging insult against . . . masculinity" (Lankford 2010, 37); "you leave me dry" sung against suddenly desolate solo guitar
1993	Queen Latifah	U.N.I.T.Y.	Rap: "I bring wrath to those who disrespect me like a dame"

Year	Artist	Song	Description
1994	Liz Phair	Go West	Dissonant tonic eleventh chords make lines like "69 in the afternoon" sound matter-of-fact
1994	Hole	Doll Parts	Female parts disembodied in Courtney Love's separately enunciated litany
1998	Natalie Merchant	Ophelia	Loudness and tension grow as song progresses from innocence to wild rebellion
1998	Alanis Morissette	Would Not Come	"If I am masculine, I will be taken more seriously" in unstable phrygian scale
1999	Bitch and Animal	Pussy Manifesto	Rap over solo drumset; "I am so sick of my genitalia bein' used as an insult"
2000	Sleater-Kinney	The Ballad of a Ladyman	"I could be demure . . . but I gotta rock! I'd rather be a ladyman" over power chords
2010	Janelle Monáe	Tightrope	"Defines a female masculinity" (Hawkins 2016, 177); second chorus vocals in parallel fifths
2016	Pussy Riot	Straight Outta Vagina	Riff on N.W.A., ode to everybody's first home; "my vagina is tough and dangerous"
2016	Beyoncé	Formation	Minor-pentatonic melody empowers Black women

embraces outspoken transgression in "The Ballad of a Ladyman" (2000): "I could be demure like girls who are soft for boys who are fearful of getting an earful but I gotta rock! I'd rather be a ladyman."

Trans identities. Theatrical drag, cross-dressing, androgyny, transgenderism, nonbinarism, and fluid gender are topics thought by conservatives in our culture to lead to chaotic ambiguity, a perception that may change as ideals are broadened and such conditions are better understood and accepted. Keep in mind, though, that trans expressions themselves, if unblurred, can uphold the binary male/female dichotomy, even if inverted, as when one transitions from one gender to *the* other. "The choice between two of *anything* is not a choice at all but rather an opportunity to subscribe to the value system that holds the two presented choices as mutually exclusive alternatives" (Bornstein 2016, 131). One celebrated nonbinary pop musician is Miley Cyrus, well known for empowering her gender-questioning fans; in 2015 she teamed up with Joan Jett and Laura Jane Grace to cover both Jett's "Different" ("live your life outside the box") and the Replacements' "Androgynous" ("unisex, evolution; tomorrow who's gonna fuss?") to benefit LGBTQ+ youth. Many genderqueers prefer to identify as, and express, no gender at all as part of an antiheteronormative political stance.

A sort of meta-genderqueer "technocultural" society of cyborg bodies (which can be seen as an outgrowth of computerized body parts, sexual prosthetics such as dildoes, and phone/online sex) is the boundary-busting creation of Sandy [Alluquère Rosanne] Stone (1995) and Donna Haraway (2003). (Note that when the Village People sing "I just touch my princess and I go crazy," they're referring to the Ma Bell device, not metaphorical royalty, in "Sex over the Phone" [1985].) Nicki Minaj recontextualized the phrase "Beam Me Up Scotty" in a song by that name (2009) as a space-traveling form of sex and plays an autotuned cyborg in the sex-based "Turn Me On" video with David Guetta (2011). As have Lady Gaga and Beyoncé, Minaj has explored many alter egos including Cyborg Barbie as well as Harajuku Barbie, Roman Zolanski, and Nicki Teresa. Janelle Monáe also has a cyborg alter ego, Cindi Mayweather, the protagonist in all of her albums: *The Audition* (2003), *Metropolis: The Chase Suite* (2008), *The ArchAndroid* (2010), *The Electric Lady* (2013), and *Dirty Computer* (2018). "Tightrope" (2010) speeds up her vocal (at 2:52–3:01) for a sci-fi cyborg quality, and therein, James Brown's "Get Up (I Feel Like Being Like a) Sex Machine" (1970) is suggested by the bright "ee" vowel sound in "scene," "green," "lead," and "machine" (0:18–0:32). Many of her tracks have sexual themes; Monáe's Prince-like "Make Me Feel" (2018) is lascivious to the nth degree with scalar microtones slithering through the lines, "a little bit of tender, an emotional, sexual bender."[38]

One common interest in twentieth-century popular music that may be considered a sort of cross-dressing is the singing of a song originally intended for one of the "opposite" gender. Many song lyrics address the gender-neutral second person, "you," in which unmarked case, historically, the listener has interpreted the love object as heteronormatively "opposite" that of the singer. (The fact that more gays and lesbians are now out than in prior decades leads listeners to consider the singer's real-life sexuality in making this inference, a factor just not recognized with earlier performers like Dusty Springfield or Lesley Gore, whose lesbianism was not a public matter at the time.) On the other hand, many songs use specific third-person pronouns (she/he, her/him, hers/his) and are thus traditionally gender-locked. To maintain a show of heteronormativity in love songs originally performed by a singer addressing the opposite sex, vocalists have had to decide whether to change personal names and pronouns in accordance with desired effect and expected norms, or to maintain them (much more frequently done by women, who have shown less anxiety about this than men, and more commonly done with folk songs than newly composed ones). Arlene Stein conveys an interesting fact: "the female rock fan learns to change the pronouns of lyrics in her head, imagining herself in the role of the active, knowing male subject. Or she simply denies her femaleness."[39] There are a number of other situations of interest, as (1) when a man would write a song for a woman to sing—thereby projecting possibly inappropriate ideas—heard with Peggy Lee's "I'm a Woman" (1962); (2) when Tina Turner recorded "A Fool in Love" (1960) after the man for whom it was written didn't appear at the studio; (3) when an opposite-sex duet would perform as a single persona (Judy Garland and Gene Kelly, "For Me and My Gal" [1942]); (4) when an instrumentalist would suggest the persona of an opposite-sex singer (guitarist Sam Andrew in Janis Joplin's "Piece of My Heart" [1968], or guitarist Jennifer Batten with Michael Jackson); or (5) when a singer "makes fun of the gendered nature of rock and roll culture" as, when the women of Sleater-Kinney sing "I Wanna Be Your Joey Ramone" (1996) (Pelly 2018, 308). The line "I got lightnin' in my pocket"

---

[38] Other than sources cited in the paragraphs earlier, the trans experience is documented in Epstein and Straub 1991, Elliott 1996, Nyong'o and Royster 2013, Serano 2016, Lester 2017, Stryker 2017, Halberstam 2018, and Perez, Friedman, and Lamothe 2021.

[39] Stein 1999, 223. A related experience of persona identification is told in Moore 2012, 185. See also Horton 1990, 14, and Hubbs 1996, 271.

just doesn't seem to mean the same things when Bonnie Raitt covers Jackson Browne's "Under the Falling Sky" (1972). Elias Krell writes about the singer Lucas Silveira (of the Cliks), who explored a range of gender-stereotyped emotions in recording many cover songs both before and after their hormone replacement therapy, suggesting "that cover songs evince a much more complex relationship to gender, sex, identity, and embodiment" (2013, 477). Table 2.3 covers a selection of songs, mostly from the rock era, made famous by one singer but then covered by another of the binarily opposite gender— the most commonly heard category of cross-dressed vocalizing. Many of these recordings exemplify the standard issue, as when Ringo Starr sings "well, I talk about boys"—not "girls"—a line he really can't adapt well in the Beatles' cover of the Shirelles' "Boys" (1963).

Related to these but not often discussed are songs in which the singer *quotes* a member of the opposite gender (perhaps voicing the entire lyric in that borrowed voice), thus possibly needing to decide whether to impersonate that implied sound.[40] Table 2.4 catalogues a few such songs. Full-fledged drag queens RuPaul (who celebrated their supermodel look in "Looking Good, Feeling Gorgeous" [2004]) and William Belli are represented here, but their kin are far outnumbered in popular-music history by partly cross-dressing rockers. Although our main focus is on music, we should mention visual appearance in terms of the long tradition of androgynous cross-dressing in entertainment history, as continuing from female impersonation in the Elizabethan stage play, opera, carnival/mardi gras, nineteenth-century comic theater and pantomime (singer Clarice Mayne was such a "principal boy" in the 1910s–1920s), and twentieth-century Philadelphia's Mummers parades, minstrelsy, burlesque, variety show (Flip Wilson), gay-bar torch song, and costumer-attended screenings of *Rocky Horror Picture Show* (a 1978 film featuring Frank-N-Furter's song, "Sweet Transvestite from Transsexual, Transylvania"). Early blues sometimes featured cross-dressing characters: Sloppy Henry's "Say I Do It" (a flaming answer song to Ma Rainey's "Prove It on Me Blues," both of 1928) made the common tie of transvestism to gay sex: "Mose and Pete lived on Greenwillow Street in Northwest Baltimore; Pete run with Mose 'cause he powdered his nose and even wore ladies' hose . . ." The same connection is drawn with Ruth Wallis's off-color novelty song, "He'd Rather Be a Girl" (*c.* 1953): "How can I

---

[40] Drag vocalization is discussed in Graddol and Swann 1989, 21, Abbate 1993, 256, Solie 1993, 18–19, Taylor 2012, 89 and 100–2, Hawkins 2016, 171, and 2002, and Bradley 2017, 224.

Table 2.3 Songs Covered by Singer of "Opposite" Gender

Cover Artist (Sex of Lead Singer)	Title (Year)	Model Artist (Sex of Lead Singer)	Sex of Lyricist; Gender of Persona	Gender Identities Changed?
Elvis Presley (m)	Hound Dog (1956)	Willie Mae "Big Mama" Thornton (f)	m	sex-suggestive verse dropped
Joan Baez (f)	House of the Rising Sun (1960)	Woody Guthrie (m)?	unknown; f	no
Bob Dylan (m)	House of the Rising Sun (1962)	Woody Guthrie (m)? Joan Baez (f)?	unknown; f	no
Animals (m)	House of the Rising Sun (1964)	Bob Dylan (m)?	unknown; f	yes
Patti Page (f)	Poor Little Fool (1962)	Ricky Nelson (m)	f	yes
Beatles (m)	Keep Your Hands Off My Baby (1963)	Little Eva (f)	m	yes
Beatles (m)	Boys (1963)	Shirelles (f)	m	yes, but . . .
Paris Sisters (f)	Dream Lover (1964)	Bobby Darin (m)	m	yes
Beach Boys (m)	Then I Kissed Her (1965)	Crystals (f) [Then He Kissed Me]	m & f	yes; agency changed as well
Aretha Franklin (f)	Respect (1967)	Otis Redding (m)	m	yes; agency changed as well
Gladys Knight & Pips (f)	I Heard It through the Grapevine (1967)	Smokey Robinson (m), Marvin Gaye (m)	m	yes
Stone Poneys (f)	Different Drum (1967)	Greenbrier Boys (m)	m	yes, but male is "pretty"
Four Seasons (m)	Will You Love Me Tomorrow (1968)	Shirelles (f)	m	no need, but a woman's predicament
Roberta Flack (f)	Just Like a Woman (1970)	Bob Dylan (m)	m	yes; agency changed as well
Judy Collins (f)	Just Like a Woman (1993)	Bob Dylan (m)	m	no; agency retained but folk context requires no lesbianism

(*Continued*)

Table 2.3 (Continued)

Cover Artist (Sex of Lead Singer)	Title (Year)	Model Artist (Sex of Lead Singer)	Sex of Lyricist; Gender of Persona	Gender Identities Changed?
Joan Baez (f)	The Night They Drove Old Dixie Down (1971)	The Band (m)	m	no; singer keeps personal name of male
Ian Matthews (m)	Da Doo Ron Ron (When He Walked Me Home) (1972)	Crystals	f	no; persona becomes gay
Bonnie Raitt (f)	Under the Falling Sky (1972)	Jackson Browne (m)	m	sex-suggestive lyric retained
Bryan Ferry (m)	It's My Party (1973)	Lesley Gore (f)	m	no; male has boyfriend
Suzi Quatro (f)	I Wanna Be Your Man (1974)	The Beatles (m)	m	no; winking rests for "man"
Suzi Quatro (f)	All Shook Up (1974)	Elvis Presley (m)	m	no; "queer as a bug"
Jayne County & Electric Chairs (mtf)	Are You a Boy or Are You a Girl (1974)	Barbarians (m) [re mods' long hair in mid-1960s]	m	no; new meaning in cultural context
Patti Smith (f)	Gloria (1975)	Them (m)	m	no; female has girlfriend
Linda Ronstadt (f)	The Tracks of My Tears (1975)	Miracles (m)	m	yes
Blondie (f)	Denis (1978)	Randy & Rainbows (m) [Denise]	m	yes; Denise now (French) Denis
Barbara Mandrell (f)	(If Loving You Is Wrong) I Don't Want to Be Right (1979)	Luther Ingram (m)	m	yes
Pat Benatar (f)	I Need a Lover (1979)	John Mellencamp (m)	m	yes, but male attitude
Tiffany (f)	I Saw Him Standing There (1987)	Beatles (m) [I Saw Her Standing There]	m	yes
Natalie Cole (f)	Pink Cadillac (1988)	Bruce Springsteen (m)	m	no need, but title = vagina
k. d. lang (f)	Big Big Love (1989)	Wynn Stewart (m)	m	no need, but title = penis
Pansy Division (m)	Femme Fatale (1995)	Velvet Underground (f)	m	yes; now "he's" a femme [fem]
Pansy Division (m)	Big Bottom (1995)	Spinal Tap (m)	m	yes; clearly gay rendering
Suzi Quatro (f)	Born to Run (1995)	Bruce Springsteen (m)	m	no; singer loves Wendy
Janet Jackson (f)	Tonight's the Night (1997)	Rod Stewart (m)	m	yes, but ménage à trois

Jeff Buckley (m)	The Man that Got Away (2000)	Judy Garland (f)	m	no
Tori Amos (f)	'97 Bonnie and Clyde (2001)	Eminem (m)	m	no; she retains "dada" persona
Robert Plant (m) / Alison Krauss (f)	Through the Morning, Through the Night (2007)	Dillard and Clark (m)	m	no; retains male perspective
Rufus Wainwright (m)	The Man That Got Away (2007)	Judy Garland (f)	m	no; JG material frequent gay source
Diana Krall (f)	The Boy from Ipanema (2009)	Astrud Gilberto (f) [The Girl from . . .]	m	yes
Blood Orange (m)	He Doesn't (Even) Know (That) I'm Alive (2011)	Janet Jackson (f)	m; f	yes
Coyote Grace (f)	I'm on Fire (2011)	Bruce Springsteen (m)	m	"she queers the erotic narrative" (Krell 2013, 487)
Amy Winehouse (f)	The Girl from Ipanema (2011)	Astrud Gilberto (f)	m	no

Table 2.4 Songs in Which Singer Quotes Member of the "Opposite" Gender

Year	Artist	Song Title	Nature of Quotation
1902	Arthur Collins	Bill Bailey, Won't You Please Come Home	Narrator quotes woman in choruses
1930	Lonnie Johnson and Clarence Williams	Wipe It Off	L. J. quotes woman in refrains, C. W. impersonates her in bawdy ode to anal sex
1931	Gracie Fields	Sally	Entire song a plea for woman to marry the singer
1961	Joan Baez	Once I Knew a Pretty Girl	Entire song in a man's voice
1966	Beatles	Drive My Car	Woman quoted in choruses; car horn but not woman impersonated
1967	Cher	You Better Sit Down Kids	She sings father's song of divorce
1974	Joni Mitchell	Free Man in Paris	Only "he said" in opening line is not in quoted man's voice
1977	Meri Wilson	Telephone Man	Drops tessitura for brief quotes of male
1978	Kate Bush	In Search of Peter Pan	Extremely high voice drops octaves halfway through prechorus to prepare quote, "When I am a man . . ."
1980	Marianne Faithfull	Why'd Ya Do It?	Most of song is in man's voice, but woman quoted: "'Why'd ya do it?,' she said . . ."
1983	David Bowie	China Girl	Ironically drops to lowest baritone to quote woman
1983	Bruce Springsteen	Car Wash	Entire song in voice of "Catherine LeFevre" [withheld until 1998]
1986	Eddie Money	Take Me Home Tonight	Employs Ronnie Spector for quote in "just like Ronnie sang, 'be my little baby, oh oh oh,' . . ."
1991	Bob Seger	The Fire Inside	At least one verse told from (hetero) woman's perspective
1994	Elton John and RuPaul	Don't Go Breakin' My Heart	Drag queen takes lines originally sung by Kiki Dee; life a masquerade
1998	Liz Phair	Only Son	Entire song in man's voice
1999	Nine Inch Nails	Starfuckers, Inc.	Spoken-sung in groupie's voice; the sung passage quotes Carly Simon
2002	Regina Spektor	Oedipus	Entire song in titular man's voice
2010	Natalie Merchant	Nursery Rhyme of Innocence and Experience	A folk-like song in a young—then older—boy's voice
2012	William Belli	Love You Like a Big Schlong	Parody of Selena Gomez sung by drag queen

surrender to a boy who wears my negligée? . . . He'll make some boy a darn good wife." Crossing over need not be done with clothes: in "Crackin' Up" (1959), Bo Diddley suffers from doing anything for his woman, even adopting what were then completely female gender roles: "I do your laundry and your cooking too; what more, woman, can a man like me do?" There is no resolution to his continuing complaints, as every phrase leads i - ii7 -V for eternally non-resolved half cadences. Paul McCartney veers into sexism thirty years later in "My Brave Face," speaking as if a man is naturally unable to keep house: "unaccustomed as I am to the work of a housewife, I've been breaking up dirty dishes and been throwin' 'em away."

Rockers' own appearances could be increasingly androgynous, progressively challenging the authenticity required by many rock critics, even while defying social repression: suits and ties for Big Mama Thornton, eyeliner and other makeup for Elvis Presley and Little Richard; the Beatles' ever-longer hair; the Shangri-Las' trousers; the Rolling Stones as trans whores in the picture sleeve and publicity for "Have You Seen Your Mother, Baby, Standing in the Shadow?" (1966); the dandified Carnaby Street fashion of London mods like the Kinks; the Mothers of Invention in dresses for *We're Only in It for the Money* (1968); the sequins and platform shoes of British glam performers such as Alice Cooper, Marc Bolan, and Lou Reed; David Bowie's dress worn on the cover of *The Man Who Sold the World* (1970) and his Ziggy Stardust costume; the cock-rock stance of Suzi Quatro; and many ostentatiously spandexed, accessorized, and otherwise genderqueer masqueraders made sensational in MTV videos (Poison, Mötley Crüe, Grace Jones, Boy George of Culture Club, Annie Lennox of Eurythmics, Prince, Kurt Cobain of Nirvana) and beyond (k. d. lang, Marilyn Manson, RuPaul, Kevin Barnes of Of Montreal, Paquita, Alaska Thunderfuck).[41]

---

[41] Rock cross-dressing is a frequent topic in scholarship; see Taylor and Wall 1976, Kaplan 1987, Frith and McRobbie 1990, 383, Gaar 1992, Whiteley 1992 and 2006, Walser 1993, Reynolds and Press 1995, Sutton 1997, Stein 1999, Auslander 2000 and 2006, Fast 2001 and 2012, Gracyk 2001, 212, Hawkins 2002, 2009, and 2016, Schippers 2002, Riley 2004, Bannister 2006, Reddington 2007, 185, Warwick 2007, 190, Brackett 2009, 215–16, Leibetseder 2012, Vargas 2012, King 2013, Arnold 2014, 24, Orenstein 2016, 162–4, Dyhouse 2017, 172, Friend 2017, 351, Kearney 2017, Powers 2017, Jasmine 2018b, Siegel 2018, and Turman 2018.

Key older forms of cross-gender impersonation, and sex-appropriate dress and behavioral attitudes, are discussed in Mulvey 1975, Gagnon 1977, 21, Rubin 1992, Kramer 1993, Kimmel 1996, Halberstam 1998, O'Brien 2002, Cameron and Kulik 2003, 6, McGoldrick, Loonan, and Wohlsifer 2007, Diamond 2008, 193–4, Carlson 2012, 150, D'Emilio and Freedman 2012, Kelly 2012, 50–1, Rutter and Schwartz 2012, 3, 43, and 121, Taylor 2012, McClary 2013, Purvis 2013, Samuel 2013, Hubbs 2014, 145–6 and 149, Thiel-Stern 2014, 71, Barmak 2016, 128, Hines 2018, and Rodger 2018.

Many of these artists confine their cross-dressing almost exclusively to visual spectacle—often banned or censored in early appearances of each sort of transgression, not referring to the practice musically. Table 2.5, though, lists a number of songs that incorporate androgyny-based ideas. The titles here represent a range of cross-dressing from Desmond Jones' theatrical drag in the Beatles' "Ob-La-Di, Ob-La-Da" (1968) to Phranc's "Tipton" (1991), which tells the story of pianist Billy Tipton's transgender expression in daily life, whereby he passed as a man even though assigned "girl" at birth. The Kinks' celebrated tale in "Lola" (1970) can be related to cross-dressing in other of their songs, such as "Dedicated Follower of Fashion" (1966, perhaps inspiring Pink Floyd's more notorious "Arnold Layne" of the following year): "He thinks he is a flower to be looked at . . . when he pulls his frilly nylon panties right up tight." In "Andy Warhol" (1972), David Bowie sings "can't tell them apart at all" in octaves to emphasize the conjoining of men's and women's traits in Warhol's films. Power chords along the minor-pentatonic scale suggest a macho phobia in Lord Tracy's "Transsexual" (2004): "they're on the silver screen, they're on the magazine, they're on the TV too." (Lord Tracy's "Submission" [1989] is downright homophobic.) Cross-dressing of some unspecified nature seems to upset PJ Harvey in "A Woman a Man Walked By/The Crow Knows Where All the Little Children Go" (2009), which opens "I went to you, a woman-man," but erupts in a scream, "where's all your woman parts?" In Phil Vassar's "Bobbi with an i," from the same year, the protagonist is a "tow-truck driving ex-linebacker who can bench-press 335," leaving no doubt as to his masculine credentials, but tavern customers on the make are warned "he might look better than you'd think" "in his pink party dress." We don't know to what degree, if any at all, transgendering impacts appearance when the singer is shocked in Aerosmith's "Dude (Looks Like a Lady)" (1987). But we do in Pansy Division's "Fem in a Black Leather Jacket" (1993): "I know a boy who catches my eye . . . he looks as good in a skirt as he does in jeans—he is a most notorious queen." From the same year, James's "Laid" gives cross-dressing ("Dressed me up in women's clothes, messed around with gender roles") an overt part to play in sex ("This bed is on fire with passionate love"). When trans dress is related to sexuality as done here, and "forbidden" clothing holds a fetishistic attraction, the otherwise-outmoded term "transvestism" is still found appropriate. Cross-dressing for its fetishistic qualities is endemic to the stiletto boots for men in "Sex Is in the Heel," centerpiece of the show *Kinky Boots* (2013): "heels tense the leg and the hindquarter region, lifting the rear and making it appear pert and ready for mating season."

Table 2.5 Songs Involving Cross-Dressing

Chart Year	Artist	Song Title	Comments
c. 1941	Ray Bourbon	My First Piece	Bawdy number spoken by female impersonator
c. 1953	Ruth Wallis	He'd Rather Be a Girl	"A boy who wears my negligée … the zipper on his pants is on the side"
1957	Billy Tipton	Plays Hi-Fi on the Piano	Female-bodied vaudeville jazz artist whose birth sex was unknown to family members
1966	Kinks	Dedicated Follower of Fashion	Man wears "frilly nylon panties"; called a butterfly (slang for male transvestite); after first verse, title sung in ironic, condescending voice
1966	Who	I'm a Boy	Boy rebels against mother dressing him as a girl; Daltrey sings in high register to imitate mother
1967	Pink Floyd	Arnold Layne	Boy masturbates in girl's underwear stolen from washlines; banned by Radio London
1968	Beatles	Ob-La-Di, Ob-La-Da	Desmond Jones makes up his/her face for a drag performance with the band
1969	Velvet Underground	Candy Says	Yule sings of transgender's hatred of her own body; turns from vulnerable diatonic iii to mode-bending ♭III at quote of Candy Darling
1969	Beatles	Get Back	"She was another man"; get back to birth gender!
1969	Johnny Cash	A Boy Named Sue	Narrator wears a girl's name; ghost rhyme at climax; "Sue" expected but singer redirects
1969	Beatles	Polythene Pam	"Looks like a man; well, you should see her in drag"
1970	Kinks	Lola	"Girls will be boys and boys will be girls"; use of ♭VII for gender surprises (see Riley 2004, 83, and Hawkins 2009, 52)
1971	T. Rex	Rip Off	Bolan sings, "I'm the king of the highway, I'm the queen of the hop"
1972	Joel Grey	Willkommen	Emcee of Kit Kat Klub in 1931 Berlin in drag makeup
1972	David Bowie	Andy Warhol	Drag queens of Warhol's films: "can't tell them apart at all"
1972	Mott the Hoople	All the Young Dudes	"Lucy looks sweet 'cause he dresses like a queen"; loud distorted guitars but yielding vocal

(Continued)

Table 2.5 (Continued)

Chart Year	Artist	Song Title	Comments
1972	Lou Reed	Walk on the Wild Side	Holly Woodlawn "[IV] shaved her legs and then [II♯] he was a she"; Lydian II♯ chord at gender switch (see Cloonan 1996, 127, Gracyk 2001, 229, O'Brien 2002, 257–8, Auslander 2006, 67–8, Gioia 2015, 241, Hawkins 2016, 53–6, and Kearney 2017, 228–9)
1976	Wayne County	Max's Kansas City	Name-checks Candy Darling, Holly Woodlawn, New York Dolls, Patti Smith; sung-spoken like Lou Reed
1977	Kinks	On the Outside	"Closet queen" in disorienting tonicizations of e dorian, d minor, minor iv chord within C major
1978	Tim Curry	Sweet Transvestite	"I'm just a sweet transvestite [high wailing alto sax] from Transsexual, Transylvania"
1978	Kinks	Out of the Wardrobe	"He's not a faggot as you might suppose . . . when he puts on that dress he feels like a princess"
1979	Frank Zappa	Broken Hearts Are for Assholes	"Whiskers sticking out from underneath of his pancake makeup and yet he was a beautiful lady"
1987	Aerosmith	Dude (Looks Like a Lady)	♯9 chord for shock: "she whipped out a gun and tried to [V♯9] blow me away"; "she had the body of a Venus, Lord, [V♯9] imagine my surprise" (see Walser 2004, 362)
1987	Eurythmics	I Need a Man	She seeks a real man who doesn't wear a dress (see Hawkins 2016, 83–6)
1988	Mylène Farmer	Sans Contrefaçon	"Pourquoi je suis pas un garçon? . . . je peux le dire, sans contrefaçon, je suis un garçon"; last three words stressed on rebellious offbeats
1988	Bangles	In Your Room	Girl tries on guy's clothes; bridge turns from major to aeolian mode to signify change
1989	Kool G Rap & DJ Polo	Truly Yours	"You're not a lady, dear; you're a square and a queer . . . winkin' your eyes to guys that wear bras" (see Blecha 2004, 119)
1990	Tack Head	Dangerous Sex	"Was it a she or was it a Herman?"; melodic (025)s

Year	Artist	Title	Description
1991	Phranc	Tipton	Transgender shown in vulnerable iii chord moving to chromatic ♭VII at "masquerade"
1993	James	Laid	"Dressed me up in women's clothes, messed around with gender roles" in upbeat major
1994	Blur	Girls & Boys	"Girls who are boys who like boys to be girls"
1998	Tribe 8	Estrofemme	"Why look like men if you hate 'em? Why can't you wear a dress?"
2001	Garbage	Androgyny	"Boys in the girls room, girls in the men's room"; unusual tonicization of leading tone in bridge
2001	Garbage	Cherry Lips	"You looked just like a girl"; dichotomy in moves from C# aeolian verses to C# major choruses
2002	Eminem	Cleanin' Out My Closet	Raps "my faggot father must've had his panties up in a bunch"
2004	Scissor Sisters	Tits on the Radio	"Black-haired tranny" sung in minor-pentatonic mode over aeolian chords
2004	Lord Tracy	Transsexual	Power chords along minor-pentatonic scale; "they're on the silver screen, . . . on the TV too"
2005	Terre Thaemlitz	Trans Portation	Electroacoustic composition in three parts (see Leibetsleder 2012, 165)
2009	Phil Vassar	Bobbi with an i	"Isn't just one of the guys in his pink party dress"
2013	Billy Porter	Sex Is in the Heel	Celebration of kinky stiletto boots for men
2013	Miranda Lambert	All Kinds of Kinds	Congressman hides cross-dressing but melody's tonic arpeggiation affirms its normality
2014	RuPaul	Sissy That Walk	Drag queen coached on strut; see Warwick 2007, 63, for comparison w Cholly Atkins

In the Beatles' "Ob-La-Di, Ob-La-Da" (1968), it's a bit inexplicable, as if an error, when McCartney seems to confuse the genders of Desmond and Molly Jones, but it's certainly intentional months later when his drafts of the Beatles' "Get Back" (1969) evolve from a rant against a certain British politician's anti-immigration stance to a song where not only did a transplanted Tucson native, Jojo, believe the grass was greener in California, but "Sweet Loretta Martin thought she was a woman, but she was another man." Both of the Beatle's boundary crossers are castigated, but they had been melodically motivated: Jojo leaves his home when he rises vocally to meet $\hat{1}\flat7$, which forces him to change location. In a later verse, the same musical event transforms Loretta's gender; neither character will return from whence they came.[42]

Some gender-troubling stories are deeper than others: the bisexual Janis Joplin was "one of the boys"—tough, hard-drinking, and outrageous, but also sensitive; all of these attributes combined in beautiful, imaginative musical experiences.[43] Joplin suffered the sort of 1960s anxiety in which straight male adolescents might have had to worry over how they crossed their legs, examined their fingernails, or carried their schoolbooks, long before such gendered behaviors might be even partially neutralized by the dominant culture. Michael Jackson, whose sexuality was ill-defined and controversial, constantly wore an ever-changing mask, including those of the werewolf and zombie, that transformed aspects of gender and race.[44] Mylène Farmer, if she must be defined according to a binary structure, chooses to be a boy in "Sans contrefaçon" (1988): "Puisqu'il faut choisir, à mots doux je peux le dire, sans contrefaçon je suis un garçon"; all of Farmer's V chords are followed deceptively by vi. Drag king Peaches (née Merrill Nisker; see *Fatherfucker*, 2003) and queen Conchita Wurst (né Thomas Neuwirth) are between genders, both sporting full beards along with a woman's makeup for simultaneous polar assertions of both masculinity and femininity.[45] Wurst is a singer of nonbinary gender with a high tessitura and gay by reputation. Their celebrated "Rise Like a Phoenix" (2014) is anthem-like in its dramatic minor-mode setting that ornaments half-cadential V harmonies with tense 4-3 suspensions for the song's most poignant lines: looking in the mirror, the singer

---

[42] Of the song's main protagonist, McCartney said during its composition, "it's a drag queen, you know." Beatles 2021a, 91, and 2021b, 01:43:29.

[43] Re Joplin's gender identity, see Taylor and Laing 1979, 377, Gaar 1992, 94, Whiteley 2000, 66, Gracyk 2001, 166–7 and 181, O'Brien 2002, 104–5, Schippers 2002, 29, Carson, Lewis, and Shaw 2004, 68–9, and Leonard 2007, 37.

[44] Jackson's androgynous gender display is the topic in Whiteley 2005, 36, 38, and 40–3, and Fast 2012. Michael's sister Janet's drag voice is discussed in Bradley 2017, 224–5.

[45] Learn more about Peaches in Leibetseder 2012 and about Wurst in Hawkins 2016.

asks, "Who can this person be?" and later, in referring to a catharsis caused by pain inflicted by another, "What you did to me." "Heterosexuality will not be taken for granted, as constructions of queer identity are made extratexturally through circulating public knowledge concerning [Wurst's] sexuality (male and gay), which may frame the narrative persona" (Rey 2018, 27). Affirmative choruses paint a transformational rebirth (at "once I'm reborn") in resolving to the major ♭III chord. The orchestra exerts contentious stress in the Tony Osborne- or John Barry-inspired score, featuring a melodramatic ritardando just before the final chorus, and a dissonant stinger in the final Perry Mason-modeled minor triad with added major thirteenth, raised eleventh, and major ninth. The song undeniably depicts one who is transformed beyond recognition in rising above tribulation, with gender and sexuality given as context only in the singer's appearance and reputation. Gender and sexuality themselves cannot be suggested musically, but the attitudes and dynamics within and surrounding them may.

Such an unusual mix of gender signifiers plays with an observing man's fetish with specific body parts, challenging him to rationalize some parts while fixating on others. Drag queen Mykki Blanco (né Michael Quattlebaum, Jr.), nonbinary singer Anohni of Antony and the Johnsons, and of course the otherworldly Nikki Minaj are further key gender-outlaw musicians.[46] In 2016, Beyoncé's major hit—her generation's anthem critiquing institutional racism, "Formation"—sampled trans rapper Big Freedia. Additional genderqueer recordings include Laurie Anderson's "Babydoll" (1989, in which she sings of the male voices in her head), Green Day's "Basket Case" (1994, in which a sex worker is referred to both as she and he), Imperial Drag's "Boy or a Girl" (1996, in which the addressee's gender is unclear, leading the singer to question his own sexual orientation), and Bitch and Animal's "Boy Girl Wonder" (2001, "he's got a real one and mine's from the store" and the dissonant ^2 and ^7 are sung simultaneously over the bass ^1 for "I'm a bender").

It may need to be stated how unacceptable trans identity and appearance were to a broad swath of Western society previous to the current century (putting

---

[46] Blanco is treated in Hawkins 2016, and Zemke and Mackley-Crump 2018; re Minaj, see Butler 2013, Smith 2014, Brown and Edell 2016, Hawkins 2016, and Gitlow 2018. For more on genderqueer voices, cyborg fusion, and a nonbinary view of gender in its historical climate, see McClary 1991, 53–4, Reynolds and Press 1995, Halberstam 1998, Cameron and Kulik 2003, 28, Hawkes 2004, Bannister 2006, Diamond 2008, 193, Hawkins 2009, Oakes 2009, Moores 2010, 189–90, Carbery 2011, Carlson 2012, Leibetseder 2012, Taylor 2012, de Boise 2015, Kearney 2017, Twenge 2017, Hegarty 2018, Kurtis and Adams 2018, and Lee 2018a.

aside for the moment such recent travesties as bathroom laws, etc.): before gays had Stonewall, the transgendered applied collective resistance to police and other bullies at the Cooper Do-Nut in Los Angeles (May 1959), Dewey's Lunch Counter in Philadelphia (April 1965), and Compton's Cafeteria in San Francisco (August 1966). Transphobia (Julia Serano prefers the term "cissexism" [2016, 184]) brought down both Olivia Records recording engineer Sandy Stone in 1977, fired for not being a "woman," and Nancy Jean Burkholder, ostracized for the same reason by the Michigan Womyn's Music Festival in 1991 (Stryker 2017, 132 and 176). Lady Gaga, who proclaimed "don't be a drag, just be a queen" in "Born This Way" (2011) (using the double-plagal I - ♭VII - IV - I progression in its chorus for a proud and bold defiance), who embodied her drag alter ego Jo Calderone and who once dressed in meat, identified with her fans by referring to them as "my little monsters" in order to destabilize binary gendering and critique homophobia.[47] Still, "many trans women turn to [sex] work because few other viable economic options are available to them" (Serano 2016, 261).

A topic of recent interest pertains to the fluidity with which a person may not maintain the same gendered identity through life, with even their "essential" traits appearing or disappearing.[48] When such a change occurs in children, it may manifest in boys having a time period from ages four to six in which they temporarily adopt female traits (Gagnon 1977, 337). Walser (1993, 109) writes of how male metal guitarists may eventually accomplish their gender through "identity work" in their music. Such a transformation, though, is much more common as a cross-dressing "tomboy" phase in young girls.[49] Musicians who have discussed their formative years as tomboys include the Cranberries' Dolores O'Riordan (see Evans 1994, 245) and the Indigo Girls' Amy Ray (see Carson, Lewis, and Shaw 2004, 119). Correspondingly, the theme makes its way into a few rock songs. In "Trouble and Strife" (1985, the title being British rhyming slang for "wife"), Everything But the Girl wonder "who would be born into a man's man's man's world?" (composer Tracey Thorn channeling James Brown at his most sexist), determining in the final chorus that "the open world of a tomboy girl is the best of life." The song ends on a major-seventh tonic chord

---

[47] Controversy as to Lady Gaga's purported genitalia was mocked in her video for "Telephone" (2009); for more on this artist, see Halberstam 2012, Leibetseder 2012, Lieb 2013, 7–8 and 129, Geller 2014, Hawkins 2014 and 2016, O'Brien 2014, Owens 2014, and Zaleski 2018.

[48] Gender fluidity is covered in Murray 1988, Stone 1995, Butler 1999, 25, Hawkes 2004, 147–8, Powell 2010, 72, Krell 2013, Lee 2013, Bornstein 2016, 63, Stryker 2017, Twenge 2017, 233–5, Gowaty 2018, and Halberstam 2018. Madonna in particular is mentioned in this regard in McClary 1991, 150.

[49] Tomboys are studied in Bancroft 1989, 158, Halberstam 1998, 5–6, 186, and 192–4, and Lakoff 2004, 40.

to convey an appropriate lack of completion.[50] Dar Williams's "When I Was a Boy" (1993) refers to the androgynous figure Peter Pan in describing tomboy behavior (with many leading tones long suspended without resolution over tonic harmony); in the last verse a man reveals that he had once been a girl. Aptly, some melodic turns and guitar textures appear very reminiscent of Judy Collins's dichotomy-embracing "Both Sides Now" (1968).

It's intriguing to ponder what the West's cultural future (both short and long term) may bring to gender, musically and otherwise. As gender, reproduction, and child-rearing responsibilities become less interdependent for more people, as marriage transforms from an assumed plan to an option, as professions and economies change in fundamental related ways, and as agency is no longer reliant on birth sex, traditional gender-specific traits will to some unascertainable degree fade in the significance they have had for centuries. No doubt many changes in gender identity will continue to play out in popular music.

---

[50] "Trouble and Strife" is discussed in Becker 1990.

3

Sexuality

Sexual Orientation

Questions of sexuality, understood as relating to sexual orientation, preferences, and behavior, "how and with whom we act on our erotic desires" (Stryker 2017, 33), are basic to the formation of human identity. Definitions for conditions such as heterosexual, gay, lesbian, bisexual, pansexual, asexual, queer, and kink are dynamically contested and confused in many ways, including

Their prevalence in various populations,
Their origins in the nature/nurture (essentialist/socially scripted) continuum, and thus their interrelationships with one's sex and gender,
Their degrees of fixity or fluidity within even non-trans-identified individuals (and the supposed prospects of conversion "therapy," i.e., the "gay cure"),
The separability of general orientation (defined by desire) and behavior (sometimes dictated less by preferences than by immediate context—e.g., imprisonment),
The frequent arbitrariness of such labels,
The patriarchal establishment of the essences of fantasy and pleasure, and differences between sexual attraction and personal emotions.

(The related notion of romance will be taken up in Chapter 4). These are the subjects, as they impact popular recorded music, to be addressed in the present chapter.[1]

---

[1] Foucault (1978), Weeks (2010 and 2011), and Diamond (2008, 2017, and 2018) have strongly influenced current thought on the importance of sexuality in selfhood and individual freedom. For more key approaches to basic definitions, see Gagnon 1977, Dean 1996, Vance 1999, Althof 2000, Williams and Stein 2002, Cameron and Kulik 2003, Dryfoos and Barkin 2006, Sedgwick 2008, Bergner 2009, Carlson 2012, Ellwood-Clayton 2012, Kelly 2012, Rutter and Schwartz 2012, Seidman 2015, Khazan 2016, and Donaghue 2018.

The interested reader may wish to explore in more depth such pertinent topics as relating to the history of social thought (including studies of race, religion, and class) on nonhetero expression; varying cultural practices across societies including sex-segregating institutions; genital

John Bancroft has identified many nonreproductive "functions or purposes of sexual behavior":

1. Assertion of masculinity or femininity.
2. Bolstering or maintenance of self-esteem.
3. Exertion of power or dominance.
4. Bonding dyadic relationships and fostering intimacy.
5. Source of pleasure.
6. Reduction of tension.
7. Expression of hostility.
8. Risk-taking as a source of excitement.
9. Material gain.
   Many of the problems of human sexual relationships stem from the participants using sex for different purposes at the same time (1989, 150).

Most of these factors will be evident in this chapter's discussion, as well as in the online Appendix, which covers the musical expression of sexual behavior in numerous such manifestations.

Because of the central importance of sexuality in defining selfhood, it can be surprising to consider that for centuries, many of these matters were shrouded in moral embarrassment or hostile outrage and not considered proper for public expression or discussion; this is especially true of gay identity. The long-held social stigma, legal restrictions against homosexuality, and related moral panics can be traced through:

Freud's "polymorphous perversity" developing into "healthy" repression and maladjusted tendencies including "inversion,"
Federal persecution in the 1950s including the expulsion of gays from military and government jobs, and attempts to censor gay-referencing literature such as Allen Ginsberg's poem, "Howl,"
Mass-arrest police sweeps of gay establishments culminating in rebellion following the raid on New York's Stonewall Inn in June 1969,
Anita Bryant's 1977 anti-homosexual jihad,
Abusive political narratives on HIV transmission,

---

responsiveness, proceptivity, receptivity, and the numerous contributory factors expressed in desire; or the possible roles of H-Y or polygenetic proteins (e.g., the "gay gene"), prenatal hormonal balance (especially in androgen exposure), or even physiological factors in orientational development.

Culture wars waged by high-profile ministers in the Moral Majority, the
    Christian Coalition, the "700 Club," and Focus on the Family,
Hate-crime murders including those of Harvey Milk, Barry Winchell, Matthew
    Sheppard, and Scott Amedure, the 2016 mass killing at Orlando's Pulse
    nightclub, and a number of then-recently killed trans women named
    in Janelle Monáe's performance at the January 2017 Women's March on
    Washington,
The Clinton administration's "Don't Ask, Don't Tell, Don't Pursue, Don't
    Harass" military policy and the 104th U. S. Congress's Defense of
    Marriage Act,
Ongoing efforts at reparative conversion therapy, and
The political struggle for gay marriage and other civil rights.

This last topic, for example, is given a tragic cast in Morrissey's "Will Never
Marry" (1990), in which a deceptively arriving vi chord follows a sad aeolian
♭VII: "I will [I] live my life as [IV] I will undoubtedly [I] die: a- [♭VII] -lone [vi]."
We will not be covering the social, cultural, psychological, and political reasons
for the suppression of sexuality here, but a history of many of the evolving and
perhaps sublimated results—including many examples in song of the avoidance
of gender-revealing names and pronouns—can be traced through the songs
listed in the online Appendix.[2]

Heteronormativity

Sexual desire and behavior between those of opposite sexes was not always the
fraught notion it can be today, given the pliancy of postmodern definitions. In
fact, plain-vanilla heterosexuality was the unmarked, indeed unstated default
condition for romantic conditions in popular song through the twentieth century
and beyond, and nonhetero sex—including masturbation—was routinely
pathologized. Gayle Rubin noted in 1984, "the only adult sexual behavior that is
legal in every state is the placement of the penis in the vagina in wedlock" (20). In
the same year, Tina Turner remarked casually that "opposites attract" in singing

---

[2] Historical studies of recent (generally post-Stonewall) decades' developments in gay and anti-gay
   politics in various Western countries and US states include Nicholson 1990, Jeffrey-Poulter 1991,
   Michael et al. 1994, Weeks 2000, 2010, and 2011, Hawkes 2004, Clark 2008, Sedgwick 2008, Rosen
   2009, Kosnick 2011, Carlson 2012, Cohen 2012, D'Emilio and Freedman 2012, Halberstam 2012, xix–
   xxi, Rutter and Schwartz 2012, Freitas 2013, Orenstein 2016 and 2020, Witt 2016, Friend 2017, and
   Twenge 2017.

"What's Love Got to Do with It." In that era, when lyrics did not reveal names and pronouns, the listener understood that a hetero relationship was being portrayed, as if compulsory. In the unusual cases in the distant past wherein a song (particularly a cover song) might suggest sexual attraction to someone of the same sex, this would be rationalized as aberrant and explained away as the lyrics being incompatible with the artist's biography, rather than ever suggesting the unthinkable homosexuality (which practices were outlawed in England by Henry VIII in 1533 in statutes not lifted until 1967; gay sex was decriminalized in Australia only in 1995 and for the most part not until 2020 in the United States). Such would have been the usual reception of some of the songs in Tables 2.3 and 2.4. "Pop culture actively promotes heterosexuality."[3] This is primarily due to the nineteenth and twentieth centuries' Western-cultural economic, political, and religious promotion of genital-exclusive heterosexuality as the "natural" and desired family-centered sex partnering necessary for reproduction and the suppression of pleasure-based sex.[4] Until the 1950s, men who lusted after men were widely considered inverts because their gender was suspected to be inwardly feminine—they "possessed a female subjectivity" (Cameron and Kulik 2003, 81). Gays were maligned as effeminate "fairies" or "pansies." Homophobia, even in self-directed anxiety, might be expressed in such acts of self-esteem maintenance or power protection as gay men adopting the "beard" of an opposite-sex companion, or even in the extreme of involvement in highly aggressive gang rape (see Sanday 1990). Gays fought their instincts; as Neil Tennant sings in Pet Shop Boys' "Metamorphosis" (1996), "What I wanted was to be a family man but nature had some alternative plans." The PSB singer's acceptance of his nature is expressed in a glorious switch from D minor to F major, "You [Dm] grow up and ex- [Dm/C] -perience this, a [Gm6/5] total meta- [E°7/C♯] -morpho- [Fsus9-8] -sis," as he comes out.

Just as significant as heterosexuality itself, the early twentieth century from Freud onward witnessed an acceptance of sexual fantasy and pleasure as healthy, and channeled by whites' puritanical societal goals into heterosexual expression, for a long time to be practiced solely within the monogamous confines of marriage, with a clear binary division of genders. These strictures

---

[3] Seidman 2015, 206. Particularly as affecting adolescents, a primary audience for popular music, see also Martin 2002, 143–4, Cameron and Kulik 2003, 141–2, Hawkes 2004, 182, and Seidman 2015, 205–6.

[4] The historical promotion of heterosexuality for cultural purposes is treated in Dean 1996, Martin 1996, Butler 1999, Padgug 1999, Hawkes 2004, Weeks 2011, D'Emilio and Freedman 2012, and Seidman 2015.

loosened over the course of the past hundred years, with masturbation and premarital sex (originally condoned first for a couple engaged to be married and later even "going steady") found universal by Kinsey in 1948–52, which research also determined that exclusively heterosexual and homosexual emotions and behaviors marked terminal points along a single continuum that saw variegated ratios of mixture of the two orientations in all individuals. Despite these unexpected findings of widespread varied sexual practices—and evolving understandings of female sexual response, contraception, and abortion, women's and civil rights, changing family forms (and cohabitation and divorce), matters of privacy, multiple forms of sexuality including heterosexual manual, oral, and anal practices, queer theory, nightlife, online offerings, sex work, sexting, and hookup culture—cultural values (particularly pertaining to the appropriateness of expressing sex-related matters publicly, as in television, films, and music) were slow to change correspondingly over the following decades.[5] Because contrasting subcultures accepted such social changes at different rates—consider, for example, liberal 1960s hippies being contemporaneous with the conservative "silent majority"—it can be expected that different musical styles will reflect varied degrees of conservative or liberal attitudes to sexuality, including qualities of heterosexuality. Such attitudes were also patriarchically phallic when spoken: romantic kissing, hugging, and intimate caressing can be expressed by men or women, even with no verbal object ("we hugged"); with more directly sexual acts, though, "men are said to fuck / screw / make love to women far more than the other way round. When women were the subject of the verb 'make love' it was more likely to be followed by the preposition 'with'; when men were the subject it was more likely to be followed by 'to'" (Cameron and Kulik 2003, 30). In different musical styles, this distinction in dominance is more—or less—maintained into the twenty-first century.

Sheila Whiteley has said, "despite the ambivalent sexuality of many of its most notable performers, it is still apparent that rock continues to provide a cultural expression of normative heterosexual masculinity" (2005, 133). This is axiomatic in the Pretenders' "Message of Love" (1981), which contains the line, "The reason we're here as man and woman is to love each other," just

---

[5] Findings in male versus female, and straight versus gay, sexual response are presented in Koedt 1973, Althof 2000, McGoldrick, Loonan, and Wohlsifer 2007, Diamond 2008 and 2017, Bergner 2009 and 2013, and Carlson 2012, 118. Changing presentations of heterosexual themes in 1960s–2010s television, stage, and film are covered in Michael et al. 1994, Martin 1996, 61, Tropiano 2002, Hawkes 2004, 166, Douglas 2010, 33, D'Emilio and Freedman 2012, Samuel 2013, Seidman 2015, 193–206, Friend 2017, Twenge 2017, 228–32, and Orenstein 2020.

as the Mindbenders had declared in "Game of Love" sixteen years earlier, "The purpose of a man is to love a woman, and the purpose of a woman is to love a man." Closeted gay composers and performers have conformed to this model, as have many out gays and lesbians. The latter group includes Me'Shell Ndegéocello, whose *Plantation Lullabys* (1994) disappointed fans and critics as "her focus was on heterosexual relationships rather than explicitly women-centered lyrics" (Mahon 2004, 136).

We've seen how the claim of heterosexual mastery, as expressed in self-esteem promoting songs like "Sixty Minute Man" (1951) and "I'm a Man" (1955), was a foundational element of early rock 'n' roll. Country music, which by and large still clings to the supposed values of middle America, nearly always exemplifies heteronormativity (except for purposes of parody). This point is well made by Jacqueline Warwick, alongside an assessment of racial standards: "Alan Jackson's 2000 song, 'Meat and Potato Man,' with its beer-drinking, football-watching and poodle-despising narrator . . ., corresponds with conceptions of white, heterosexual masculinity as normal and unmarked" (2009, 353). Nadine Hubbs cites the dark side of abusive heterosexual relationships in country songs through the common woman-battered-by-drunk-partner genre (2014, 73), but short of that extreme, country women are often portrayed as subservient to their men, right to the present day. In rock music, hetero relationships have also been the norm. Such sex is basic to Led Zeppelin, as we've seen in their performances geared to the heightening and then releasing of sexual tension. A dark side exists in rock as well, especially in blues, heavy metal, and other depictions of domestic violence, date rape, and even gang rape (see Willie Mabon's "I Don't Know" [1952], Sweet Honey in the Rock's "Joan Little" [1976], Judas Priest's "Eat Me Alive" [1984], and Tribe 8's "Frat Pig" [1995]), as opposed to gentler pop and Latinx forms that have focused on intimate romance. In recent years more explicit portrayals of hetero sex would appear in Black, R&B, soul, and hip-hop productions (see Color Me Badd's "I Wanna Sex You Up" [1991], Snoop Dogg's "Pay for Pussy" [1998], and Janet Jackson's "Moist" [2004]).[6] Some rockers, notably Frank Zappa, are notorious for satirizing hetero sex; his "Make a Sex Noise" (1992), one example of many in which he portrays orgasm sonically, is "a blush-inducing sequence where Zappa invites four Irish girls up on stage to

---

[6] Heteronormative pop and rock approaches are the focus of Waksman 1996, Halberstam 1998, Stein 1999, Gracyk 2001, 206, Schippers 2002, Walser 2004, Fast 2005, Auslander 2006, 60–1 and 211–15, Vargas 2012, McClary 2013, Kearney 2017, Berrios-Miranda, Dudley, and Habell-Pallán 2018, and Lankford 2010.

prove that Irish people are, contrary to myth, sexy" (Watson 1994, 498). Satire in popular music has roots in the early blues, as with Ida Cox's "One Hour Mama" (1939), "an irreverent attack on male sexual prowess" (Carby 2015, 43). Glam rockers may have exhibited Whiteley's "ambivalent sexuality" in their "outsider" dress and stage acts, but some of these men "talked about how many women they fucked on tour" and otherwise—as in song—objectified women as their objects of choice (Schippers 2002, 22–3). Beginning in the 1980s, women rockers, such as Suzi Quatro, PJ Harvey, and Madonna, could be as aggressively hetero as were men, and rocking men such as Bruce Springsteen and Prince could be hetero yet sensitive, as discussed in Chapter 2 as related to gender performance. There is no need to further demonstrate here the prevalence and nature of heterosexual identity in pop/rock music; the online Appendix provides hundreds of such illustrations.

Same-Sex Attraction

Some 2 percent to 20 percent of the general US population (studies vary widely) is mostly or wholly attracted to same-sex individuals, with women generally more practicing or fantasizing than men. Researchers' disagreements about how homosexuality might result from a combination of polygenetic and environmental influences lead to very different theoretical and political interpretations. Clearly this question is problematized by nonbinary considerations regarding both sex and gender, in addition to a growing number of youths' rejection of sexuality-based labels altogether, but we shall proceed with coverage of gay (man to man) and lesbian (woman-to-woman) orientations constituting by far the usual forms of same-sex attraction throughout the rock era, with further caveats to be noted as will follow. Historically, homosexual behavior has been viewed in the West variously as an appetite of choice (as discussed by Plato); a sin (as were all nonreproductive sex acts practiced since the ascendancy of Christianity); a capital crime into the nineteenth century (receptive sodomy and bestiality treated as similar offenses whereas an adult man penetrating an adolescent boy was typically acceptable); the consequence of a medical condition involving gender deviance (in the neuropsychiatric theory of inversion, a "woman's soul enclosed in a male body" [Hekma 1989, 178]); the conduct of a category of people—a "repository of whatever is symbolically expelled from hegemonic masculinity, the items ranging from fastidious taste in home decoration to receptive anal pleasure" (Connell 1995, 78); and the basis of a healthy identity with full civil rights (as determined, if tremulously, in the early twenty-first century).[7]

Same-sex attraction may be forced by constrained opportunity, as demonstrated in sex-segregated populations such as boarding schools, armed forces, and correctional institutions. In "Jailhouse Rock" (1957), when Elvis Presley sings "Little Joe was blowin' on the slide trombone" and "Number 47 said to Number 3, 'you're the cutest jailbird I ever did see,'" it does not suggest (even farcically) that either Little Joe or Number 47 is normally gay—although the prime numbers put at least two of these three characters in a small minority group (!)—but only that hetero sex is prohibited by the setting. "Lord, if you can't send me no woman, please send me some sissy man," as Kokomo Arnold sang in "Sissy Man Blues" (1935). Heterosexual Black men are said to be on the down low if they have sex with other men (particularly when they are penetrated) (McGoldrick, Loonan, and Wohlsifer 2007, 429). Whereas acceptance of homosexuality has increased in the general population since about 1990, with the average age of gays fully coming out dropping to adolescence, homophobia remains stronger in some religious and ethnic groups, and economic classes, than others. Thus, for example, Black Christian churches typically have a large role in maintaining homophobia as basic to Black masculinity and therefore to hip-hop culture. Kool G Rap & DJ Polo, for instance, insult with slurs, "you're lookin' more sweeter than a Playboy bunny . . . you're not a lady, dear, you're a square and a queer . . . winkin' your eyes to guys that wear bras," in "Truly Yours" (1989). In hip-hop, homophobia can extend to whites as in the notoriously anti-gay language of Eminem ("Marshall Mathers" [2000]: "Slim Anus, I don't get fucked in mine like you two little flaming faggots"; see also "Cleanin' Out My Closet" [2002]).[8]

Acceptance of gay life in music belongs to a reticent century. Aside from occasional risk-taking blues figures like Bessie Smith, the world of Broadway

---

[7] Useful histories of social attitudes toward homoerotic behavior and corresponding selfhood are found in Henry 1948, Foucault 1978, Gerard and Hekma 1988, Laqueur 1990, Trumbach 1991, Michael et al. 1994, Dean 1996, Halberstam 1998, Tropiano 2002, 1–12 and 63, Hawkes 2004, Diamond 2008, Weeks 2010 and 2011, D'Emilio and Freedman 2012, Kelly 2012, Taylor 2012, and Seidman 2015. The likelihood that a person's sex and gender (essentially, those of men as opposed to women) determine very different forms and degrees of homosexuality is explored in Rutter and Schwartz 2012. Diamond 2008 (214–15) allows that "we might imagine hundreds of different subcategories representing different mixes of same-sex proceptivity and same-sex arousability." Hawkins 2016 (205–6) cites six categories of gender alone.

[8] See Zemke and Mackley-Crump 2018, 131–8, and also West 1993, Stephens and Phillips 2003, 24, and Smith 2014, 364–5, on relevant Black culture; and Stephens 2005 and Kimmel 2008, 163, on white.

(Cole Porter, Leonard Bernstein, and Stephen Sondheim), and London's West End (Nöel Coward), pop gay performers were not at all out before the gay liberation movement in the 1970s. Recall that performers like Liberace or Little Richard could engage in then-outrageous gender play, but as with drag costuming, this in and of itself revealed nothing definitive about their sexuality.[9] It was likely beyond comprehension to most in the 1950s that truly homosexual performers could subject themselves to the public eye. In a 1972 interview, theater-bred David Bowie revealed his gay side, yet despite his outlandish stage dress and deportment (including mimed sex with guitarist Mick Ronson), his lyrics and music seem almost completely unrelated to his underlying sexuality ("Lady Stardust" [1972] is one exception; see Auslander 2006, 136). Musical theater was a leading venue for gay expression when it was still not accepted elsewhere; in "I'm Gay," from the show *Let My People* Come (1974), an imitative duet suggests either the splitting of a psyche or perhaps two separate male lovers who both compose letters home, as the lead persona comes out to his parents in writing. In previous years, homosexuality had been largely a subject of musical ridicule; Ruth Wallis's "Queer Things" (*c*. 1953) and Steve Greenberg's "Big Bruce" (1969) are representative. In December 1967, BBC-1 banned Scott Walker's "Jackie" for its reference to "queers." Disco, which emerged in gay clubs and attained its broadest popularity in the 1977 film *Saturday Night Fever*, was attended by a homophobic backlash that culminated in a hateful 1979 record burning in Chicago.[10] Gay pride was celebrated with 1970s songs by the Village People, but at the same time, gay sex was often harshly ridiculed by Frank Zappa in explicit, often sadomasochistic terms ("Punky's Whips" [1978], "Sy Borg," "Broken Hearts Are for Assholes," "Bobby Brown" [all 1979], "Harry-as-a-Boy," and "He's So Gay" [both 1984]). For full context, we've already noted that derision was Zappa's attitude to many aspects of hetero sex as well.[11]

Musical homophobia remained strong in the 1980s, as with Guns n' Roses' hostile "One in a Million" (1988), "with its notorious rant about 'immigrants

---

[9] The public view of Little Richard's sexuality is studied in Steptoe 2018.

[10] (Possibly latent) homoeroticism in disco, heavy metal, glam and post-glam, queercore punk, house, and diva performance and their audiences (both gay and straight) is explored in Attig 1991, Gaar 1992, 173, Walser 1993, 115–16, McRobbie 1994, 20, Tomlinson 1998, 196, Bennett 2001, 119, Griffiths 2002, 52–4, Whiteley 2005, 131, Auslander 2006, 137, 170, and 232, Brackett 2009, 351, Kopkind 2009, 356–60, Taylor 2012, 123, 126, and 133–9, Hajdu 2016, 181, Hawkins 2016, 6, 78, and 197–9, Wald 2016, 282–4, and Lee 2018b, 150–5. The significant overlap between musical comedy and other forms of pop is placed in a gay and gender-related context in Hawkins 2009, 109.

[11] Zappa's gay-bashing songs are well covered in Watson 1994, Courrier 2002, Miles 2004, Lowe 2006, and Schmalenberger 2018.

and faggots'" (Gracyk 2001, 234; see also Blecha 2004, 119). Dire Straits mock the homophobe who would say, "see the little faggot with the earring and the make-up" in "Money for Nothing" (1985). Queercore band Anthrax loaded their chorus of "Forbidden Love" (1987) with transgressive tritones and cross-relations as if to closet any horrifying malefactors: "[^♭7/♭VII] Is this the love, the forbidden love, careful what you [^7/V] say—give yourself away; [^♭7/♭VII] Is this the love, the forbidden love, take your love a- [^7/V] -way." Even into the 1990s, Screeching Weasel could perform the sarcastic, post-punk "I Wanna Be a Homosexual" (1992), the bridge of which opens derisively, "Call me a faggot, call me a butt-lovin', fudge-packin' queer, I don't care." Whereas the lyrics in Pet Shop Boys' "The Truck-Driver and His Mate" (1996) convey no sense of shame about the gay relationship revealed there, the music departs from its conventional harmony at the end of the verse, landing with apparently fault-finding backing-vocal non-chord tones for a dissonant alternation of F♯ and G over the A minor chord, emphasizing the devil's tritone with F♯ clashing against the tonic C, itself an ego lost within the "wrong" vi chord. The tritone of ^♯4 against ^1 is also the guitar's emblem for "the queerest of the queer" transgressive gay sex in Garbage's "Queer" (2007). To be sure, such aural dissonances do not portray anything about gay sex itself, but only the strong aversion to it that is expressed in the lyrics.

Still, twentieth-century song lyrics were rarely themselves "out": the object of Paul Jabara's "Disco Queen" (1978) could be imagined to be either man or woman. Fred E. Maus explores this situation further in the case of Pet Shop Boys:

> Like much communication about homosexuality, [Neil] Tennant's lyrics are often double-voiced, carrying special meanings for insiders while remaining differently meaningful for others as well. 'To Speak is a Sin' [1993], for instance, can be heard as a sad song about an evening in a pub, but it evokes, quite precisely, experiences of cruising in gay bars . . . when heard by listeners in whom such experiences can be evoked. . . . This ambiguity creates deniability.[12]

When Mick Jagger French-kissed Ron Wood on "Saturday Night Live" in October 1978 or Bruce Springsteen would routinely meet Clarence Clemons full on the lips centerstage, this was typically interpreted as affected support for gays and audacious blood-brother friendship rather than a sign of gay lovemaking.

---

[12] Maus 2001, 383–4. See also Hubbs 1996, 268, on Morrissey's deliberate obfuscation through a lack of pronouns.

So, even considering references to gay characters in many of his lyrics, first-person gay bonding narratives in Springsteen's outtakes "My Lover Man" (1990) and "This Hard Land" (1983) challenge—but do not overcome—fans' perception of his straight personal life and that of his songs' vocal personae.[13] In fact, Springsteen's defiant embrace of gay tokens may be seen as the super-confident expression of a strong, macho figure. Still,

> Springsteen's 2009 tribute to deceased band member Danny Federici, "Last Carnival," continues the queer lyrical themes explored throughout his career. "Last Carnival" acts as a sequel to 1973's "Wild Billy's Circus Story" by showcasing Federici on accordion as the listener is taken on a journey through the seedy and glorious (and gay) life of a traveling carnival. The narrator alternately searches for his "handsome Billy" and "darlin' Billy," sadly mourning "the thing in you that made me ache." As Springsteen sings a dirge for his departed bandmate, the line between friend and lover is noticeably blurry. (Fanshel 2013, 378)

And whereas gay imagery became commonplace in music videos, most songs illustrated by them did not necessarily support exclusively gay interpretations when considered apart from any visual story: see, for example, Pet Shop Boys' "Domino Dancing" (1988) (Hawkins 2002, 135) and Madonna's "Vogue" (1990) (Dhaenens 2016, 532). The much later lyrics of Le1f's "Wut" (2012), on the other hand, fully uphold a video setting that includes a gay lap dance (Hawkins 2016, 133–4, and Dhaenens 2016, 541).

Gay themes in early pop/rock music did appear in some early avant-garde song lyrics, as in the Velvet Underground's "Sister Ray" (1968, Lou Reed's precursor to his "Walk on the Wild Side," 1972). Larger audiences were found for gay texts in the 1980s by the Smiths, Frankie Goes to Hollywood, Bronski Beat, and the Communards; by 1999, the Magnetic Fields' "When My Boy Walks Down the Street" (1999) could bring a gay romance to a fully public setting ("the street") and audience (Butler 2007, 241). Some songs themselves unrelated to gay sexuality were appropriated as anthems early in the Gay Pride movement simply for their conquering of adversity, affirmation, and their powerful "messages of unity and celebration" (Hajdu 2016, 181); these include Gloria Gaynor's "I Will Survive" (1978; note how her melody droops in descent but then rises to $\wedge 2$ in triumphant inner strength) and "I Am What I Am" (1983), Sister Sledge's "We Are Family" (1979), Sylvester's "You Make Me Feel (Mighty Real)" (1978), Cyndi Lauper's "True Colors" (1986), and Aretha Franklin's "A Deeper Love" (1994).

---

[13] Particularly regarding these Springsteen songs, see Fanshel 2013 and Hawkins 2016, 167, and 181–4.

But Tom Robinson's "(Sing If You're) Glad to Be Gay" (1978) is remarkable for its explicit embrace of the cause. Later songs attained anthem status by explicitly advocating gay ideals or opposing homophobia, such as Garth Brooks's "We Shall Be Free" (1992) or Macklemore & Ryan Lewis's "Same Love" (2012) (see Dhaenens 2016, 532–6). Pansy Division's "Some of My Best Friends" (2009) is antagonistically antihomophobic in its line, "I might not be gay, but I know this much is true, I'd rather fuck an asshole that be one just like you."

A frequently cited attribute of gay performance is camp, a mannered, over-the-top aesthetic that adds theatrical eccentricity for an ironic element of decadent fun. When religious groups bizarrely labeled kids' cartoon character Sponge Bob as "pro-homosexuality" in 2002, it was likely the lovingly friendly toon's spirit of pollyannaish tolerance and the hyperbolic surrealism with which animators would exaggerate his silliest behaviors that evidenced a camp sensibility widely misattributed to sexual orientation (which itself is never suggested in the program). Camp may be an outgrowth of both drag dress and the "element of parody in gay men's adoption of hypermasculine styles" such as mustaches and leather in San Francisco's 1970s Castro Street (Connell 1995, 218). In 1969, Monty Python practiced musical camp in "The Lumberjack Song" to reveal that a rugged logger was incongruously a drag queen ("I wear high heels, suspenders and a bra; I wish I were a girlie just like my dear Mama" [later changed to "Papa"]), with possible implications for his sexuality.[14] Parodic camp frequently spoofs the virile character, often a cowboy (following Andy Warhol's 1968 film, *Lonesome Cowboys*): see Pansy Division's "Cowboys Are Frequently, Secretly Fond of Each Other" (1995), and the Supreme Fabulettes' "A Drag Queen is a Cowboy's Best Friend" (2013), but also the trucker as in the Foo Fighters' video for "Keep It Clean (Hot Buns)" (2011). If someday one were to regard nonheterosexual identities as normal and not deviant, camp performance conceivably might be observed and suffered as sexuality's blackface, and so we might predict a possible future rejection of camp as a socially repugnant exertion of dominance.

In the previous chapter, we touched on the debate as to whether "masculine" or "feminine" music can be produced and identified as such. Even more subject to controversy is the question as to whether *sexual orientation* can be suggested

---

[14] Musical camp is discussed in relation to subverted gender and homosexuality in McRobbie 1994, 19 and 86, Hawkins 2002, 134 and 165, 2009, 6–7, 27, 113, and 148–50, and 2016, 13–14, 134–5, and 159, Cameron and Kulik 2003, 99–103, Dickinson 2004, 175–6, Whiteley 2005, 133, Bannister 2006, xxv, Busse 2006, 260, Middleton 2007, 116, Leibetseder 2012, 59–75 and 150, Taylor 2012, 67–80 and 129–41, Vargas 2012, xiv, Harper-Scott 2013, 147, King 2013, 96–7, Lieb 2013, 90–1 and 129, Gioia 2015, 240, and Hawkins 2016, 42, 106–7, and 199.

musically. At times, the synthesizer has been taken as a gay signifier—"Kurt Loder, writing for *Rolling Stone* in 1983 about the 'new British Invasion' derided synthpop groups as 'poofs,' 'fops,' 'dandies' and 'preening poseurs'" (Peraino 2015, 292–3), but such generalizations are subject to the same objections raised in Chapter 2 about the synthesizer's being taken as an emblem of masculinity. Often, when music is heard as "gay" or "queer," what's really being expressed is stereotyped qualities of gender, rather than sexuality, as true in describing the "weak and effeminate" sound production of 1930s crooners (McCracken 2015, 26). Is it proper to think of gayness, for instance, as expressible in deviance from musical norms? Such an assumption seems to lie behind many analyses.[15] To the contrary, Susan McClary (2006, 206 and 2013, 33), for one, rejects the notion. Janis Ian points out that *all* artists are to a degree outsiders, regardless of their sexuality (Carson, Lewis, and Shaw 2004, 35), so those who agree with her might find factors other than sexual orientation to guide music typically away from, or toward, its norm-signifying impulses.

Aside from the possible question of such an approach intersecting with homophobic tendencies, one must recognize that deviance from norms is in the nature of most music (with some trance-invoking minimalism or maximally— or arbitrarily—controlled musical factors outside our consideration). All tonal music potentially creates interest by mixing relationships that both comport with and defy expectations based on what are understood as typical tension-based behaviors in pitch, rhythm, texture, dynamics, and formal relations. As for music depicting homosexuality as opposed to heterosexuality, perhaps the reliance on deviance as a key marker would change in degree from decade to decade, depending upon growing social tolerance; one can't expect "Bakhtin's carnivalesque grotesque realism" (Taylor 2012, 140) to express gayness more than—say—the contradiction of any norm, sexual or otherwise, in any or all decades. But some *heterosexual* relationships such as in adultery (a frequent situation inspiring pop music) might be similarly portrayed as forbidden and thus deviations from norms. As argued previously regarding some examples of homophobia-carrying dissonances, it seems that music can well portray deviation, but not "gayness." Music can express some qualities (aspects measured

[15] See, for example, Watson 1994, 358, Hubbs 1996, 273–7, Gracyk 2001, 206–7, Miller 2003, Auslander 2006, 90, Rycenga 2006a, and Vargas 2012, xiv–xv. Hawkins 2016, 20, 143, and 149–50, can be clear in separating (while relating) "genderbending" and sexuality, but elsewhere in the same source (pp. 44–5, 58, 109, 136–50, 173–6, 190, 199, 214, and 218–19), "queerness" (an attribute or function of sexuality?) seems to be equated with camp's heightened expressivity, as if pain itself is a marker of sexual orientation. Maus 2006, 201, discusses Michael Stipe's own related views.

dynamically: big, smooth, sad, quick), but not others (the color orange).[16] Simon Frith says, "The disco version of eroticism and ecstasy is not, itself, homosexual, but the aesthetic uses of these experiences did reflect gay consciousness" (1981, 246). In Springsteen's "My Lover Man" (1990), if one were to replace the title with the words "My lover, Anne," at each appearance, the song would simply be accepted as a tender love song. As with camp, creating and discerning music as "gay" may be perceived as a defensive coping mechanism, whether practiced by songwriter, performer, or listener. From Ma Rainey's lesbian-proclaiming "Prove It on Me Blues" (1928) (see Carby 2015, 41) to Morrissey's "ambisexuality" (Hawkins 2009, 93), Garbage's self-reflexive songs of queer identity (Hawkins 2016, 89), and Nicki Minaj's embodiment of the *ménage à trois*, questions of musico-poetic relationships and the differences between artist and portrayed persona should be carefully considered when examining the musical representation of sexuality.

Frank Ocean is a popular gay singer-songwriter. His "Self Control" (2016) might serve as an example for an analysis of the treatment of gay sexuality. After an intro, the first verse opens with the line, "I'll be the boyfriend in your wet dreams tonight." While the addressee might conceivably be a woman, the wet dream is more often associated with a nocturnal emission of semen than of vaginal fluids (and more typical in adolescents than adults). The song's last line could be a reference to gender: "You're spitting game" is a phrase meaning flirting that originated in hip-hop culture, normally taken to signify a guy chatting up a girl, but the idiom could easily be appropriated by gays. So the song's only potential references to gender are somewhat ambiguous, as are other lyrics, which may suggest that the singer fantasizes about a bygone lover or "the one that got away." When he sings "I'll sleep between y'all," perhaps he pictures himself in the imagination (but not the actual presence) of that past (potential) lover who is now with another. Let's proceed as if Frank is singing about an ex-boyfriend who kept his self-control when the singer lost his (a moment portrayed in the song's greatest melismas), in a memory living only in the bygone summer during which the singer had exited the closet. Three musical facts are of interest: (1) The ever-repeated harmonic loop, the doo-wop progression, I - vi - ii - V, is as conventional as could be. But singularly, halfway through the second cycle (after I - vi, at 0:55), the first verse gives way to the chorus, which moves in

---

[16] Everett 2012 provides a comprehensive literature survey of various mechanisms by which music can be expressive.

a rotated form, ii - V - I - vi, then marking every transition from verse to chorus (again occurring between vi and ii at 2:07) and back (1:18, and to the outro at 2:32). So there's a very unusual mis-phasing between chord loop and formal sections. (2) All chords are destabilized with jazzy sevenths; the major-major I7 chord reverberates in the outro's iii chord (both sonorities suggesting an intimate vulnerability in the "damaged" ego of IM7) introduced in the new loop, I - iii - ♭VII - vi. (3) The vocal parts (the solo singer double-tracks at the unison or polyphonically in places, and in four-part singing at 3:19) vary in contrasting (a) heavily autotuned choruses against "straight" verses, (b) the normal tessitura of verses against the first chorus's sped-up vocal and the second chorus's very low register, and (c) a greater degree of reverb against lesser (true of guitars as well as of vocal). Such contrasts could have fit with clear narrative depictions of past and present, but "Self Control" does not neatly divide perspectives of time; all of Ocean's juxtapositions are jumbled in a dreamlike fantasy. Whereas these bittersweet lost possibilities might relate to a gay relationship, or one—never consummated—between a straight and a gay, all of these factors could apply to a heterosexual liaison as well, resulting in a recording to which a wide audience can relate.

The long persecution and sacrifice of gays have led to a culture of tragic literature: Oscar Wilde's novel, *The Picture of Dorian Gray*, James Baldwin's novel, *Giovanni's Room*, Tony Kushner's play, *Angels in America*, Ang Lee's film, *Brokeback Mountain*, and Craig Hella Johnson's oratorio, *Considering Matthew Shepard*, are a few examples. The tradition obtains in popular music as well. Rod Stewart's "The Killing of Georgie" (1977) is a two-part song: a Dylan-like ballad conveying the tale of the tragically unintentional homicide in a repeated plagal riff devoid of any real harmonic motion (but damaged each time I is replaced by iii), its drama conveyed in Stewart's vocal alone, followed by an apotheosis— the key having fallen a fifth from B♭ to E♭—repeating a plea borrowed from the Beatles' "Don't Let Me Down" (1969). The tribulations in Morrissey's "Billy Budd" (1994) may be less severe than Georgie's on the surface (the singer's rejected job application, the object's distressing lack of freedom), but the listener likely positions Billy as namesake of the title characters of both Melville's novel and Britten's opera, a sailor hanged for accidental manslaughter.

Two songs by Rufus Wainwright are of interest in this regard. In "Gay Messiah" (2004), he assumes the role of John the Baptist (as "Rufus the Baptist"), itinerant preacher and prophet foretelling the arrival of a gay redeemer. The messiah is reborn out of life as a porn star first appearing in the gay clubs of

Fire Island, "baptized in cum," who absolves those who confess their sins. Just as John was sentenced to beheading by Herod, Rufus will kneel and give his head to those powerful enough to demand it, a farcical rewriting of annihilation. In "Perfect Man" (2012), Rufus paints himself as a sailor on the Flying Dutchman, a ghost ship—possibly that of pirates—doomed to wander the seas eternally in a fruitless search for the ideal lover. In some versions of the myth, told in Heine's novel and Wagner's opera, the sailor is allowed to make port one night every seven years to attempt finding salvation in a faithful wife. Wainwright's singer compares himself to the tragic "Sisi," the assassinated nineteenth-century Austrian empress Elisabeth. In his corner are the likes of Pirate Jenny (in Weill/ Brecht's *Die Dreigroschenoper* a harassed maid who, after foretelling the act, takes revenge on a whole townspeople by ordering pirates to kill them all then riding away in their freighter), Lady Jane Grey (the subject of Schönberg's op. 12/1: England's sixteenth-century queen deposed after nine days on the throne, then beheaded), and "Nina . . . a sweet nymphomaniac" (perhaps a cryptic reference to Nina Simone?, who along with Lotte Lenya was well known for her interpretations of "Pirate Jenny"). With this crew, Wainwright forever travels "over it, over it" through metrically halting and chromatically wild "red herrings," falling repeatedly over a lamento bass as he cruises "Rufus Street" in all of Europe's parks in futile search of his lifelong ideal, a literate lover, the "perfect man" who he ultimately suspects haunts him without hope of resolution. The music in both of these songs could easily support heterosexual versions of the same tragic tales. Table 3.1 presents a selection of songs treating gay sexuality. While it is not comprehensive, it presents a true picture of changes over time in terms of homophobia, acceptance, and forthright language as opposed to euphemistic evasion.

In a press conference on August 24, 1966, a journalist asked John Lennon and Paul McCartney about two Beatles songs of the previous year, thus: "In a recent article, *Time* magazine . . . referred to 'Day Tripper' as being about a prostitute and 'Norwegian Wood' as being about a lesbian. I just wanted to know what your intent was when you wrote it, and what your feeling is about the *Time* magazine criticism." McCartney japed preposterously in response, "We were just trying to write songs about prostitutes and lesbians, that's all." The notion of lesbianism (invisible through much of twentieth-century Western culture) did not exist before the seventeenth century; nineteenth-century doctors "conflated nymphomaniacs, prostitutes, and lesbians"; "the abiding image of the male-attired self-identified woman-loving-woman" became widely recognized in

Table 3.1 Songs Portraying Gay Themes

Chart Year	Artist	Song Title	Comments
1928	Sloppy Henry	Say I Do It	"Mose and Pete . . . two could be seen runnin' hand in hand"
1928	Ma Rainey	Sissy Blues	"My man got a sissy, his name is Miss Kate"
c. 1941	Ray [later Rae] Bourbon	My First Piece	"It was hard, [laughs] very hard, but he was so patient and so gentle"
c. 1953	Ruth Wallis	Queer Things	Off-label novelty song; "they knew he liked the best man better than the bride"
1968	The Kinks	David Watts	"He is so gay and fancy free," avoids the girls in the neighborhood
1969	Steve Greenberg	Big Bruce	Ridicules gay character ("he got arrested for passing three-dollar bills") delivered in mincing spoken voice
1972	Lou Reed	Make Up	"Now we're comin' out, out of our closets"
1973	Bruce Springsteen	Lost in the Flood; Wild Billy's Circus Story; Incident on 57th Street	"Wolfman fairies dressed in drag"; "The hired hand tightens his legs on the sword swallower's blade"; "Them barefoot boys . . . kissed each other goodbye" (see Fanshel 2013; Hawkins 2016, 181)
1974	*Let My People Come* cast	I'm Gay	Son coming out of closet to parents; sung as an imitative duet to suggest split persona
1974	Steely Dan	Through with Buzz	"Maybe he's a fairy"
1975	Queen	Bohemian Rhapsody	"Pulled my trigger, now he's dead," shot with slow dropping bass gliss (see Whiteley 2007)
1977	Elton Motello	Jet Boy Jet Girl	Fifteen-year-old boy has sex with older man
1977	Rod Stewart	The Killing of Georgie	Singer's friend, in these "so-called liberal days," rejected by parents after coming out
1978	Carl Bean	I Was Born This Way	Predates Lady Gaga's celebrated anthem by decades; "I'm happy, carefree and gay"

(Continued)

Table 3.1 (Continued)

Chart Year	Artist	Song Title	Comments
1978	David Allan Coe Band	Fuck Aneta Bryant	"Who the hell is she? Tellin' all them faggots that they can't be free" (see Hubbs 2014)
1978	Tom Robinson Band	(Sing If You're) Glad to Be Gay	Creepy minor mode like "Leaping Lesbians"; verses of harassment by (British) police, press, individual queerbashers (see Cloonan 1996)
1978	Sylvester	You Make Me Feel (Mighty Real)	Gay anthem with powerful aeolian chorus, "[♭VI] you [♭VII] make me [I] feel [♭VI] migh- [♭VII] -ty [I] real"
1978	Village People	Y.M.C.A.; My Roommate	"They have everything for you men to enjoy, you can hang out with all the boys"; He "keeps me up at night"
1978	Frank Zappa	Punky's Whips	Rapid vocal trill on gay ecstatic "squirm"
1979	Sugarhill Gang	Rapper's Delight	Some gay bashing; idea of dancing, "I'll put TNT in your behind", predicts later explicit anal sex
1979	The Vectors	Death to Disco	"Whose little girl dancing with a fag?"
1979	Frank Zappa	Sy Borg; Doing Work for Yuda	Gay sex with a doll; Gay anal sex
1981	Depeche Mode	What's Your Name	David Gahan sings, "Hey, you're such a pretty boy" (see Peraino 2015, 289)
1981	Prince	Controversy	"Am I straight or gay?"
1982	Grandmaster Flash	The Message	Homophobic references to prison sex
1982	Frank Zappa	Valley Girl	Homophobic rant on Moon's teacher
1983	La Cage aux Folles cast	I Am What I Am	Confidently rising arpeggios, "your life is a sham 'til you can shout out loud . . ."
1984	Frankie Goes to Hollywood	Relax	Song about aborting orgasm just before point of inevitability; artists gay but song not explicitly so
1984	Frank Zappa	Harry-as-a-Boy; He's So Gay Why?; Smalltown Boy; Need-a-Man Blues	Spoken pantomime about man driven gay by women's lib (!); Gay anal sex
1985	Bronski Beat		Anti-homophobia: "contempt in your eyes as I turn to kiss his lips"; "The sweetest thing of all is men loving men loving men"

1986	Alaska	¿A quién le importa?	Lesbian/gay anthem; chorus a strongly directed motion through full fifths circle
1987	George Michael	I Want Your Sex	Singer is gay but musically in closet; sings to woman (indicated by backing vocals)
1987	Swinging Erudites	Walk with an Erection	Ridicules gay character
1988	Guns N' Roses	One in a Million	Homophobic rant on spread of AIDS
1988	Frank Zappa	Jezebel Boy	Client wants blowjob from male prostitute
1989	2 Live Crew	If You Believe in Having Sex	"[Ld Vocal:] Bulldaggers! [Response:] Suck Pussy! [LV:] All faggots! [R:] Suck dick!"
1990	George Michael	Freedom! '90	Coming out in chorus expressing inevitable truth in double-plagal falls
1990	Morrissey	Will Never Marry	Tragedy of lonely life before gay marriage
1991	Thompson Twins	Come Inside	"When all the doors are open wide, I'll be yours and maybe you'll be mine"
1992	Garth Brooks	We Shall Be Free	Explicitly supportive of gays
1992	Screeching Weasel	I Wanna Be a Homosexual	Homophobic punk rant in ironic power chords for "lisp" "limp wrist," "mincing"
1993	Nirvana	All Apologies	"What else could I say? Everyone is gay"
1993	Pansy Division	The Cocksucker Club	Man discovers he is gay
1993	Pet Shop Boys	Can You Forgive Her?; To Speak Is a Sin	Man in castrating relationship wonders if he can perform what the woman needs; Gays now free to live as themselves
1993	Senseless Things	Homophobic Asshole	Singer complains that hate speech makes no sense; main riff has tritone over tonic
1994	Blur	Girls & Boys	"Girls who are boys who like boys to be girls who do boys like they're girls . . ."
1994	Lemonheads	Big Gay Heart	"I don't need you to suck my dick"
1994	Morrissey	Billy Budd	Singer rejected for being gay; double-plagal progression for preordained event
1994	Bruce Springsteen	Streets of Philadelphia	Fatalistic $\wedge 3$–$\wedge 2$–$\wedge 1$ melody over singer and friends wasting away of HIV infections

(Continued)

Table 3.1 (Continued)

Chart Year	Artist	Song Title	Comments
1995	Pansy Division	*Pile Up*	Many songs explicitly about gay sex
1995	Robert Preston	Gay Paree	"there's also bound to be rough trade"
1996	Me'Shell Ndegéocello	Leviticus: Faggot	Homophobic father and gay son; Ominous minor-pentatonic guitar
1996	Pet Shop Boys	Metamorphosis	Repressed gay gloriously emerges from closet as d minor replaced by F major
1998	George Michael	Outside	"Let's go outside in the sunshine" for coming out (see Hawkins 2016)
1998	Bruce Springsteen	My Lover Man	"Come into my arms and fall, my lover man" (see Fanshel 2013; Hawkins 2016)
1999	Magnetic Fields	When My Boy Walks Down the Street	"He's going to be my wife"; verses conventional but bridge timeless, weightless without drums and bass
1999	Pet Shop Boys	In Denial	Feminine inner voice advises gay singer
2000	*Bare: A Pop Opera* cast	Epiphany	Gay man's religious upbringing pushes him to renounce his desires
2000	Jeff Buckley	Dream Brother	Man kisses man on tritone ("another")
2000	Eminem	Stan; Marshall Mathers; Criminal	Fan's gay fantasy; Homophobic statements in several songs
2001	Deep Dickollective	Mariposa Prelube	Rap about homophobia; "we wear the masks of them sodomite fudgepackers"
2003	Pansy Division	No Protection	Man wants unprotected gay sex
2003	Amy Winehouse	Stronger Than Me	Antifeminist; "All I need is for my man to live up to his role. . . . are you gay?"
2004	Green Day	American Idiot	"Maybe I'm the faggot America"
2004	Rufus Wainwright	Gay Messiah	The head of Rufus the Baptist being a gay receptacle
2005	Anal Traffic	Two Pumps and a Squirt	"Just take your cock and stick it right up me!" on minor-pentatonic scales
2006	Morrissey	At Last I Am Born	Comes out with timpani and snare on defiant rising aeolian progression

Year	Artist	Song	Description
2006	Peaches	Two Guys (For Every Girl)	"I wanna see you work it guy on guy"
2009	Gossip	Men in Love	"… with each other" line in stop time
2009	Pansy Division	*That's So Gay*	Several songs about gays
2009	Bruce Springsteen	Last Carnival	Carnival a metaphor for dangers of gay life for male singer and Billy
2011	Foo Fighters	Keep It Clean (Hot Buns)	"Think I'm in the mood for some hot man muffins"
2011	Lonely Island	3-Way (The Golden Rule)	"It's not gay when it's in a three-way; with a honey in the middle"
2012	*A Letter to Harvey Milk* cast	What a Shanda	Gay sex goes against God's plan; Lesbian is a waste of womanhood
2012	Macklemore & Ryan Lewis	Same Love	Against conversion therapy and hip-hop's homophobia; for gay marriage
2012	Rufus Wainwright	Out of the Game; Perfect Man	"You're only a young thing, 'bout to sleep with a sea of men" (see Hawkins 2016)
2013	Cakes da Killa	Goodie Goodies	"Hit me on Grindr so I know where to find ya"
2013	John Mayer	Who You Love	Support for gays
2013	Pet Shop Boys	Love Is a Bourgeois Construct	"I've been hanging as a fairy riff raff" (see Hawkins 2016)
2014	Le1f	Boom	"LGBT cuties all over the world"
2015	*Fun Home* cast	Let Me Introduce You to My Gay Dad	Allison's dad was gay

Radclyffe Hall's 1928 novel, *The Well of Loneliness*, and the heterosexual norm led to the twentieth-century idea that lesbians were either "femme" (identifying with women) or "butch" (identifying with men).[17] As an example of the latter distinction, the Swiss band Les Reines Prochaines sing "I wanna be a butch 'cause butch are strong and sensitive!" in "I Wanna Be a Butch" (1999).

Popular music performed by lesbians such as Dusty Springfield (who came out early, in 1970, and sang her own song called "Born This Way" [1990]: "in this world there's a love that's unspoken . . . learn to love yourself, respect yourself, say 'that's the way I am'"), Lesley Gore, Janis Ian, Joan Armatrading, k. d. lang, Phranc, and the two members of the Indigo Girls has rarely if ever reflected the artists' sexual identities or proclivities (especially before the mid-1990s, a period when nearly all gays and lesbians stayed in the closet). Maxine Feldman lamented in an aeolian "Angry Atthis" (1971), "I hate not bein' able to hold my lover's hand 'cept under some dimly lit table; . . . we've run half of our lives from that damn word, 'Queer!'" Other singers, however, have proclaimed their orientation as a feminist and morale-boosting political statement: Sweet Honey in the Rock's anthem, "Every Woman" (1977), has the chorus, "Every woman who ever loved a woman, you ought to stand up and call her name: Mama, sister, daughter, lover." Olivia Records-founding singer Cris Williamson, queercore bands like Tribe 8, "riot grrrl"-inspired artists like Bikini Kill and MEN, and cover band Lesbians on Ecstasy further exemplify artists exercising power in their sexuality.[18] Lesbians such as Holly Near have performed at concerts and other events on the women's circuit, "a loose affiliation of record companies, concert promoters, and related businesses that focused on a determinedly lesbian audience" (Berman 1997, 128). Lesbians, once out, can feel free to perform songs about women that were created by men (as does Melissa Etheridge when singing

---

[17] The first quote ("conflated . . .") is from Dean 1996, 6, the second ("the abiding image . . .") from Weeks 2011, 101. Other historical information on lesbianism (one sense of "tribadism"), instances of same in literature, film, and television, prevalence, and the relevant relationships between identity and acts, is provided by Smith-Rosenberg 1975, Rich 1980, Califia 1983, Perry 1988, van der Meer 1988, Laqueur 1990, 53, Traub 1991, Rubin 1992, Butler 1993, Sayrs 1993–4, Michael et al. 1994, McRobbie 1997, Halberstam 1998 and 2012, Vance 1999, Tropiano 2002, Weston 2002, Cameron and Kulik 2003, Hawkes 2004, 170, Whiteley 2005, Clark 2008, Diamond 2008, Douglas 2010, Weeks 2010, D'Emilio and Freedman 2012, Dabhoiwala 2012, Leibetseder 2012, Rutter and Schwartz 2012, Bergner 2013, Hubbs 2014, Thiel-Stern 2014, Seidman 2015, Barmak 2016, Orenstein 2016, Twenge 2017, and McDonnell 2018.

[18] Thoughts on lesbianism in music are presented in Petersen 1987, Gaar 1992, Solie 1993, McDonnell 1997, Burns 1999–2000, Cusick 1999b, Hisama 1999, Stein 1999, Auslander 2000 and 2006, O'Brien 2002, Carson et al. 2004, Cusick 2006, Rycenga 2006b, Middleton 2007, Warwick 2007, Leibetseder 2012, Taylor 2012, Lieb 2013, Smith 2014, McCracken 2015, Hawkins 2016, Jasmine 2018b, and Phillips 2018.

[in 1995] Bruce Springsteen's "Thunder Road" [Carson, Lewis, and Shaw 2004, 108]), provocative straight women may sing in men's voices to suggest a lesbian identity (Suzi Quatro's "All Shook Up" [1974]), a hetero singer may pose in support for the gay cause (Katy Perry's "I Kissed a Girl" [2008]), or a lesbian *listener* might have a gay reading of a heterosexual's song (as with Jennifer Rycenga's take on Kate Bush's "Running Up that Hill" [1985] [1997, 212–14]). Recently relaxed mores allow Nicki Minaj to rap playfully with Gucci Mane, "Can I squeeze your boobs? Let me see your boobs" ("Girls Kissing Girls," 2016).

Table 3.2 offers a list of lesbian-situated songs. All were not necessarily created with that intent. For instance, whereas singer-songwriter Brandi Carlile is in fact a lesbian, her "Jospehine" (2007) was originally written by bandmate Tim Hanseroth in reference to a county in the Oregon Cascades by that name. Nevertheless, it is easy and not inappropriate to interpret this love song about a lesbian relationship. Carlile's "If She Ever Leaves Me" (2019) was also written by a man (Jason Isbell), but expressly to create a lesbian cowgirl waltz. Meg Christian's recording of "Leaping Lesbians" (1976, written and first recorded by Sue Fink, who plays a Lurch-worthy harpsichord on Christian's performance) was created in 1977 as a tongue-in-cheek rebuttal to Anita Bryant's ugly crusade at a time when gay sex frightened the majority culture. The song is a camp novelty, opening with a horror movie's mock warning, a slow, suspenseful "tiptoe" arpeggiation up the minor tonic octave, tremolo on the German sixth and quick stepwise descent from $\hat{5}$ to $\hat{1}$ to prepare for the frightening howl, "Here come the lesbians!" It's made even more alarming by the tritone-heavy wordless cry, leaping up the octave, $\hat{1}$ - $\hat{8}$, only to drop to a wailing $\hat{\sharp}4$ to warn, "Don't look in the closet!" Tom Robinson's cabaret-like "(Sing If You're) Glad to Be Gay," which followed Fink's song by a year, contrasts the same creepy, Grinch-evoking minor-mode quality in sarcastic verses about queerbashing with a major-mode chorus ("Sing if you're happy that way") that is all too fleeting, dissolving after a shocking "Hey!" on V into the original minor-mode depression. The hopeful major is merely a failed part of the overall tragic arpeggiation, i - III - V - i, along the lines of the gay tragedies mentioned previously.

Minor and major are also contrasted in Gloria Gaynor's "I Am What I Am" (1983, a song from *La Cage aux Folles*), which alternates an initial major mode ("damaged" by the opening I - iii move, which seems to acknowledge the singer's major-seventh vulnerabilities) with an instrumental minor-mode lamento bass tattoo (0:38+) that is itself immediately replaced by a vibrantly rising major-mode defiance (0:43-0:45). This buoyant $\hat{5}$ - $\hat{6}$ - $\hat{7}$ - $\hat{8}$ - $\hat{2}$ rise rhymes with

Table 3.2 Songs Portraying Lesbian Themes

Chart Year	Artist	Song Title	Comments
1923	Alberta Hunter	Someone Else Will Take Your Place	"There are five or six women long to take your place"
1928	Ma Rainey	Prove It on Me Blues	"An affirmation of lesbianism" (Carby 2015, 41; see also Davis 1999, Halberstam 2007, and Leibetseder 2012)
c. 1935	Lucille Bogan	B. D. Woman's Blues	"Comin' a time, [Bull Dyke or Bull Dagger] women, they ain't gonna need no men"
1951	Willie Mae Thornton	No Jody for Me	She has no truck with Jody, a universal male character (see Steptoe 2018, 71–2)
1961	Chavela Vargas	Paloma Negra	Woman breaks singer's heart (see Vargas 2012, 106)
1971	Maxine Feldman	Angry Atthis	Aeolian lament of having to live in the closet, but "no longer afraid of being a lesbian"
1973	Alix Dobkin	View from Gay Head	Refined, courtly piece with strings, cadential trills; "it's a pleasure to be a lesbian"
1973	Elton John	All the Girls Love Alice	Hard rock for unsatisfying boys; softer for "getting your kicks in another girl's bed"
1974	Meg Christian	Valentine Song; Ode to a Gym Teacher	"Evenin' kisses, woman, . . . wakin' up still together"; Young girl fantasizes about her female teacher in her lowest vocal register
1975	Patti Smith	Redondo Beach	Song about a lesbian hangout
1975	Cris Williamson	Sweet Woman	"A little passage of time 'til I hold you and you'll be mine, sweet woman," in low alto
1977	Meg Christian	Leaping Lesbians	Camp creepy tiptoes in minor mode; "here come the lesbians"; tritone for "closet"
1978	David Allan Coe Band	Whips and Things	"Pussy-eatin' Pamela"
1980	Diana Ross	I'm Coming Out	Confident "There's a new me coming out"
1981	Sheila Hylton	The Bed's Too Big without You	"When she left I was cold inside"; minor triads on ♭vi – ♭vii – i repeated
1981	Frank Zappa	Goblin Girl	Camp creepy minor tiptoes for spooky witch

1982	Alaska	Bailando	Lesbian and gay anthem
1983	Gloria Gaynor	I Am What I Am	Coming out in rise from inner to upper voice
1984	Jane Siberry	Dancing Class; Mimi on the Beach	Singer pairs up with beautiful girl; Rise to climax in bridge as waves heighten for "Mimi and me"
1988	Michelle Shocked	If Love Was a Train	"...I'd throw my body on her tracks"
1992	Indigo Girls	Galileo	Singer wonders when truth will come to her
1993	Bikini Kill	Alien She; Rebel Girl; New Radio	"I am her Siamese twin connected at the cunt"; "They say she is a dyke"; "Come here, baby—let me kiss you like a boy does"
1993	Tribe 8	Lezbophobia	"You got lesbophobia, ... homoparanoia"
1995	CeBe Barnes Band	She's a Winner	"She's a winner, she's a dyke" (see Kearney 1998)
1995	k. d. lang	Sexuality	"Kiss away the ones who say the lust you feel is wrong"; cadence from "Nature's Way"
1995	Jill Sobule	I Kissed a Girl	Whammy bar suggests her world is rocked
1995	Tribe 8	Neanderthal Dyke; Manipulate	Screed against feminist theory; "I just wanna slap around my girlfriend"
1996	Ani DiFranco	Shameless	"I covet another man's wife"
1996	Me'Shell Ndegéocello	Mary Magdalene	Singer promises woman a life of pleasure; no climax but alternation of i with ♭VII (see Burns and Lafrance 2002)
1996	Tribe 8	Checking Out Your Babe	"She's strapped it on and wants to bone ya"
1996	2 Live Crew	Bulldagger Stole My Bitch	"She'd rather suck pussy, she don't want no dick!"
1996	Suzanne Vega	Stockings	Passionately desires woman friend
1996	Weezer	Pink Triangle	Nazi symbol for gays worn by woman
1997	Indigo Girls	It's Alright	"You hate me 'cause I'm gay"
1997	Janis Ian	Ride Me Like a Wave	Title whispered in doubled voice; frisson in suspended cymbal rolls, in surrender
1998	PJ Harvey	Catherine	Phrygian loss in broken heart
1998	Lords of Acid	Pussy	"Lay your little pussy right next to mine"
1999	Les Reines prochaines	I Wanna Be a Butch	"... 'Cause butch are strong and sensitive" (see Leibetseder 2012, 11)

(Continued)

Table 3.2 (Continued)

Chart Year	Artist	Song Title	Comments
2000	Holly Near	Rock Me in Your Arms; Simply Love	Alto voice for romance with "pretty woman"; "Simply my love for a woman"
2001	Bitch and Animal	Best Cock on the Block	Song about a lesbian's dildo
2001	Melissa Etheridge	The Different	"The dark and the wild and the different" may refer to lesbianism, but unclear
2003	Me'Shell Ndegéocello	Andromeda & the Milky Way; Love Song #3	Flowing river and garden as symbols of vulva for cunnilingus
2003	Angie Reed	*Presents the Best of Barbara Brockhaus*	"Fun is always on the tip of her tongue" (see Leibetseder 2012, 33)
2004	Melissa Etheridge	This Moment	"Can I slip into you?"
2005	50 Cent	Hate It or Love It	"Coming up I was confused, my mommy kissing a girl"
2006	*Bad Girls* cast	Every Night	A lesbian love song
2007	Brandi Carlile	Josephine	"Take me back, Josephine"
2007	Girl in a Coma	Clumsy Sky	Lesbian duet
2007	Of Montreal	Bunny Ain't No Kind of Rider	"Saw her . . . kissing girls, what a shock"; "to me you're just some faggy girl"
2009	Nicki Minaj	Go Hard	"I only stop for pedestrians, or a real real bad lesbian" (see Lieb 2013; Smith 2014; Hawkins 2016)
2009	Rihanna	Te Amo	"Te amo, te amo,' she says to me"
2010	Nicki Minaj	Girls Fall Like Dominoes	"Everytime that I come out it's just girls gone wild" (See Smith 2014)
2011	Lady Gaga	Born This Way	Gay pride, "God makes no mistakes"
2011	MEN	Who Am I to Feel So Free	"We found options that were better than a man—radical surgery, prosthetic sex"
2013	Janelle Monáe	Q.U.E.E.N.	"Am I a freak for watching Mary?"
2013	Kacey Musgraves	Follow Your Arrow	Gay support: "Kiss lots of boys or kiss lots of girls if that's something you're into"
2015	*Fun Home* cast	I Leapt Out of the Closet	Alison came out as a lesbian and four months later her father killed himself
2019	Billie Eilish	Wish You Were Gay	"All you do is look the other way"
2019	Highwomen	If She Ever Leaves Me	"If she ever leaves, it's gonna be for a woman with more time"

her ^2- ^3 - ^4 - ^5 - ^6 - ^7 - ^8 - ^2 ascent from inner voice to outer for "time to open up your closet" (1:52–1:53), an idea perhaps reborn in Wurst's "Rise Like a Phoenix" (2014). There's no such drama, and nothing either major or minor in Holly Near's validation of bonding with a woman in "Simply Love" (2000), but simply a haunting aeolian-mode tune over diatonic yet poignant non-chord tones. In "Sexuality" (1995), k. d. lang frees lesbian love from the bounds of social opprobrium ("kiss away the ones who say the lust you feel is wrong"). Her bridge does not end on a masculine-powered V, but is caught in a tension-filled dissonance: "un- [Gm] -leash your sexu- [Am] -ality on [B♭M7 - 6/5 - 4] me," invoking the same phrase ending heard in Spirit's "Nature's Way" (1970), "it's nature's way of telling you something's wrong"—as if the tension of social pressure feeds into the couple's sexual climax. Suzanne Vega represses her passionate desire for a woman in "Stockings" (1996), but a woman loving a woman is simply a straight-ahead situation for a love song in "Every Night," from the show *Bad Girls* (2006). The trope of a man's bemoaning the "waste" of an attractive woman on others of her gender is the Yiddish-intoned topic of "What a Shanda" (from the show, *A Letter to Harvey Milk* [2012]): "What a shame, what a shanda, a gorgeous face like hers she's gonna squanda on some schlumpy girl who dresses like a guy?"

Other Sexualities

"When asked if he was bisexual, singer David Johansen said, 'No man, I'm trisexual; I'll try anything'" (O'Brien 2002, 257). Recall that Freud theorized that no one has a fixed sexuality at birth, that all are "polymorphously perverse" and essentially pansexual prior to (a) indoctrination with the Oedipus complex and (b) the repression of socially unacceptable expression. Kinsey, too, saw bisexuality as a common orientation and practice, and it became moreso from the 1970s through 2015. Bisexuality and pansexuality are forms of identity or orientation that seem to sex researchers to be about twice as prevalent in women as in men (and more common among the trans population [Lester 2017, 159–60]); "libertine" artists such as Lord Byron, Vaslav Nijinsky, and Bessie Smith proclaimed themselves bisexual in so many words long before Janis Joplin, David Bowie, Elton John, and Me'Shell Ndegéocello would. Many performers, such as Freddie Mercury (who had both male and female lovers), whose career took place in highly homophobic times, declined to discuss their own sexuality publicly, and so it would be inappropriate for others to assign definite labels. Michael Stipe has said, "there wasn't really a category for me and I didn't like the third sex, it didn't feel comfortable calling myself bisexual," but Fred E. Maus hears suggestions of "bisexual eroticism" in Stipe's songs like "Pretty Persuasion" (1984) (Maus 2006, 200–2). Elsewhere, in "King of Comedy" (1994), Stipe sings "I'm straight, I'm queer, I'm bi" through a weirdly distorting Leslie speaker. Living Colour, in "Bi" (1993), sing, "There's a category if you're straight or gay; you're a wild-card gambler and you like it both ways," implying there's no specific third such division. In "Venus as a Boy" (1993), Björk fantasizes about loving a boy who has the beauty and sensitive desires of Venus, as if the object's gender is of no consequence; the song's chord chain (a repeated loop simply of Eb minor and F minor triads) goes nowhere, reveling in quite sensual feminine images. A heady fantasy without certain gender objects flows through the chorus of Blur's "Girls & Boys" (1994): "Girls who are boys who like boys to be girls who do boys like they're girls who do girls like they're boys." Here, the vocal ornamentation of Cb as upper neighbor to Bb fits the tonic G minor chord but seems to need some lubrication when suspended as a double-dissonance on top of the neighboring C minor chord. Researchers are finding larger populations of bisexual than exclusively homosexual individuals in terms of both arousal and behavior, and given the apparent rising prevalence of bisexuality, many iGen'ers are turning against labels for sexual orientation entirely.[19]

A few songs relate stories of bisexual characters. Katell Keineg's "Leonor" (1997) is a narrative ode to bisexual Argentine painter Leonor Fini. As relayed in verses, Fini lived with two men for forty years while openly enjoying sexual encounters with women. A double life is suggested in the chorus, in which the titular first name is sung three times, each in a double-stopped voice that begins on ^7 - ^8 - ^9 at the unison but moves to the sustained perfect fifth, ^1 over ^4. Fini's anti-patriarchal portraits of strong, often mythological women are captured in the line, "the image of the female self subverting the male's dialogue with his dick." "Leonor" uses the off-color bVII chord to portray the dark side of misogyny she had suffered. Her idiosyncratic approach to life is further captured in the unconventional verses, which comprise lines of a regular four bars each but lack any regularity in syllable counts or accent patterns. Additionally, couplets rhyme in the first two verses, but that feature disappears in the freer third and

---

[19] On the nature of bisexuality, see Diamond 2008, 2017, and 2018, Bergner 2009, Weeks 2011, Rutter and Schwartz 2012, Samuel 2013, Seidman 2015, and Twenge 2017. For discussion of bisexual musicians, see Braziel 2004.

fourth. These portrayals of bifurcation and eccentricity can be considered in relation to bisexuality, while they are not necessarily tied to matters of sex at all.

Lady Gaga's "Sexxx Dreams" (2013) tells of a bisexual, but we can't be sure whether it's the singer or her lover of unspecified sex who has a boyfriend. The double-stopped singer is alone (all supporting instruments silent in stop time) when singing "When I lay in bed I touch myself and think o' you," so there's a nice musical emblem of the solitary nature of masturbation, but there is no obvious musical portrayal of bisexuality. A similar obscurity colors Boy George's "Love and Danger" (2013), in which he sings, "She's waiting for you, but so am I, ambiguous, so beautiful, that's life." The Clovers' much earlier "Love Potion Number Nine" (1959) is the tale of an impotent man ("I was a flop with chicks") who takes the risk of receiving a fortune teller's magic potion. But perhaps he overindulges or the potion works too well, as the singer's lust is so uncontrolled, he becomes pansexual, "kissin' everything in sight." In the Departure phrase of verse 3, the over-ardent singer imprudently kisses a highly offended traffic cop (for humorous effect), who symbolically crushes the singer's arousal and erection ("He broke my little bottle of love potion number nine"), the title sung in stop time over a dramatic retransitional V, rendering the singer impotent once again. "Love Potion" portrays a pansexual episode, but the musical drama, appropriate as it is, could work in exactly the same way for a multitude of nonsexual themes.

Some consider themselves asexual. While this label would of course apply to those too young (as with boy bands) or conceivably too old to be genitally sexual beings, it also describes those of any age with no sex drive or interest in sex.[20] Most mainstream pre-rock 'n' roll music, such as Tin Pan Alley fare and Appalachian folk music, reflects its puritan age by repressing sex as a topic. Later, folk-derivational punk and "music of the mind"—such as many examples of psychedelia, progressive rock, and new wave—might seem to illustrate asexuality because sex is not their immediate issue. The "soulless," "robotic" synthesizer, already characterized differently in the pages earlier, has been tied to asexuality; Judith Peraino's discussion (2015, 308–9) of the Human League's album, *Reproduction* (1979), is an example, but her essay goes on to show with subtlety how androgynous "synthpop provided a sustained meditation

[20] Asexuality, with implications for sex and cultural differences, is a topic in Martin 1996, 16, Bland and Doan 1998, 115, Dickinson 2004, 175, Ellwood-Clayton 2012, 181, and Barmak 2016, 35. Musical ramifications are explored in Pini 1997, Tomlinson 1998, Gendron 2004, Whiteley 2005, Bannister 2006, Lankford 2010, Lieb 2013, and Gioia 2015. As for asexual, "innocent," children, Pat Califia 1983, 87–8, maintains that children are sexual to the extent permitted by the ignorance imposed on them by adults.

on sexuality detached from identity, desire dislocated from gender [exposing] the tension between complex human emotions and the mechanical social interface—the 'controllers'—that are gender and sexuality" (313–14). Natalie Merchant's "Ophelia" (1998) opens in celibacy, as "Ophelia was a bride of God"; the track grows in loudness and other tension as the title character's wild rebellious past is contrasted with her newfound nun's innocence. Abstinence, of course, is a theme running strongly throughout pop history, from the Shirelles' "Will You Love Me Tomorrow" (1960) through Billy Joel's "All You Wanna Do Is Dance" (1976), Janet Jackson's "Let's Wait Awhile," Jermaine Stewart's "We Don't Have to Take Our Clothes Off," and Georgia Satellites's "Keep Your Hands to Yourself" (all three from 1986), Taylor Dayne's "Don't Rush Me" (1988), Monica's "The First Night" (1998), and Mercy's "Duffy" (2008), to Khalid's "Talk" (2019).

More overtly an expression of asexuality, Murray Head's "One Night in Bangkok" (1985) has a chess player oblivious to the fleshy temptations around him declare, "I get my kicks above the waistline, Sunshine." Johnny Rotten notably derided love as an overrated "two minutes of squelching." For some, no doubt the chilling sex-related nature of AIDS transmission dampened sexual expression in the 1980s and 1990s. Rave culture promoted closeness without erotics; the "arrested orgasm" in the music of its clubs "creates a 'plateau of bliss that can neither be exceeded nor released,' leaving ravers in a state of liminality, suspended between ascension and climax, between childhood and adulthood" (Tomlinson 1998, 201). Björk may be autosexual but is ultimately indifferent in "Isobel" (1995), whose droning melody—largely based on stable ^1 and ^5— lacks structural tension as she sings, "My name Isobel, married to myself; my love Isobel living by herself. In a heart full of dust lives a creature called lust." Regina Spektor's "Oedipus" (2002) casts the singer as a male whose mother, "not at all a sex machine," "liked to keep her body clean, clean, thought the world to be quite obscene." (Compare the fireman's preferences in the Beatles' "Penny Lane" [1967].) Personal politics can take asexual forms: Stan Hawkins writes of Morrissey's "claims to asexuality" as part of an anti-hero persona that "promotes celibacy" in ridiculing macho masculinity (2002, 73–4). Citing Camille Paglia, Hawkins has also said that Lady Gaga's "absence of 'genuine eroticism' . . . signals the end of the sexual revolution, hence the death of sex. . . . 'Gaga, for all her writhing and posturing, is asexual'" (2014, 20–1). Doris Leibetseder, on the other hand, finds Gaga's music problematic in relation to her posed sexuality: in "Born This Way" (2011),

Gaga holds on to the idea of a fixed identity; her words sound very similar to the argument of "homosexuality is in the genes" and lead to false essentialist biologism. Categories and essentialisms are not queer at all. So she still is confusing us, because her identity in her performances is queer and fluid, but in her lyrics, she tells us a different story. (2012, 78)

Whereas "queer" had long been a derogatory slur against homosexuals, this descriptor has been rehabilitated for countless nonexclusive forms of sexuality, sex, and gender identities since the gay liberation movement of the 1970s and increasingly in and beyond the 1980s, sometimes through campaigns such as Queer Nation. The "queer" label is applied according to the bearer's desires: it may mean gay, but it may more often signify a rejection of all essentialist pigeonholing identity labels, a carnivalesque unsettling, and a "twisting, lampooning and dismantling of hegemonic culture."[21] While Ani DiFranco "uses the word 'bisexual' in response to an interviewer's question about what she calls herself, she says that she really prefers the word 'queer'. She says 'queer' is 'an open-ended word. It means, like, the kind of love I experience is not the kind of love that's on TV'" (Carson, Lewis, and Shaw 2004, 111). Perhaps because of the regressive sexual politics at work in hip-hop, Nicki Minaj has made contradictory statements about the nature of her sexuality, but she "articulates a queer identity that panders to sexual promiscuity and flexibility" (Hawkins 2016, 112) and, in "Girls Fall Like Dominoes" (2010), "openly raps about delighting in the attention from women fans and admiring their bodies" (Smith 2014, 367). Despite Stan Hawkins's interesting analyses that rely on colorful engineering as "markers of queerness" for "articulating traits of gender and sexuality in pop tracks and videos" (2016, 218), we believe that such traits are not expressive of sex or gender per se, but only of the potentially camp deviations from cultural and musical norms that may be expressed thereby, a stance parallel to others taken in several discussions in these pages.

Today's sexologists understand how—like gender identity—sexual orientation can be contingent and fluid, sometimes unexpectedly so, perhaps radically destabilized over an individual's lifetime. Of course, we are all sexual in new

---

[21] Taylor 2012, 38. Further discussion of queer meanings is found in Carson 2004, Diamond 2008, Hegarty 2018, and Rodger 2018. Musicians and their performances identified as queer, such as with Anal Traffic, the Apostles, Azealia Banks, Kevin Barnes, Mykki Blanco, Michael Jackson, Zebra Katz, Lady Gaga, Le1f, Lesbians on Ecstasy, Mika, Nicki Minaj, Morrissey, Pansy Division, Tribe 8, and Conchita Wurst, are topics in Hubbs 1996, Hawkins 2002, 2014, and 2016, O'Brien 2002 and 2014, Rycenga 2006a, Halberstam 2012, Leibetseder 2012, Taylor 2012, Burns and Lafrance 2014, Colton 2014, Iddon and Marshall 2014, Owens 2014, Smith 2014, McCracken 2015, Lee 2018a and 2018b, Rey 2018, and Zemke and Mackley-Crump 2018.

degrees and ways as we attain puberty; in Doris Day's "Secret Love" (1954) her love object changes from her own hand to a separate lover, metaphorically, as she loses her virginity: "Once I had a secret love that lived within the heart of me [in a breathy low register for the 'heart' of her love]; all too soon my secret love became impatient to be free," ending with a new maturity, "at last my heart's an open door and my secret love's no secret anymore." Barbara Mason sings of readiness to give up her virginity in "Yes, I'm Ready" (1965) with a consistently sharp intonation portraying a naïve inexperience that will presumably come to an end. But the gender of one's object choice may change over time as well. One important study showed that, to different degrees, "both lesbian and heterosexual women became physically aroused by visual images of both men and women. In contrast, men's responses fell in line with their self-described sexual orientations" (Diamond 2008, 8). Thus, it is thought that women may be more open than men to widening their explorations of polyamorous attractions through their lives, while not necessarily changing their views of themselves.[22] Lisa Diamond writes that "women's sexual behavior is more strongly shaped by social factors (such as her level of education, economic opportunity, social attitudes) than is the case for men. [It may also be that it is] more socially dangerous for men than for women to explore same-sex desires" (2016, 252). Hélène Cixous supports this view in her use of "the ocean as a metaphor for female subjectivity; unlike the masculine trait of fortifying the self against invasion, female consciousness oozes out beyond the self to embrace the world" (Reynolds and Press 1995, 284). (Fluidity in a man is a rare early topic in the Clovers' "Love Potion Number Nine" [1959], in which the magical liquid stimulates the singer's change of sexual orientation.) In "I Spent My Last $10.00 (On Birth Control and Beer)" (1997), Two Nice Girls bring a bisexual fluidity to country music. Before the singer meets Lester, she had "hated the thought of kissing a man." But after, her new adventure results in the song's title and certain complications: "my life was so much simpler when I was sober and queer . . . for there's certain thrills that lesbian love simply cannot supply like payin' for abortions from sperm gone awry."

Two songs are particularly apt in expressing a woman's fluid sexuality. In "In or Out" (1997), Ani DiFranco sings above her assertive strumming, "some days the line I walk turns out to be straight; other days the line tends to deviate," but

---

[22] In addition to Diamond 2008 and 2018, work on fluid sexuality, some based on longitudinal studies, is also presented in Murray 1988, Dean 1996, Butler 1999, Althof 2000, Hawkes 2004, Bergner 2009 and 2013, Carlson 2012, Halberstam 2012, Kelly 2012, Bergner 2013, and Lefkowitz and Vasilenko 2014. Music studies that acknowledge fluidity of sexuality include Hawkins 2009, and Zemke and Mackley-Crump 2018.

Table 3.3 Songs Portraying Themes of Unfixed Sexuality

Chart Year	Artist	Song Title	Comments
1935	Kokomo Arnold	Sissy Man Blues	"Lord, if you can't send me no woman, please send me some sissy man"
1959	Clovers	Love Potion Number Nine	The elixir makes the singer attracted to men as well as women
1968	The Kinks	David Watts	Asexual object "is of pure and noble breed"
1983	The Smiths	This Charming Man	Morrissey has an asexual reputation
1985	Murray Head	One Night in Bangkok	Asexual: "I get my kicks above the waistline, Sunshine"
1987	Apostles	Forbidden Love	Queercore band features tritone and cross-relation
1993	Nirvana	All Apologies	"What else could I say—everyone is gay"
1994	R.E.M.	King of Comedy	"I'm straight, I'm queer, I'm bi"
1995	Björk	Isobel	Lust locked in a dusty heart; "married to myself"
1995	Pansy Division	Smells Like Queer Spirit	Nirvana take-off: "Here we are now, so fellate us; roll it on now, lubricate us. . ."
1996	Weezer	Pink Triangle	"Everyone's a little queer"
1997	Ani DiFranco	In or Out	"I've got one membership to more than one club"; "some days the line I walk turns out to be straight, other days the line tends to deviate"; bVI - bVII - i basis
1997	Katell Keineg	Leonor	Song about bisexual Argentine surrealist painter Leonor Fini
1997	Two Nice Girls	I Spent My Last $10.00 (On Birth Control and Beer)	Bisexual: "My life was so much simpler when I was sober and queer"; "there's certain thrills that lesbian love simply cannot supply"
2003	Peaches	I U She	"I like girls and I like boys"; group sex, SM
2005	Anal Traffic	Six Beer Queer	Queercore band sings of guy who turns to men when he's drunk
2007	Garbage	Queer	Guitar tritones for "queerest of the queer"
2012	Nicki Minaj	High School	Adolescent's bisexual experimentation
2013	Boy George	Love and Danger	Man sings, "She's waiting for you but so am I"
2013	Lady Gaga	Sexxx Dreams	Asks girl to meet for sex when boyfriend is away
2015	Flo Rida	G.D.F.R.	"Your girl just kissed a girl; I do bi chicks"
2019	Ariana Grande	Thank U, Next	Singer fluidly moves from series of men to a woman

she resists classification: "you can't put me up on any shelf," because "I've got more than one membership to more than one club." Whereas the song's tonality is a (sharp) F♯ aeolian, the regular alternation of tonic with ♭III, the relative (high) A major, suggests a dual affinity; the song ends without commitment, containing members of both i and ♭III. In Ariana Grande's "Thank U, Next" (2019), the singer expresses gratitude for what she has learned from her exes Sean, Ricky, Pete, and Malcolm, but now has found love with—and even foresees marriage to—a woman, Ari. Fluid change of orientation is constantly suggested harmonically: the G♭M7 - F7 - B♭m7 - D♭7 loop alternates the briefest tonicizations of B♭ minor with those on G♭ major, with a fickle lack of commitment to either goal. Perhaps the postmodern West is slowly transitioning (despite reactionary steps backward) into an age where orientation and sexual behaviors, gender, and embodiment of sex—much of it not linked to reproduction—is to be freely flexible and so openly celebrated without eliciting moral judgment. Table 3.3 provides a selection of songs that open the treatment of sexuality to bi- and nonbinary, queer, and fluid identities. Prince seems to have led the charge against binary sexuality in "Controversy" (1981): "Am I black or white, am I straight or gay? Controversy! . . . I wish there was no black and white, I wish there were no rules." In "Pink Triangle" (1996), Weezer makes such a wish in a more selfish context when desiring love with a lesbian: "Everyone's a little queer; oh, can't she be a little straight?"

We have now covered all elements of sexual identity as expressed by musical performers, portrayed in songs themselves, and alive in listeners. Chapter 4 will contextualize these factors in an examination of erotics as conveyed throughout the recorded history of pop/rock music, a time of growing exploration, frankness, and intensity.

Pop/Rock Erotics

In examining the topic of erotics in our musical repertoire, we aim to address matters of sexual attraction, fantasy, lust, romance, ecstasy, arousal, and orgasm—the behaviors of sexual beings. As Chapters 1 through 3 have set with some thoroughness the theoretical foundation for this particular investigation, the present chapter will remain light in its references to the work of others and present more exclusively analytical matters pertaining to music recordings.

Physical Attraction

Good looks. In Western societies, physical beauty is prized as the primary motivator for sexual attraction. This plays out in popular music, with all sorts of bodily attributes appreciated. In some quarters, twenty-first-century standards demand a large derrière: see Mos Def's "Ms. Fat Booty" (1999) ("ass so fat that you could see it from the front"), Big Sean featuring Chris Brown's "My Last" (2011) ("she a seven in the face, but a ten in the ass"), 2 Chainz featuring Drake's "No Lie" (2012) ("Movie bought my boo tits and a bigger ass"), or Meghan Trainor's "All About That Bass" (2015) ("My mama . . . says boys like a little more booty to hold at night"). While perhaps not as outré as these examples may be on the surface, other songs would lead listeners to recoil for other reasons, such as with the naïvely quaint quality of innocent country earnestness in examples such as the Bellamy Brothers' "Do You Love as Good as You Look" (1981) ("judging from the cover, I'd love to read the book") or Thomas Rhett's "Look What God Gave Her" (2019) ("how perfect he made her"). Along with the booty, other individual traits have always been held up as enticing, as in the body parts mentioned in LL Cool J's "Around the Way Girl" (1990) ("I want a girl with extensions in her hair") and Deana Carter's "Did I Shave My Legs for This?" (1996), or very often in attire, as with Cake's "Short Skirt/Long Jacket" (2001), or in material possessions, as with Missy Elliott with Nas's "Hot Boyz" (1999) ("Is that your car, . . . can I be your date?"). For many, a Brazilian wax has become de rigeur, sometimes for practical reasons: in "Gangsta Bitch" (2001), Eve shares, "gotta keep the cat smooth so . . . it's good and wet." Sometimes, as in Drake's "Final Fantasy" (2018), a woman's natural beauty can't be improved upon: "I like best when you're fresh-faced and no foundation." Despite the fact that women have generally been empowered through recent decades in how their bodies are depicted sexually, female singers can still show a victimized anxiety over the impermanence of physical allure, as when Lana Del Rey laments "will you still love me when I'm no longer" "Young and Beautiful" (2013).

But popular song also celebrates qualities of character as factors in the mating ritual; Marv Johnson sings "nature didn't give you such a beautiful face" in "You Got What It Takes" (1959), and similar sentiments are professed by the Crystals in "He's Sure the Boy I Love" (1962), by Bob Dylan in "Ugliest Girl in the World" (1988), and by Prince Royce in "Corazón Sin Cara" (2010). This appreciation for deeper qualities is not always sincere; (lame) comedic irony is mined in insults proclaiming that a downright ugly partner will ward off competing males in such songs as the Maddox Brothers' "Ugly and Slouchy (That's the Way I Like 'Em")" (1957) and Jimmy Soul's "If You Wanna Be Happy" (1963). Irony itself is ugly in Mickey Gilley's "Don't the Girls All Get Prettier at Closing Time" (1976) and the White Stripes' "I'm Lonely (But I Ain't That Lonely Yet")" (2005), and is twisted like a boomerang when we learn in the end that the object regards the subject with equal disdain in the Monks' "Nice Legs Shame About Her Face" (1979).

Beauty resides in the mind, for worse or better, in Right Said Fred's "I'm Too Sexy" (1991) and Elliott Smith's "Pretty (Ugly Before)" (2004). The way physical beauty dominates how people see each other (a topic introduced in Chapter 1) is deplored in Beyoncé's "Pretty Hurts" (2014) but seems to be elevated in the following year's reactionary "Body Was Made" by Ezra Furman. In many songs, it's not what you've got but how you use it, as when a glance captivates the heart in Ana Gabriel's "Ay Amor" (1987) ("Miradas casuales qu aumentan latidos").

Roberta Flack's recording of "The First Time Ever I Saw Your Face" (1969) presents a poignant perspective on first impressions. Its extremely slow tempo (starting and ending at exactly one beat per second) and non-percussive instrumentation (string bass plucked at slow intervals, classical guitar lightly arpeggiated, sparse piano, and the second verse's emotive bowed cello plumbing depths replaced by the third verse's softly sustained string quartet) support Ewan

MacColl's thoughtful, reflective lyrics that treat the beauty underlying first sight, first kiss, and first sex. The unexpected nature of the singer's stunned attraction to first light is well portrayed in the opening chord presented in medias res, as the verse begins not with the stable I, but with an unprepared ii chord. The metaphor of the morning sun rising "in your eyes" is set with ascending melody, and the melismas on the delicate iii chord for bright eyes, trembling hands, and beating heart convey a vulnerable tenderness. The ♭VII chord portrays the same "dark," endless essence suggested by Flack by concluding each verse's melody on a dreamy ^5 rather than the solid ^1, even in the coda that negates a structurally achieved perfect authentic cadence. All of these points underlie a sensitive representation of erotic attraction.

Fantasy. Table 4.1 lists a selection of songs from the pop/rock era in which physical attraction is based in fantasy. In some cases, the object is a known, absent lover; in others it is purely imaginary. In a few instances, fantasy is part of an actual loving encounter. A number of the later songs have a strong suggestion of, or overt mention of, masturbation, but this never overshadows the nature of fantasy as a sexual component.

Fantasy is at play in a wondrous excitement in Stephen Sondheim and Leonard Bernstein's "Tonight," as sung by Marni Nixon in *West Side Story* (1961). Here, a tonic pedal that underlies the alternation of I with a major II chord (rooted in the present rather than looking forward to an expected V) underlies a motif that has suggested dreamy bliss at least since 1828 with the final strophe of Schubert's setting of "Gute Nacht." Anticipatory examples of such a state are heard in Jennifer Lopez's "Waiting for Tonight" (1999) and Jason Derulo's "In My Head" (2009). More often, memories of past love spur the imagination into reverie. Such is the case with Elvis Presley's "Are You Lonesome To-night?" (1960), the Shangri-Las' "Remember (Walkin' in the Sand)" (1964), Van Morrison's "Brown Eyed Girl" (1967), Leonard Cohen's "In My Secret Life" (2015), and Kid Rock's "First Kiss" (2015).

Bob Seger and the Silver Bullet Band's "Night Moves" (1976) is a retrospective coming-of-age narrative about first-time teenage sex, presented as memories that stimulate an older person's fantasy. With music suggesting tensions complementary to those in the lyrics, the song is a validation of past teen sex and its bittersweet role in memories held in an adult present. Early verses map the dynamics of fumbling young partners fruitlessly attempting to satisfy one another sexually. Here, chords long repeat a static double-plagal loop (I - ♭VII - IV - ♭VII - I), contrapuntal triads lacking forward harmonic drive.

Table 4.1 Songs Based in Erotic Fantasy

Year	Artist	Song Title
1957	Billy Williams	I'm Gonna Sit Right Down and Write Myself a Letter
1958	The Everly Brothers	All I Have to Do Is Dream
1959	Bobby Darin	Dream Lover
1962	Roy Orbison	Dream Baby
1963	The Beach Boys	In My Room
1964	The Paris Sisters	Dream Lover
1968	Big Brother and the Holding Co.	I Need a Man to Love
1971	The Temptations	Just My Imagination (Running Away with Me)
1976	England Dan and John Ford Coley	Nights Are Forever without You
1976	Kenny Nolan	I Like Dreamin'
1977	Leo Sayer	When I Need You
1977	Conway Twitty	I've Already Loved You in My Mind
1978	Atlanta Rhythm Section	Imaginary Lover
1980	Prince	Dirty Mind
1983	Mtume	Juicy Fruit
1987	LL Cool J	I Need Love
1987	Belinda Carlisle	Heaven Is a Place on Earth
1992	Indigo Girls	Ghost
1993	Björk	Venus as a Boy
1995	Elastica	Car Song
1995	Mariah Carey	Fantasy
1996	Poe	Fingertips
2000	LL Cool J	You and Me
2001	Janet Jackson	Love Scene (Ooh Baby)
2005	Dave Matthews Band	Dreamgirl
2011	Wale feat Miguel	Lotus Flower Bomb
2012	Usher	Scream
2012	Paul McCartney	I'm Gonna Sit Right Down and Write Myself a Letter
2014	Robin Thicke	You're My Fantasy

The refrain (1:04–1:15) similarly loops an expanded dominant preparation (vi - V - IV - V - vi), tantalizingly teasing but not setting free a passing V.

In contrast to such frustration, the "Night Moves" bridge (see Figure 4.1) opens with a promising moan and reaches a retransitional V at 2:57–3:00, thrusting and forward-moving energy appearing at the moment of formal concision. Seger emphasizes the climax, painfully exacerbating the dissonance of having "waited on the thunder." Intervals above the bass feature fourths that act progressively freely, at first prepared and resolving into consonant fifths, then entering freely, and

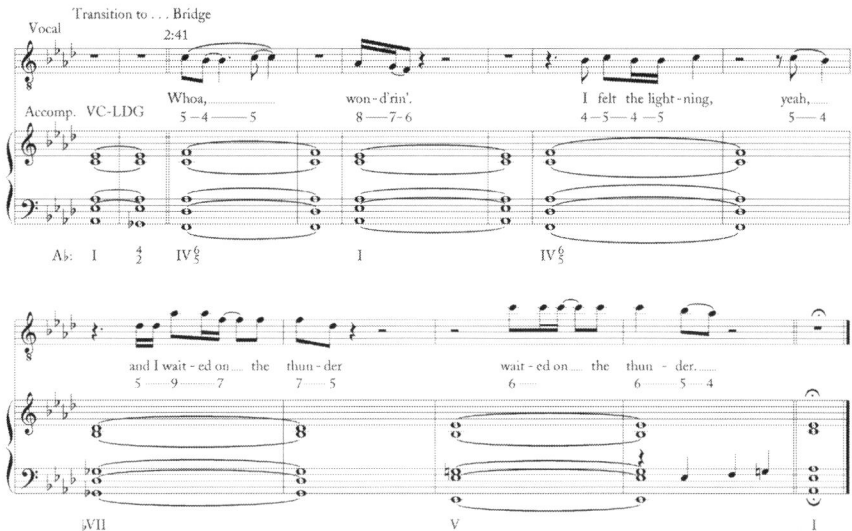

Figure 4.1 "Night Moves" (Bob Seger), bridge.

ultimately left unresolved above the retransitional V. Above the ♭VII chord, Seger sings in rising register an apparent arpeggiation of IV, increasing the dissonance while suggesting an unrealized double-plagal resolution. When V then appears, Seger's highest vocal register bursts through with a passing motion from ^3 to ^1, anticipating ("waited on") members of the coming tonic for a tense blurring of present dissonance and anticipated resolution. Of a related anticipatory experience, Alfred Kinsey says, "Memories of past experience, the anticipation of renewed experience, and the contemplation of new types of activity are such significant factors in his arousal that it is usually difficult for a male to reach orgasm in masturbation without the aid of some sort of fantasy" (Kinsey 1948, 165). Seger's rising vocal anticipations map a central dynamic of orgasm and relate to the fantasy narrative as a simultaneous mix of past, present, and future.

Following Seger's climax, a post-coital tempo-free passage is followed by a final verse (3:09+) that—instead of repeating the chord pattern heard in earlier verses—simply alternates I - IVM7, and a refrain (3:25–3:43) that alternates vi - IV7, now with no V passing in between, such tension having been released in the bridge. "Night Moves" maps the sexual act, with constrained tension followed by release and then timeless torpor; the speaker then shifts to the adult present. Throughout, fullness was not achieved in the past. But now it's uncertain whether the wished-for thundering fullness can exist in the future, given the speaker's bittersweet approach to the ideals he'd held as a teen. Do sounds of thunder remind him that he is still waiting? Or perhaps the entire narrative represents an adult fantasy. Regardless of such polysemy, his reflection indicates that although the teen years are not the place for fullness, they were, to borrow William Wordsworth's line, "life and food for future years."[1]

Lust. Lustful desire has always been a rock staple, at one time presented openly only in R&B as opposed to a then-sanitized pop radio fare. By the 1960s, though, lust became a respectable topic in Motown and in many other styles of decades beyond. Strong sexual passions, often driving a singer to the point of madness, might be aroused by the mythical Lorelei (as in both Roxy Music's "Editions of You," 1973, wherein alto sax, electronic organ, and Moog speak for the bewitching trio, and for the lovesick sailors of the Pogues' "Lorelei," 1989). Arrows represent the phallic directedness of desire in both the Jimi Hendrix Experience's "Voodoo Chile" (1968) and Kate Bush's "The Sensual World" (1989), the pair opposing male and female tendencies that seem to bridge Odysseus and Penelope with the tenderness of Molly's soliloquy with Leopold in Joyce's *Ulysses*. A rising direction is observed or promised in Sly and the Family Stone's "I Want to Take You Higher" (1969), Brandy's "Afrodisiac" (2004), and Adele's "Send My Love (To Your New Lover)" (2015), but lust is positioned lower among contrasted vocal registers to express inner desire in Def Leppard's "Women" (1987). Dogs in heat are the unsavory image presented in Isaac Hayes's "The Feeling Keeps on Coming" (1973), Ted Nugent's "Stranglehold" (1975), 2 Live Crew's "Me So Horny" (1989), and—why not?—Missy Elliott's "Dog in Heat" (2001). Lust drives tense music, with dissonant singing often shouted or treated with vocal fry, in the Beatles' "I Want You (She's So Heavy)" (1969), U2's "Desire" (1988), Janet Jackson's "My Need" (1997), Lucinda Williams's "Still I Long for Your Kiss" (1998), Mary J. Blige's "Feel Like Makin' Love" (2003), Christina Aguilera's "Sex for Breakfast" (2010), and Don Omar feat. Natti Natasha's "Dutty Love" (2012).

Strong lust is located in the rocking male drive heard just a bit ahead of its time in the Kinks' "All Day and All of the Night" (1964). Here, Dave Davies's rough power chords in an aggressive rhythm burst through an otherwise muted strumming with the primitive minor-pentatonic figure, G5 - F5 - Bb5 - G5. These roots are doubled by bass and by brother Ray's insistent vocal melody. In the prechorus ("the only time I feel all right . . ."), the Bb5 chord pivots modally from the tonal center of G to that of D, ushering in the chorus's transposition

---

[1]   Thanks to Katie Kapurch for the Wordsworth connection.

of the (025) pattern up a fifth to the highest regions of the guitar neck for Ray's urgent plea in a vocally harmonized cry as the title is repeated as if involuntarily, from uncontrollable emotion.

Heat is a core component of lust, notably in Motown; Martha and the Vandellas' "Heat Wave" (1963) catches the singer wondering what's happening as she is taken over by the devil, or perhaps whether "this is the way love is supposed to be?"; minor-mode confusion in verses is replaced by major-mode understanding in choruses. Diana Ross growls multiphonically as her heart is rent by a "burning sensation" in "Love Is Like an Itching in My Heart" (1966). The reader might wish to compare how heat rises in Tom Jones's "Love Me Tonight" (1969), Karyn White's "Romantic" (1991), Prince and the Power Generation's "Cream" (1991), The The's "Dogs of Lust" (1993), and Nelly's "Hot in Herre" (2002). A number of songs positively combust into open flame: hear the cross-related Am - F♯m (verse) and DM - BM (chorus) chords in the Doors' "Light My Fire" (1967), the burning rhythm guitar and tremulant-heavy organ solo in the Pointer Sisters' "Fire" (1978), the trebly lead guitar bullets in Rod Stewart's "Body Wishes" (1983), the dissonant anticipatory V7 with ♯9 among minor-pentatonic pitches sung by Madonna in "Burning Up" (1983), the heavy vocal reverb in Bruce Springsteen's "I'm on Fire" (1984), the soft, sustained backing vocals against staccato synths in Kenny Rogers's "Morning Desire" (1985), the competing rhythms of vocal placement, hand percussion, and bass-drum pattern in LL Cool J and Jennifer Lopez's "Control Myself" (2006), the veering from aeolian to major mode in the Jonas Brothers' "Burnin' Up" (2008), the sustained dissonance of ^7 stuck on both I and vi chords in Kings of Leon's "Sex on Fire" (2008), the similarly dissonant ^5 suspended over IV in John Mayer's "Edge of Desire" (2009), the fast hypnotic 808 snare beat with closed hi-hat offbeats, and vocal rests punctuating the word "desire" in Madonna's "Girl Gone Wild" (2012), and the passionate vocal melismas in the chorus of Alicia Keys's "Girl on Fire" (2012).

Romance. Love songs have always been the bread and butter of pop; evergreen moments in this genre include the yearning melody and ramping-up formal structure of the Ronettes' "Walking in the Rain" (1964), the six different fragile major-seventh chords in Joni Mitchell's "Help Me" (1974), references to the Beatles' electric twelve-string that summon a romantic past in Karen Carpenter's "Making Love in the Afternoon" (rec. 1979, rel. 1996), and the breathy delivery and echoing of key lines in Alicia Keys's "Un-Thinkable (I'm Ready)" (2010). The tendency, reflecting a cultural myth of evolutionary psychology, has been to ascribe physical drives more to men and emotional desires—as in the examples mentioned earlier—more to women. Men, moreover, are said to deny feelings other than anger entirely, "thus the misogynistic emphasis on carnality in male sex songs" (Rutter and Schwartz 2012, 58). Consider the ways men hide their feelings of romantic loss in the Everly Brothers' "Crying in the Rain" (1962), the Temptations' "I Wish It Would Rain" (1968), and Smokey Robinson & the Miracles' "Tears of a Clown" (1970). In these songs, male singers rely on disguises (rain or a greasepaint's phony smile to camouflage pain's tears) to shield their emotions. Traditionally, men are allowed to brag about heroic predation and conquest, and although women must suppress their sexual urges, the latter express their emotions through idealist fantasies. Early-adolescent girls sing of romance and epiphanies like "magnified moments [such as] first dates, first looks, first meetings, as well as break ups," and so on (Williams and Stein 2002, 143). Still, pop/rock music has allowed cis-gendered heterosexual men to present an interest in the feeling side of romance's magnified moments. Writing in 1987, one critic notices a shift in the content of music videos related to romance:[2]

> It is significant that recently more male stars have been creating romantic songs with corresponding videos. Earlier, . . . the romantic video tended to be the province of female stars like Cyndi Lauper ("Time After Time" [1983]), Stevie Nicks ("If Anyone Falls" [1983]), Heart ("What About Love?" [1985]), etc. The male star in such videos, like Lionel Richie in "Hello" [1983], used to be an exception. But in 1983-4 the type had been virtually taken over by the male star and is often top of the [MTV] countdown. Besides Phil Collins's "One More Night" [1985], Foreigner's "I Want to Know What Love Is" [1984], and Paul Young's "Everytime You Go Away" [1985], already mentioned as in the top slot for several weeks, there was Bob Dylan's "Tight Connection to My Heart (Has Anybody Seen My Love)" [1985], Simple Minds' "Don't You (Forget About Me)" [1985], Julian Lennon's "Too Late for Goodbyes" [1985], and Paul McCartney's "No More Lonely Nights" [1984]. (Kaplan 1987, 96)

Long before the video age, cis-gendered heterosexual male singers had professed romance, even through glorification of the "magnified moment." The bridge of the (female) Crystals' "Then He Kissed Me" (1963) was given lush, ecstatic violins; the Beach Boys' similar arrangement for "Then I Kissed Her" (1965) buried the same violin part deeper in the mix and presented smoother backing vocals than those in the original—the Crystals evinced excitement, the Beach

---

[2]   A fuller and more nuanced understanding of romance as a gendered phenomenon can be had from, in addition to the sources cited earlier, Firestone 1970, 150, 166, Person 1988, 267, Shepherd 1991, 167–8, Martin 1996, 60–2 and 93, Halberstam 1998, 5–6, Stein 1999, and Warwick 2007, 145–6.

Boys, warmth. "This Magic Moment" was made a hit by men: first by the Drifters (1960), with rapidly bowed, *frémissement* violin tremolos, then by Jay & the Americans (1968), with the disguise of a sensitive lead vocal (note the dynamically delicate moment at "and then it *happened*" at 0:34) brushed aside by pushy backing singers and martial brass).

When it comes to rejecting heterosexual romance in favor of other pursuits, women musicians have also disrupted the love-obsessed stereotypes to which they have been assigned. Cyndi Lauper certainly liberated listeners from such sexist portrayals with "Girls Just Want to Have Fun" (1983). "Manipulate" (1995), by the LGBTQ+ punk-band Tribe 8, features lyrics to the effect "that a woman's love is not all gentle and perfect, because she also likes to manipulate her girlfriend and wants to objectify her, although she knows that this is wrong" (Leibetseder 2012, 177–8). These lyrics evidence how sex can be associated with shame, a topic covered in Chapter 1.

Pop songs revel in the earliest romantic memories; for one thing, the (pre-) adolescent audience is key and is reflected in memories of budding feelings—and anticipations of a grown-up future—in such songs as Claudine Clark's "Party Lights" (1962), Millie Small's "My Boy Lollipop" (1964), the Beach Boys' "When I Grow Up (To Be a Man)" (1965), Jay and the Techniques' "Apples, Peaches, Pumpkin Pie" (1967), and the Intruders' "Cowboys to Girls" (1968). It seems no accident in retrospect that this innocent genre bloomed in the post-Elvis/Berry/Lewis era of sanitized radio fare. The occasional later hit drawing from this circumstance, such as Tommy Cromwell & the Young Rumblers' "I'm Seventeen" (1990), often features more emotional complexity. The youthful romantic ritual of dating is explored in Manfred Mann's "Do Wah Diddy Diddy" (1964), Blink-182's "First Date" (2001), Luther Vandross's "Take You Out" (2001), Taylor Swift's "Fifteen" (2008), Keith Urban's "Sweet Thing" (2008), and Gloriana's "(Kissed You) Good Night" (2011); all of these encounters seem to have gone much better than Joan's did in the Beatles' "Maxwell's Silver Hammer" (1969); perhaps she should have kept to her test tubes.[3]

The worlds of romantic misadventure and casual sex, and often country-styled despondency as well, collide in the sometimes anonymous one-night stand, a rock staple. Alluded to in regarding the "walk of shame" discussed in Chapter 1, this genre is represented in dozens of titles included in the online

---

[3] I'm indebted to Cevin Soling for pointing out to me the masturbatory imagery in "Maxwell'"s test tubes and in the "lagoon" of "She Came in Through the Bathroom Window," both songs from the Beatles' *Abbey Road* (1969), in a September 2019 conversation.

Appendix. Among those, Earth, Wind, and Fire's romantically set "Reasons" (1975) has been a perennial wedding favorite for many oblivious to its lyrics, all about a one-night stand.

For a deeper look into pop romance, the Toys' idyllic "A Lover's Concerto" (1965) will serve. The dream of a utopian past is suggested in numerous ways. The tune is a pop-rendered 4/4 setting of what was originally a 3/4 minuet theme taken from the Anna Magdalena notebook associated with Bach. The instrumental introduction circles through piano arpeggios like those in the soloist's entry in the Tchaikovsky Piano Concerto in Bb minor, a wildly popular warhorse of the romantic nineteenth century: Van Cliburn's award-winning performance of this work topped *Billboard*'s *pop* album charts for seven weeks in 1958. For the Toys, this opening passage is a dramatic foil against the gentle song proper that gets underway once the stormy dorian mode opens out to the bright rainbow of the major mode. (The dorian i - ii - i7 progression seems to exploit one distinctive mark of the British invasion, announced in the Zombies' "She's Not There" from mid-1964.) In continuing to find past-related imagery, one might imagine a suggestion of the Elizabethan sonnet in the opening line's iambic pentameter, "how GENtle IS the RAIN that FALL[eth] SOFT." An eighteenth-century vocal ornament, the mordent, graces several words including "falls" (0:20) and "this" (0:53–54). A polyphonic trio of trumpets and trombones in the neo-Baroque instrumental break (1:21+) realizes the contrapuntal potential of a previously very active bass line for a final nod to the romanticized musical past.

Still examining the "Concerto," songwriters Linzer and Randell alter Bach's harmony to introduce a tender iii chord on the word "rain." This may be an homage to the bridge of the Shirelles' "Will You Love Me Tomorrow" (1960), where IV twice collapses into the weak iii, notably for the word "broken."[4] Vulnerability is also carried in soprano Barbara Harris's unsupported vocal, with its narrow tone despite deep vibrato, that can err innocently on the sharp side (as at "to you," 0:51–0:52). A periodic antecedent—consequent formal construction transcends the gentle opening of each verse to find strong closure in the projection of idealized eternal love. Such hope for the future is expressed in the rising melody, and especially in the profusion of rising half-step modulations (a Linzer-Randell trademark), from C to Db and to D in verses, first motivated

---

[4] The fragility of the iii chord (and its cousin, IM7) is key to the "dizzy dancing" aura of Joni Mitchell's "Both Sides Now" (made a hit in 1968 by Judy Collins), a mature perspective on the illusion of love's fantasy. In a related way to that seen in "Will You Love Me Tomorrow," the "broken" iii in alternation with a more hopeful IV portrays the unsafe exposure of deficiency in the bridge of the Beatles' "Nowhere Man" (1965).

by the entry of backing vocalists, continuing through E♭ and E to F in the coda. In "A Lover's Concerto," all of these relationships support the fanciful and clichéd notion of a gentle, never-ending romance begun on a memorably magic, pastoral day.

Lascivious Ecstasy

While lots of bumps and grinds from bass drum and brass, and fast wiggles from trumpet trills were obvious examples of lewd text painting in David Rose and His Orchestra's "The Stripper" (1962), it was the arousal suggested in its sliding trombone that seems to have launched a thousand ships. That portamento implied lascivious intent or aroused reaction in a slide on "shiverin'" in Peggy Lee's "I'm a Woman" (1963), chromatic lines and sliding trombone in Peter and Gordon's "Lady Godiva" (1966), stepwise-falling chords, G - F♯7 - F in the Beatles' "Sexy Sadie" and slide guitar over grinding rhythm section in their "Why Don't We Do It in the Road" (both 1968), chordal descents of A - A♭ - G - F♯ minor in Britney Spears's "Perfect Lover" (2007) and E - D♯ - D - C♯ minor in her "Womanizer" (2008), and nth-degree microtones that fall the distance between ^7 and ^6 with *five* distinct pitches in Janelle Monae's "Make Me Feel" (2018). The strip club, once zoned as a seedy, secret retreat for "gentlemen" and shamelessly referred to by the 2 Live Crew ("Strip Club," 1990) and Kiss ("Take It Off," 1992), became a who cares setting for the twenty first century; the online Appendix contains thirteen such references, from Mr. Cheeks, Eminem, Paris Hilton, Ray J & Yung Berg, Flo Rida, Waka Flocka Flame, Chris Brown, Nicki Minaj, R. Kelly, AC/DC, Zebra Katz, Migos, and Dita von Teese. Even the lap dance comes in for casual mention in Montell Jordan's "Let's Ride" (1998), Ludacris's "What's Your Fantasy" (2000), T-Pain's "I'm N Luv (Wit a Stripper)" (2005), and Panic at the Disco's "But It's Better If You Do" (2006).

The predatory leering male gaze, traced in note 25 of Chapter 1, is behind the undressing by eyeballs central to a number of 1950s hits: a wolf whistle is performed in the Four Lads' "Standing on the Corner" (1956); Lieber and Stoller write for competing soloists in both Coasters records, "Young Blood" (1957) and "Three Cool Cats" (1959), wherein the listener wonders which singer's ogles can turn most threatening. Frank Zappa's "Find Her Finer" (1976) and Liz

Phair's "Jealousy" (1994) have differently styled takes on fantasies aroused by girl watching.

Arousal and frisson. In 1960, Connie Francis sang "I hear your voice and something stirs inside of me" in "My Heart Has a Mind of Its Own." This involuntary reaction to sexual stimuli powers Janet Jackson as well when she sings "Every time you whisper in my ear I get aroused" in "Moist" (2004). A first experience of this sort of rapture is captured by Etta James in "Something's Got a Hold on Me" (1962). To set the scene, she opens with an unmeasured, dry recitative intro with shouted tumbling strains: "Sometimes . . . I get a feelin' that I never, never, never, never had before, no, no," as emphatic as any gospel number—in fact, the song's outro could be compared to that of the Southern Tones' "It Must Be Jesus" (1954). James's verse portrays this new feeling by deviating from an implied prototypical twelve-bar blues structure that had been prepared by two phrases of standard I - I - I - I, IV - IV - I - I chord changes supporting four bars of text that repeat in bars 5–8. Normally, this pattern would be completed by a third four-bar phrase moving V - (IV) - I - I, but here James gives us another *sixteen* bars that begin by tonicizing an unfamiliar tonal area ("[I] I got a feeling, I [I♭7] feel so strange, [IV] everything about me seems to have changed"), repeat this quickened half-phrase idea in bars 11–12, and then lead in bars 13–16 to her realization in a rising series of tingling, enlightened "oh!"s that "it must be love!," an explanation that her backing singers had been trying to impress upon her since the verse's first line.

This early 1960s expression is hardly the uninhibited outpouring of Donna Summer's "Love to Love You Baby" (1975)—James is relatively classical, as opposed to Dionysian—but she does sing in the bridge, "I shake all over."[5] Such sexually suggestive shaking and tingling is expressed in many rock numbers: in 1983, the Rolling Stones shake the whammy bar as they sing, "feel the prickles runnin' up and down your back" in "Tie You Up (The Pain of Love)"; in "Temptation" (1985), Prince sings "purple electricity whenever our bodies touch" in a high falsetto over the scratching of a distorted guitar; and Jennifer Hudson and backing singers harmonize, "I can't describe all of my heart . . . it tingles here, tingles there, ooh it tingles everywhere" in "I Can't Describe (The Way I Feel)" (2014). The Stones' whammy bar is an homage to "Shakin' All Over" (done first in the UK by Johnny Kidd and the Pirates in 1960, produced similarly in America by the Guess Who in 1965, and given a less tingly but more

---

5   The Chiffons' "One Fine Day" (1963) has a similarly excited though classically contained bridge retransition ("you'll come to me when you want to settle down, oh!").

aggressively demonic performance by the Who in 1970). In the Pirates' original "Shakin," guitarist Mick Green opens with two effects: a minor-pentatonic tumbling strain, then percolating descending arpeggiations: "When you move in right up close to me [guitar's tumbling strain], that's when I get the shakes all over me [tumbling strain repeated]." Then whammy! for "quivers down the backbone" and other cited tremors, before the arrangement hits stop time for the song's title. (At Leeds, Townsend plays the tumbling strain and whammy, and Entwistle takes the percolating part.) Table 4.2 provides a few more examples of pop/rock frisson; note the multiple references to butterflies. The table's twenty-year gap between 1965 and 1984 seems representative of the literature (just barely inside these dates, Bob Lind's mellow "Elusive Butterfly" [1966] and Deniece Williams's delicate "Black Butterfly" [1984] are hardly related to sexual excitement), but an explanation for the void is elusive.

Sexy vocalizations. The hearing of whispers is arousing in many songs from Brenda Lee's "Sweet Nothin's" (1959) on. Such unvoiced talking is a lascivious vocal technique in more than a score of songs given in the Appendix, from Jimi Hendrix Experience's "Foxy Lady" (1967) to Jane Birkin & Serge Gainsbourg's "Je T'Aime" (1969), the Bells' "Stay Awhile" (1971), and Sylvia's "Pillow Talk" (1973), and is combined with vocal fry for stronger seduction in Sheena Easton's "Sugar Walls" (1984), Madonna's "Erotica" (1992), Jennifer Lopez's "Come Over" (2001), and Britney Spears's "Breathe on Me" (2003). Christina Aguilera's "Come on Over (All I Want Is You)" (1999) is interesting in the way the singer's psyche is divided into an overt lead vocal and double-tracked interjections of whispered come-ons from an underlying subliminal id, a more physically sexual being.

Whispers assume the inarticulate form of heavy breathing in many rock performances. Gene Vincent may have started this off in his "Be-Bop-a-Lula" and—moreso—in "Woman Love" (both 1956). In the Beatles' *Sgt. Pepper's Lonely Hearts Club Band* (1967), John Lennon's improvised panting in the bridge of "A Day in the Life" expresses innocent exhaustion, but sex is clearly the root of this sound at the end of "Lovely Rita." Marvin Gaye borrows a woman's voice for heavy breathing in "You Sure Love to Ball" (1973), but featured artists perform the sound themselves in Suzi Quatro's "Daytona Demon" (1973), the Staple Singers' "Let's Do It Again" (1975), Slade's "Thanks for the Memory (Wham Bam Thank You Mam)" (1975), Eugene Wilde's "Gotta Get You Home Tonight" (1984), and Tone Loc's "Wild Thing" (1988). In "Soft and Wet" (1978), Prince presents a different sort of multiply-voiced rapture than does Aguilera in "Come on Over"; with Prince, it's the mechanical synthesizer backing that

Table 4.2 Pop/rock Frisson

Year	Artist	Song Title	Means of Expression
1953	Eartha Kitt	C'est Si Bon	"Un espoir merveilleux qui donne le frisson" sung on a high, long-sustained fifth scale degree; later vocal fry in ecstatic "ummmm"
1954	The Drifters	Honey Love	"It thrills my spine"; frisson ends with orgasmic vocal fry on "oooh"
1954	Jo Stafford	Make Love to Me!	Double-tracked soprano/alto duet for "When you're near, so help me dear, chills run up my spine" with high brass stabs
1955	Alma Cogan	Never Do a Tango with an Eskimo	"You can bet your life you're gonna get a chill", then stop-time tongue rolls, "brrrrrrrr" for cute frisson
1960	The Drifters	This Magic Moment	Rapidly bowed violin section for "magic" frisson
1962	Shelly Fabares	Johnny Angel	"How I tingle when he passes by" not depicted in tame music
1962	Shirley Jones	Being in Love	"My first love heroically ran the streetcar; I tingled at every clang clang" not expressed in the tame music
1964	Omar Sharif and Barbra Streisand	"You Are Woman, I Am Man"	Ends with her vocal-fried "oh" before "there's some thrills and chills goin' through me"
1965	The Supremes	I Hear a Symphony	Tremolo violins on sustained fifth scale degree for frisson
1965	The Beatles	It's Only Love	Fast tremolo in highly treble rhythm guitar for "my inside just flies, butterfly"
1984	Prince	When Doves Cry	Wild synth pitch bend follows "Touch if you will my stomach, feel how it trembles inside"
1987	Stephanie Mills	I Feel Good All Over	Lead singer's rapid tremolo throughout, choral shivering overlapping imitation and direct modulations; ends with soft high-register piano arpeggiations
1987	Whitney Houston	So Emotional	"Ain't it shocking what love can do" represented in rapid high-register staccato sixteenth notes in synths
1990	Living Colour	Under Cover of Darkness	Sharply pitched accents in slap bass for "I'd like to [send] sparks of passion up your spine"
1991	Mariah Carey	Emotions	"I like the way I feel inside" sung on impossibly high fifth scale degree

1991	Divinyls	I Touch Myself	Chorus's jump of fifth and drop of a sixth for repeated "oh no" is stylized, not pictured, frisson
1999	Mariah Carey	Bliss	Intro's celeste with heavy reverb and two mellow slow-tremolo guitars continue under whisper-sung vocal
2001	Michael Jackson	Butterflies	Subtle tremolo on vocal parts for "butterflies inside, inside and I," enabled by digital processing
2001	Alicia Keys	Butterflyz	Fluttering expressed in strong contrasts of vocal dynamics
2002	Ashanti	Baby	"Your kisses make my lips quiver"
2002	Counting Crows	American Girls	Lead guitar's quick and long trill alternation of scale degrees 3 and 2 for "little shivers"
2006	Ne-Yo	Sexy Love	"She makes the hairs on the back of my neck stand up"

contrasts sharply against the whispers and heaving of multiple passionate vocal parts.

Related is the moaning frequently expressive of sexual abandon; investigation of the Appendix suggests it may be heard just as often as whispering. Elvis Presley's vocal fry and various breathy "boogifications" make for a sexy "Such a Night" (1964), but the moaning in this performance lacks the thrust of Clyde McPhatter and the Drifters', and of Johnnie Ray's earlier recordings (both 1954) of the same song. Owners of Ray Charles's "What'd I Say (Part 1)" hit single (1959) who turned over their 45 found that "Part 2" had the Raelettes respond to all of Charles's ecstatic vocalizations alternating "eh" and "oh" in a rhythmic acceleration unmistakable in its sexual imagery.[6] The same soloist/response arrangement fills the 45-second intro to K5's "Passion" (1997). A related alternation is heard in 1960 when Tina Turner's gravelly screeches and sultry groans are answered by husband Ike's amp-tremolo guitar stabs in "I Idolize You." Both the vocal groans and string glissandi in John Fred & His Playboy Band's "Judy in Disguise (With Glasses)" (1967) seem a parody of this effect. Female moans are supplied alongside male artists' work in Rod Stewart's "Tonight's the Night (Gonna Be Alright)" (1976), Prince's "Lady Cab Driver" (1982), and Jackyl's "Dirty Little Mind" (1992). In "Caligula" (1999), Macy Gray warns, "Hush, the neighbors hear you moanin' and groanin', but I just can't help it 'specially when we be bonin'." The sensual moan is particularly orgasmic in Brigitte Bardot's "Moi je joue" (1964) and in Donna Summer's "I Feel Love" (1977), which anticipates Prince's contrasts mentioned earlier with its passionate vocal against its heavily electronic drum machine and synthesizers.

Ecstasy and fever. Several songs in Table 4.2 include an ecstatic melodic emphasis on ^5. This position connotes distance from ^1 that typically resolves by falling (as it typically must when in the bass). Listen to how the Penguins' lead singer repeatedly alternates ^5 with its less stable upper neighbor ^6 in the dramatic "oh-oh-oh, oh!" retransition of "Earth Angel (Will You Be Mine)" (1954); the same melodic relationship erupts in Jerry Lee Lewis's "Great Balls of Fire" (1957) ("you're mi-ne, mi-ne, mi-ne, mi-ne"). In "Caught Up in the Rapture" (1986), Anita Baker enters the chorus with a rising vocal melisma on "ah," set on ^6 - ^7 - ^8 - ^2 - ^3 - ^5, following the scale until leaping up to the high ^5 as she is "caught up in the rapture of love." The fifth scale degree is set in an inner register in Missy Elliott's "X-Tasy" (2001), where it quickly gives way to the

---

[6] "Boogification" is Richard Middleton's term for the physical variables in Elvis's vocal production (1990, 19). The feature is considered closely in Everett 2007, 119–22.

Figure 4.2 "X-Tasy" (Elliott–Mosley–Keys), opening of first verse.

dissonant ^4 (which is repeated, still dissonant, an octave higher for "high"), on each of the downbeats but the first in the excerpt given as Figure 4.2; backwards percussion and lots of heavy reverb and filter sweeps complete the effect. The dissonant ^4, in another way, plays a major role in establishing a blissful melodic climax in Paul McCartney & Wings's "My Love" (1973). Here, the singer's initial peak, a high ^3, is reached several times in the song, first as a dissonant seventh in a half-diminished ♯iv chord (on "my love does it *good*," 0:29). But the ode ends rhapsodically, on the same text, by pushing up unexpectedly to a singular, timeless-by-fermata higher ^4 (3:44–3:46), which then falls deliriously through the resolving ^3 to a final ^1. Other ecstatic outbursts are key to Little Richard's falsetto shrieks of "ooh!" in "Tutti-Frutti" (1955), to the violins' entry pushing to V following the line, "he kissed me in a way that I've never been kissed before" in the Crystals' "Then He Kissed Me" (1963), to a stop-time title over a dissonant IV/5 chord in Madonna's "Crazy for You" (1985), to Whitney Houston's rapid tumbling strain ending the bridge of "I'm Your Baby Tonight" (1990), to the dissonant fully diminished seventh chord on "ecstasy" in R. Kelly's "Sex Me" (1993), to the repeated vocal ornaments on a fully diminished seventh chord in "I can't get enough of a-you in me" in TLC's "Let's Do It Again" (1994), and to the meshing of compressed and distorted vocal and guitar lines in PJ Harvey's "No Girl So Sweet" (1998).

A fevered pitch is to be taken literally in the heat of ecstasy in many pop songs: it's the titular focus of "Fever," as sung by Little Willie John (1956), Peggy Lee (1958), and Madonna (1992), and in a new incarnation of the same title by Kylie Minogue (2002). Temperature runs high in Elvis Presley's "Burning Love" (1972), Gary Glitter's "Do You Wanna Touch Me?" (1973), and Quincy Jones's "Body Heat" (1974); with specificity, it reaches 103° in Foreigner's "Hot Blooded" (1978). Lust-ignited fever provokes tumbling strains in both Warrant's "Machine Gun" (1992) and Adele's "Rolling in the Deep" (2011). Pressure from introductory electric bass octaves and fiery lead vocals from Steve Winwood drive the Spencer Davis Group's "Gimme Some Loving" (1966). Winwood's opening line, "Well my temperature's rising," is already burning up, but it continues to climb in a push of minor-pentatonic chords: "[I] So glad we [bIII] made it, [IV] so glad we [bVI] made it." The Knack must have been impressed by this prechoral ramp, because "My Sharona" (1979) (also in the key of G) opens with identical bass octaves before replicating the Davis Group's rakish minor-pentatonic development, "[I] never gonna stop, give it up, such a dirty mind, I [bIII] always get it up for the touch of the younger kind; [IV] my my [bVI] my aye-aye [bVII] whoa! ma ma ma my Sharona."

Doctors are consulted, but sex is the only cure for such intense deliria, as we are told by Gene Vincent in "Woman Love" (1956), the Young Rascals in "Good Lovin'" (1966), and the Sylvers in "Boogie Fever" (1975). Tina Charles gives us "Dr. Love" (1976); Kiss, "Calling Dr. Love" (1977); Graham Parker, "Lady Doctor" (1978); Little Feat, "Rock and Roll Doctor" (1978); and the Thompson Twins, "Doctor! Doctor!" (1984). Physicians are deemed useless in Bon Jovi's "Bad Medicine" (1988) and Billie Eilish's "My Strange Addiction" (2019). One beautiful depiction of the need for erotic salvation is Marvin Gaye's "Sexual Healing" (1983). Frustration comes through in held-back rhythmic placement in the refrain, "And when I get that feeling I want [pause] sexual healing," and even moreso in the repeated attempts of V to find I, only to be trapped by deceptive motions to vi every time. Tonic harmony is only approached by less aggressive, inverted V chords, perhaps as a means to administer to "weaker," "feminine" fantasies. Robin Thicke's "Sex Therapy" (2010) is a similarly slow and smooth R&B groove, with a soft celeste and also with chords that never resolve tension in a V - I cadence, instead repeating an aimless loop of Ab minor - Eb - G minor - F minor sonorities.

Sometimes medicine is dispensed in the form of a mythical aphrodisiac; in "Venus" (2013), Lady Gaga offers, "Have an oyster, baby; it's aphrodisy." The most lasting pop aphrodisiac, though, is undoubtedly the one prescribed in the Clovers' Lieber and Stoller-penned "Love Potion Number 9" (1959). As with Etta James discussed earlier, the song opens with an affect of accompanied recitative, without rhythm in the piano/bass accompaniment, as the singer tells us he took his "troubles" to the gypsy, his problem being perpetually "flop"py impotence. The spellbinding, exotic setting is set musically in the bridge, when Madame Ruth concocts the draught ("She bent down and turned around . . ."), when IV is tonicized, unusual in an overall aeolian key. The lyrics are captivating throughout, with an entrancing assonance of consonants L, V, and N in the first refrain, "se*lli*n' *li*tt*l*e bott*l*es o*f Lo*ve Potio*n N*umber *Ni*ne," and unusual rhymes climaxing in the bridge ("wink / sink / ink / drink"), which section ends with assertive monosyllables on a repeated ^5: "I held my nose, I closed my eyes, [and gulp!] I took a drink."

(The Inevitable) Orgasm

Coming is coming. In "Can't Help Falling in Love" (1961), Elvis Presley sings, "Like a river flows, surely to the sea," channeling a sensitive perspective on the inevitability of romance (an inevitability grounded in the cadential six-four that concludes every refrain, and the long string of bass fifth descents in the bridge's retransition). In rock, though, such a sense of undeniable urge is frequently applied to the onset of something far more physical, as suggested when Kacey Musgraves sings "running like a river trying to find the ocean" in "Love Is a Wild Thing" (2018). Masters and Johnson discuss their Phase I of a man's orgasm as such a sudden awareness of impending loss of control:

> In the human male a sensation of ejaculatory inevitability develops for an instant immediately prior to, and then parallels in timing sequence, the first stage of the ejaculatory process. . . . From onset of this specific sensation, there is a brief interval (2 to 3 seconds) during which the male feels the ejaculation coming and no longer can constrain, delay, or in any way control the process. This subjective experience of inevitability develops as seminal plasma is collecting in the prostatic urethra but before the actual emission of seminal fluid begins.[7]

Thus Devo cram eleven rising "yeah"s into the space of nine semitones, ^3 up to ^8, in both the middle and end of "Uncontrollable Urge" (1978), and Björk sings "I can sense it, something important is about to happen, it's coming up," in "Big Time Sensuality" (1993). In "To My Bed" (2017), Chris Brown knows "we ain't gonna make it to my bed." Attempts to postpone the impending release are made in Selena Gomez's "Slow Down" (2013) among other examples.[8] Boston's "We're

---

[7] 1966, 215. See also Bancroft 1989, 78. Bancroft 2009 finds that the anticipation of orgasm can reward with as much pleasure as does the release (64).

[8] Stamina against premature ejaculation is the topic of Julia Lee & Her Boy Friends' "Don't Come Too Soon" (1950), the Dominoes' "Sixty Minute Man" (1951), Ruth Wallis's "Long Playing Daddy" (*c* 1953, discussed in this book's Introduction), Frankie Goes to Hollywood's "Relax" (1984), Patti LaBelle's "Something Special (Is Gonna Happen Tonight)" (1986), BWP's "Two Minute Brother" (1991), and TLC's "Don't Pull Out on Me Yet" (1999).

Ready" (1986) barely contains a beautiful build-up to orgasmic climax and an even more satisfying denouement. Along the way, soft muted electric guitar arpeggiations and sustained backing-vocal "ooh"s, sometimes with imitative gentle neighbors (on "simplify" in the second verse, from 0:57), are replaced by a rock-hard distorted guitar, insistent snare offbeat and crash cymbal (1:03) that bring—"come what may, come what may"—multiple vocal parts and a distorted guitar riff to readiness in power chords: "we're ready! We're ready! We're ready! Yeah!" A free guitar solo erupts into two parallel parts, pushing to an inevitable circle of fifths (1:31) and soft afterglow.

Sexual excitement brings the release of bodily fluids just prior to orgasm. Prince compares the inner release of flowing hormones to external moisture: "Pheromone, rush over me like an ocean . . . pheromone, when your body's wet," in "Pheromone" (1994); the same year, in "Flower," Liz Phair is typically frank: "every time I see your face I get all wet between my legs." Whereas this sexual event was not referred to in pop music before the 1970s except in masked metaphors such as tears and rain, it becomes boldly familiar in pop of the large twenty-first century, often in that by top divas: Sylk-E. Fyne with Chill, "Romeo and Juliet" (1998) ("hot sex on a platter just to get you wet"); Rihanna, "Umbrella" (2007) ("it's raining, raining, ooh baby it's raining, raining; baby come into me"); Janet Jackson, "2nite" (2008) ("my body's here, I'm soaking wet"); Ludacris, "My Chick Bad" (2010) ("pussy stay wet, sex so good"); Nicki Minaj feat. Lil Wayne, "High School" (2012) ("pussy so wet I'mma need goggles"); Madonna, "S.E.X." (2015) ("Oh my God, soaking wet"); Rihanna, "Sex with Me" (2016) ("you know I'm saucy and it's always wet"); Lil Yachty, "Dirty Mouth" (2017) ("they nicknamed her 'Juicy' 'cause she keep a wet pussy"); Rich the Kid, "Drippin" (2018) ("that pussy keep me focused—she a water, water, water"); and perhaps most notoriously Cardi B feat. Megan Thee Stallion, "WAP" (2020) ("bring a bucket and a mop for this wet-ass pussy"). Oddly in-your-face barely metaphors are presented to us by Rufus Wainwright in "Between My Legs" (2007): "Now that you're away, I'm out there without you when I shed a tear between my legs" and by the cast of *Me and My Dick* in "Land of the Dicks" (2009): "Cocks from far and wide, oh, they lay down at my side; I take them in and wipe their tears away."

Ejaculation. In 1935, Lucille Bogan boasted, "I got somethin' between my legs that'll make a dead man come" ("Shave 'Em Dry"); Mick Jagger throws out a line stolen from this hyperbole at the end of the Rolling Stones' "Start Me Up" (1981). "Blowing my top" (in both the Dominoes in "Sixty Minute Man" [1951] and Anisteen Allen in "Fujiyama Mama" [1955]), "keep on churnin' 'till the butter comes" (Wynonie Harris's "Keep on Churnin'" [1952]), "bang, bang, shoot, shoot" (the Beatles' "Happiness Is a Warm Gun" [1968]), "skyrockets in flight" (the Starland Vocal Band's "Afternoon Delight" [1976]), "gonna have us a champagne jam" (Atlanta Rhythm Section's "Champagne Jam" [1978]), "I'm melting, I'm melting" (Michael Jackson's "Don't Stop 'Til You Get Enough" [1979]), "a happy ending" (Sharon Brown's "I Specialize in Love" [1982]), "firing your load" (AC/DC's "Deep in the Hole" [1983]), "I told him, 'I am the flower, you are the seed'; we walked in the garden, we planted a tree" (Heart's "All I Wanna Do Is Make Love to You" [1990]), "I'm hearin' thunder" (2Pac's "Me and My Girlfriend" [1996]), "put your icing on my cake" (Christina Aguilera's "Nasty Naughty Boy" (2006), "this is when my buzzer goes" (Amy Winehouse's "You Know I'm No Good" [2007]), and "now I've got your honey all over my tummy" (Lucinda Williams's "Honey Bee" [2008]): these are some of the metaphors that often clarify the cause of groaning that accompanies variously male and female musical orgasm. Many other songs of the past few decades are more explicit: In 1977, Richard Hell and the Voidoids observed that "Love Comes in Spurts"; the following year, Lou Reed (in "I Wanna Be Black") exercised multiple racist tropes in singing "I wanna be Black, have natural rhythm, shoot twenty feet of jism too." The Lonely Island has Andy Samberg and others rap "Jizz in My Pants" (2009); that same year, Eminem had the same oops experience in "We Made You." ZZ Top's stop-time whammy bar produces a "Pearl Necklace" (1981), Joe offers, "I'd put a string of pearls right in your hand" in "All the Things (Your Man Won't Do)" (1996), and dresses get cum-stained in Prince's "Head" (1980), Vanity's "Pretty Mess" (1984), Nickelback's "Figured You Out" (2003), and Beyoncé's "Partition" (2013). "Busting a nut" became a hip-hop thing in 1987 (LL Cool J's "Kanday") (see also 2Pac, Lil' Kim with Da Brat, Ice Cube, Snoop Dogg, Nicki Minaj), and, simply, "nutting" did so in 2014 (YG, "Do It to Ya"; see also Wu-Tang Clan, Lil Yachty, and Cardi B). Beyond its portrayal as a seed, the procreative nature of semen leads to "shoot a child in your mouth" in Lil Nas X's "Montero" (2021) and, a year later, "they swallowed all my children" in Kevin Gates feat. Juicy J's "Thinking with My Dick." Often set with extreme musical excitement, classically with a highly ornamented retransition on a bridge-ending V harmony, ejaculation is set with pounding triplets at that point in Etta James's "I Just Want to Make Love to You" (1961) and traded vocal pitches erupting in an arpeggiated V9 chord, glissandi and shouts in the Beatles' "Twist and Shout" (1963). In "Don't Say No Tonight" (1985), Eugene Wilde adds to such a frenzy with a pump-up modulation.

No rock artist has explored the many deviations of the sexual experience as thoroughly and often as Frank Zappa. Despite censorship of a handful of particular words by his label in early releases, Zappa has routinely been explicit in covering the many sorts of penchants and behaviors that result in orgasm. In "Brown Shoes Don't Make It" (1967), he and the Mothers of Invention evoke Antheil, Varèse, and Ives as well as the Beach Boys, a dorian shuffle, a Merrie Melodies cadence, a stripper's grind, an Austrian Landler, and a rag blues to enscript a full-blown pedophiliac fantasy as savored by a degenerate middle-aged denizen of city hall, evidence of the composer's frequent observation that hypocritical super-patriotic lawmakers control the entire population due to frustration caused by their own deviant predilections.[9] The seven-minute tableau sandwiches Fred's fantasia (1:22–6:06) in between an exposition criticizing social conformity and the bureaucrat's return home to an uninspiring wife, with a final ballet mécanique coda emblematizing his lust for power. The inner masturbatory episode opens with a modern-jazz-based non-resolving dissonance of a slowly repeated B major triad over open fifth of C and G while a string bass passes again and again from Db through C to B. Imaginary sexual intercourse is made audible with repeated non-pitched throaty thrusts of "hratche-pulche" (2:07+) and out-of-control screams of "Baby, baby." We enter more deeply into the pol's depraved world with rock's first twelve-tone passage (2:13+), set for string quartet, piano, piccolo, muted trumpet, horn, and bass clarinet—a perfect device within a tonal context for the groundless nature of unconscious reverie. Orgasm is composed-out in an agitated transition (4:04–4:27) of timpani, string tremolos, brass fanfares, full-register woodwind outbursts, and the anticlimax of a record player's dying motor. It's interesting to note that the album on which this track appears, *Absolutely Free*, was released at just about the same moment as was another avant-garde orchestra's outburst-as-orgasm in the Beatles' "A Day in the Life" on *Sgt. Pepper's Lonely Hearts Club Band*.

In LaBelle's "Lady Marmalade" (1974), women (Patti LaBelle, Nona Hendryx, and Sarah Dash) sing a number written by men (Bob Crewe and Kenny Nolan) about a sex-working woman who brings a man to orgasm. (Further complicating the song's artistic provenance, whereas both songwriters were white, most of the song's session players—notably producer and electric pianist Allen Toussaint, Hammond organist Art Neville, Fender bassist George Porter, Jr., and drummer Joseph Johnson—were Black.) Set in the milieu of New Orleans prostitution, the

[9] Zappa's own thoughts on "Brown Shoes," originally appearing in *Keyboard* magazine in 1987, are found in Courrier 2002, 116–17.

protagonist is a "mocha chocolata creole," her exotic gumbo (again, cooked from a recipe by white male songwriters) stirring together many tonal languages: (1) a dorian i - IV/1 intro features a syncopated minor-pentatonic guitar-and-bass riff; (2) dorian verses and choruses are flavored with aeolian accents (in the prechorus's minor iv chords); and (3) an instrumental break veers from major-mode horns in contrary motion to a minor key's V, ending with a strong minor-pentatonic tumbling strain with bass again doubled by guitar. The major V triad in the retransition (1:52–1:55), coming only after the introductory motto, first verse and prechorus, chorus, second verse and prechorus, second chorus, and break, is the song's first dominant harmony and is stressed with syncopated brass stabs. The john encountered in prechorus 1 just begins to "freak," his V-arpeggiating orgasm suggested ("Hey, hey, hey!") at this retransition and produced at the end of verse 3 as the "savage beast" roars "more, more, more" (2:25–2:29), a culminatory phrase not present in the first two verses. The event is recapitulated in the client's home-based memories of verse 4. Just as emphatic as the ejaculation, however, is Marmalade's presence, as her name is sung at 1:20 an octave higher than previously, and in the third utterance, at 2:42, she projects a great lead vocal slide, C♯-D-F. The song's multiple climaxes prove the lady's power is responsible for the guy's pleasure.

Waves. Multiple orgasm was discussed in Chapters 1 and 2 as being a woman's property, often portrayed as waves. Above, in connection with "Tonight" from *West Side Story*, the alternation of I with a major II chord (over an unchanging ^1) was taken as a token of dreamy euphoria. Such was promised, in waves of repeated bliss, in the chorus of Phil Phillips with the Twilights' "Sea of Love" (1959). A more sensitive, less predictable rhythm of gently lapping waves is heard in the unusual metric changes of Jimi Hendrix's "Drifting" (1971); PJ Harvey's "Water" (1992) is in 5/4 throughout, producing a hypnotic flow for the central message, "I'm walking down into the sea." The Beatles' "A Day in the Life" was mentioned earlier for its suggestion of male climax; a contrasting composition is heard in Heart's "Soul of the Sea" (1976), in which a frantically awakened middle section interrupts the slower song proper. It is not set off by male orchestral climax, but by slow wave-like strings over a chromatic choral descent and then slide-guitar trills (3:00). No partner—particularly no man—is present for this instance of masturbation; there is "no rain, no seed, no silence." Retransition to the original key and acoustic twelve-string guitar occurs over the sound of actual ocean surf: "Mama ocean, hold me to you; rock me on your waves." (As a moaning woman comes in Prince's "Orgasm" [1994], a sample of ocean waves makes the nature of the climax obvious.) Also in 1976, Patti Smith opens "Chiklets" by instructing acoustic guitarist Lenny Kaye to "keep it really sexy, and like dark, you know, like a really damp cave"; he obliges with wave-like repetitions of a minor-pentatonic riff ending with a tumbling strain. In Stephanie Mills' "I Feel Good All Over" (1987), there are many small peaks throughout, with the singer's rapid tremolo, choral shivering in overlapping imitation, and direct modulations, but the stop time at 4:11 allows for a major climax. Lots of instability over the bass ^5 ends with frisson-inducing waves over soft, rapidly repeated high-register piano arpeggiations.

Some songs about lesbian love picture the waves that can describe a woman's multiple chills and orgasms, as opposed to the single climb-and-crash climaxes enjoyed by men. Jane Siberry's "Mimi on the Beach" (1984), Janis Ian's "Ride Me Like a Wave" (1997), k.d. lang's "Love's Great Ocean" (2000), and to a lesser degree the Indigo Girls' "Ghost" (1992) share such watery ebb-and-flow imagery. Siberry's epic opens with a seadog's shantey-like alternation of open fifths on E (I5) and D (bVII5), then wavelets appear in multiple internal rhymes like "I stand and scan on the strand of sand," always repeating in a wave-like two-note neighbor motion. Tensions rise in prechoruses ("But the day was faultless . . .," 2:35+) that present layers of shining-sea vocal strands and move to repetitive choruses (2:52+) that recall the opening melodic neighbor motions and crest in a chromatic tension-breaking chord progression, B minor to Eb major (iii - bVI, 3:02-3:04) that returns to the G major tonic for the ensuing verse 3 by common-tone modulation.[10] Thus, the V chord typical of male-based climaxes in retransitional events is avoided. In verse 3 (3:07+), pointillistic repeated staccato keyboard eighths, and watery whammy-bar bends and shimmering trebly circular figures in electric guitar (3:34+) also suggest the pleasurable play of light on tiny swells and surges as Mimi paddles into position on her surfboard. A new sort of climax builds during the spoken-word bridge (4:43–5:17), which picks up energy through a newly repeating pedal, a gradually rising guitar line amidst a "Sargasso Sea" of vague mystery, increasing vocal intensity, and a repeated goal—"Stand up, Mimi, stand up, Mimi, stand up!"—as the singer coaches her lover to erection and as a breaker takes shape. Again, the peak is not based in a

---

[10] The cresting Bm - Eb major progression, highly unusual in this repertoire, represents the neo-Riemannian "LPL" hexatonic pole transformation found by Richard Cohn (2006) to represent the Freudian uncanny in Wagner's *Parsifal*. As a result, "Mimi"'s tonal structure is built on an arpeggiation of equal major thirds, progressing Bm - Eb - G, slithery in its voice-leading transforms, rather than the dramatically propulsive "male" I - V - I division.

man's hyperclimactic V chord and leads not to the verse's tonic but sideways to the opening's searching submediant, E.

Ian's "Ride Me Like a Wave" similarly avoids the retransitional dominant (except once, ending the instrumental break, although this is minimized in live performance as recorded for *Breaking Silence*). Many mildly tense V7-*shaped* chords (A7, F♯7, D7), however, do appear amid the sustained, unresolved bossa nova dissonances of major and minor suspended seventh, ninth, and eleventh sonorities, and the frisson of rolling suspended-cymbal accents. Like Siberry's play of internal rhyme, Ian uses initial assonance to set up wave-like accents: "[Am9] Dry me with de- [Am9/G] -lusion and de- [FM7] -sire; ride me like a wave," with title doubled by a whispered voice for a sense of ocean spray. As with the gay-based songs discussed in Chapter 3, there is nothing inherently lesbianic in the music that accompanies lines in the poetic text such as "lead me to your harbor" (could there be?), but there may be suggestions of the shapings of women's sexual response in its dynamics. In related ways, vaginal juices seem to be the "river" for which Me'shell Ndegéocello wishes in "Andromeda & The Milky Way" and "Love Song #3" (both 2003), and they certainly are in "the waves of passion" of Janet Jackson's "Moist" (2004), although it is likely a hetero love depicted swimming there.

Many topics related to erotics touched on tangentially thus far could be explored more deeply in and of themselves within the pop/rock canon, among them erogenous zones, specific masturbatory and copulatory behaviors, abstinence and promiscuity, cheating, paraphilia, fetishes, sex toys, pregnancy, sex work, and issues of consent and assault, but more than a book could be filled on these topics alone. We'll leave these suggestions here with the hope that the Appendix would serve well to support any such investigations.

A Brainiac Amour

Command, Surrender, and Improvisation
in Patti Smith's "Land"

Patti Smith is among the most creative poet-musicians of the past half-century. Lauded for her National Book Award-winning memoir of 2010, *Just Kids*, which details her life with Robert Mapplethorpe, Smith continued until the onset of the pandemic to take the stage about a hundred times each year. She and her rock 'n' roll band present a wide range of ever-changing story songs spanning a recording career that (except for a small-pressing single in 1974) began in 1975 with the album, *Horses*. We focus here on one composition from that record, the nine-minute song "Land," as a locus of her rich poetic imagery and her improvisatory skills as they interact with musical elements—particularly formal structure. Smith's oeuvre, especially her song "Land" and its improvisational performances, addresses that process of creating human desire through embodied orgasmic destruction that exists both inside and outside the identification of male and female forms. Along these lines, "Land" functions as both the projection of the performer's autoerotic fantasy—and the mirrored creation of it for the audience commanded to surrender to a similar masturbatory experience. Through "Land," Smith offers progressive, visionary perspectives on gender and sex as she negotiates the themes of command and surrender, seemingly opposed sexual motifs whose roles are imbued with a blurriness similar to Smith's own genderqueer performance.[1]

This study of Smith began with transcriptions of improvised poetic texts from audio tapes of the twelve earliest available live performances of "Land," from 1975 and 1976, and of thirty available videos of the same from recent

---

[1] Theodore Gracyk: "When Patti Smith's raised arm reveals armpit hair on the cover of *Easter* (1978), it sharply deviates from the overtly 'feminine' display of her torso. . . . Her gender is thus revealed to be a contingent element of her identity" (2001, 204).

Table 5.1 Live Performances of "Land" by the Patti Smith Group Studied for This Chapter, 1975–2017

May 11, 1975: "War Is Over" concert, Central Park, New York

December 26, 1975: The Bottom Line, New York, late show

December 27, 1975: The Bottom Line, New York, late show

January 9, 1976: Paul's Mall Jazz Workshop, Boston

February 7, 1976: Huntington Beach, California

March 9, 1976: Ford Theater, Detroit

March 24, 1976: Avery Fisher Hall, New York

March 25, 1976: Georgetown University, Washington, D.C.

March 27, 1976: Tower Theater, Upper Darby, Pennsylvania

March 28, 1976: Symphony Hall, Boston

May 11, 1976: "Old Grey Whistle Test," BBC-TV, London

October 3, 1976: Conserthouse, Stockholm

June 25, 2005: Royal Festival Hall, London

October 15, 2006: CBGB, New York

November 22, 2011: Olympia Theater, Paris

August 31, 2012: Piazza del Campo, Siena

December 1, 2012: Rams Head Live, Baltimore

February 27, 2013: Neptune Theatre, Seattle

June 22, 2013: Herodion Theatre, Athens

June 24, 2013: Ancienne Belgique, Brussels

July 2, 2013: Zitadelle Spandau, Berlin

February 12, 2014: Apostel Paulus Kirche, Berlin

January 26, 2015: Rio Theater, Santa Cruz

May 29, 2015: Parc del Fòrum, Barcelona (fragment)

July 13, 2015: Tollwood Sommerfestival, Munich

July 21, 2015: Kulturzentrum Tollhaus, Karlsruhe

July 24, 2015: Festival les Nuits de Fourvière, Lyon

August 2, 2015: Krizanke, Ljubljana

August 15, 2015: Slottsskogen, Gothenborg

October 21, 2015: Olympia Theater, Paris

November 10, 2015: Beacon Theater, New York

December 30, 2015: The Fillmore, San Francisco

January 2, 2016: Rio Theatre, Santa Cruz

Table 5.1 (Continued)

January 8, 2016: The Wiltern, Los Angeles

June 23, 2016: Ana Tiyatro, Istanbul

July 1, 2016: Hyde Park, London

July 4, 2016: Wiener Arena, Vienna

July 10, 2016: Ruissalo, Turku

October 20, 2016: Teragram Ballroom, Los Angeles

October 23, 2016: Hollywood Bowl, Los Angeles

April 9, 2017: State Theatre, Sydney

April 17, 2017: Hamer Hall, Melbourne

In the body of the text, particular shows will be referred to by date only.

years, 2011–17, all listed in Table 5.1.[2] We took this approach to textual analysis because Smith endows "Land" every night with a whole new set of thematic stories, settings, and images, informed by William Blake and other notable poets and musicians, as well as storytellers both real and fictional. Indeed, Smith's performances are much like Blake's illuminations in *Songs of Innocence and Experience*, each copy a one-of-a-kind formed of the same engraving, but whose coloring is unique because of the handmade process of painting.[3] Similarly, Smith's changing stories are always intertwined with the song's fixed underlying structure, and these associations continue to reveal her near-oracular stature as an improvisational artist. Smith said *c.* 1975, "When I perform, I just sort of mingle everything that I'm into at the moment. About a year ago it was the legend of Scheherazade and Patty Hearst. But it keeps changing all the time" (Heylin 2005, 194). Smith relates herself to the folkloric character Scheherazade, the narrator in the frame story of the collection of Middle Eastern and South Asian tales known as *One Thousand and One Nights*.

Smith's Scheherazade association offers meaningful insight into her improvisational performance of sexual subject matter, especially motifs associated with sexual violence and survival. Once upon a time, the story goes, King Shahryar is wronged by an unfaithful wife and her lovers, who are all punished with death; feeling particularly retributive, the king continues to

[2] Dozens of audio cassettes were auditioned at the Rock and Roll Hall of Fame Museum and Archives in Cleveland, thanks to a generous research fellowship held in July 2016, with the assistance of Daniel Goldmark, director of the Center for Popular Music Studies at Case Western Reserve University. The later videotapes studied were those shared by fans on YouTube in June–July 2017.

[3] I am indebted to Katie Kapurch for this observation.

rape and murder a new wife night after night—until the daughter of the king's advisor and a well-read scholar herself, Scheherazade, devises a plan. On her wedding night, Scheherazade spins an improvised tale until dawn, but leaves it unfinished, intriguing the king just enough to grant her a reprieve so she can continue the story the following night. This process goes on until 1,001 nights have passed, at which point the king grows protective of Scheherazade, whose life is spared. In December 1975, Smith—just such a storyweaver—said of "Land"'s early material:

> I started the first "Land"—this was Upstairs at Max's Kansas City—with a recitation of a New York poem from "Witt" [Smith's second book of poetry]. Then, as I got more confident, it was Scheherazade: "Welcome to the Palace of a Thousand Sensations . . ." Then it got real sadistic, I don't know how that happened [short laugh], and got mixed up with a dream I had when I was 16 about a hallway plastered with six-foot posters of nuns and me running along burning holes in their groins with a cigarette. Then it was Arabia, Mexico, U.F.O.'s, razors, jackknives, horses and in some notes I wrote last Dec. 16— the 701st birthday of the great Persian mystic poet Jalal ad-Din Rumi—Jim Morrison, Janis Joplin, and Jimi Hendrix. Twenty versions got lost when I lost a notebook I had been writing in for three years. The way I'd write versions of it—I learned this from Genet, who wrote in prison so he could turn himself on and masturbate—I'd sit at the typewriter and type until I felt sexy, then I'd go and masturbate to get high, and then I'd come back in that higher place and write some more. But no matter how much, how many times I tried to transform the song in my notebooks, I always landed in my immediate environment. (Hiss and McClelland 1975, 29–31)

These kaleidoscopic references, for which Scheherazade is a touchstone, speak to the wide range of source materials for various presentations of "Land." They reveal the composer's mystical romance with words and a sexual relationship with her text, along with the roles of contemporaneous news, concert location, and audience interaction that nightly motivate allusions to her "immediate environment." On May 28, 1975, in a New York concert broadcast on WBAI, Smith performed an encore, referring to Scheherazade while introducing her cover of the Quin-Tones' "Down the Aisle of Love" (1958). With thematic subject matter consistent with her fictional predecessor's exigence for storytelling, the song is a wedding (and perhaps funerary) celebration containing the line, "A choir of angels sent from above when we walk, oh, walk down the aisle of love," whose image also informs a scene that occurs midway through "Land."

Like Frank Zappa's "Brown Shoes Don't Make It" (1967), discussed in Chapter 4, "Land" is a multi-section tableau. Its basic idea is the fantasy of a rape and murder involving ambiguous sex and gender, usually triggered by an inanimate talisman, which leads to orgasm in a frenzied cover of Chris Kenner's 1962 R&B garage-rock staple, "Land of 1000 Dances," a title suggestive of Scheherazade's "One Thousand and One Nights" and the likely basis for Smith's own title, "Land."[4] The many named dances (the pony, mashed potato, twist, and watusi) are followed by a resurrection and secondary climaxes.[5] "Land" centers on the rape orgasm, a violational transcendence that unleashes both the horses of Revelation and Smith's preoccupation with the Babel story. Horses are linked both to the pony dance that opens "1000 Dances" and to the galloping of unstoppable sexual climaxes. Babel is cited as a mythic example of human transgression in the form of a God-threatening tower, punished by a prohibition against communication. For Smith, sex is a primal form of both transcendence and communication. The song "Land," then, reflects many perspectives on sex, which are especially evident in Smith's portrayal of orgasm as a little death, improvisation as a vehicle for expressing the sex-related dichotomy of command versus surrender, nonconformist representations and readings of gender, the role of reciprocal communication in Smith's conception of sex, and the power of rock 'n' roll in bringing sexual imagery and embodied responses to the level of a communal force.

Background: Words and Music, Fantasy and Sex

Born in 1946, young Patricia was intrigued by her mother's inventiveness in creating stories. Seeing double due to strabismus, and her high-temperature deliriums from a bout with scarlet fever, had a lasting impact on the child's widening imagination, resulting for example in the hallucinatory visions captured in the *Horses* song "Kimberly" involving her sister as a child. Exposure in her teens to Blake, along with Arthur Rimbaud, reinforced such mythic and

---

[4] In the March 28, 1976, performance of "Land," Smith intones, "I cannot foresee the king . . . I saw you in the palace, . . . in the palace of a thousand sensations; in a land of a thousand dances there are lots of girls dancing around the Christmas tree . . ."

[5] Smith repurposes the resurrection story in 1978 with the album title, *Easter*, there announcing the artist's return to concertizing after a fall from the stage had broken her neck.

impressionistic percepts.[6] An early expression of her sexual imagination was her coining of the phrase "brainiac amour," by which she described a libidinal urge based on verbal relations that underpinned her fantasized affair with the sensual poetry of the gay Rimbaud: "I discovered Rimbaud and I realized that you can be entertained by words sexually in some place other than your sex organs [a concept reverberating with Freud's theories documented in Chapter 1]. I discovered what I call 'brainiac amour'—when you fuck with the mind." Smith is later paraphrased in the same interview: "Rimbaud predicted that, once liberated, women would be poets [and] would discover strange and unfathomable things that would make them shake and [come in] their pants" (Cohen 1976).

Smith wished to carry out Rimbaud's prediction by masturbating, like Genet, to inspire her poetry. In a much earlier interview, from December 3 or 4, 1972, for KQRS Radio in Minneapolis, Smith said that around 1966, "somebody would say a . . . word like 'platinum' and all of a sudden that word . . . would shine, you know, and I couldn't get the word out of my head and . . . I realized that I was really, really courting language, I was havin' this real romance with the word, you know, and as St. John says, . . . 'in the beginning was the word.'"

(It is unknown whether Smith would have known Žižek's concept of phallicism as the often shiny nature of the fetishistic object that "does not fit," as covered in Chapter 1.) Smith, however, sees the masturbatory experience that is rooted in shared art as potentially reciprocal: "I can jerk off best to Rimbaud, just because he's perfect. . . . I really hope people jerk off to my records. . . . I'm trying to write porno rock 'n' roll in an illuminated way, so that not only will you wet your pants but your mind will crack like an egg" (Cohen 1976). Verbal play is a particularly masturbatory vehicle for Smith: "The Word is just for me, when I'm alone late at night and I'm jerkin' off, you know, pouring out streams of words" (Shapiro 1975). Not coincidentally given this context, Rimbaud's name and the phrase "brainiac amour" appear among the "Land" lyrics.[7]

Smith's recollections of her masturbatory practices, especially the requirement of subject matter with rich personal and artistic substance, suggest a foundational

---

[6] Smith tells of her concentrated fascination with Blake in the 2004 song, "My Blakean Year," the refrain of which suggests that life is a "woeful schism" between the glorious and the painful: "One road is paved in gold, one road is just a road." The image of a schizoid path, as clarified below, is central to the emerging story in "Land."

[7] Smith's romance with Rimbaud, originating in her 1964 reading of *Illuminations* (1874) and continuing with *A Season in Hell* (1873), runs deep: Among her earliest performances in various small venues in 1972–5 (revived in 2007–8 and 2016) were her "trashy" poetry readings entitled "Rock 'n' Rimbaud." She discusses this theme in the KQRS interview. Definitive Smith setlists are found at http://setlists.pattismithlogbook.info.

theory in sexology studies. Alfred C. Kinsey found that two-thirds of females require the psychologic stimulation of fantasizing to masturbate to orgasm, whereas one-third reach orgasm through physiologic stimulation alone. Males, by contrast, fantasize much more frequently to attain erotic arousal (1953, 164–5, 667). John Bancroft summarizes studies that have since reevaluated Kinsey's findings, finding in one case that "there was no significant difference in gender effect between [visual and non-visual sexual stimuli], which challenges the assumption [. . .] that females are less influenced by visual stimuli" (2009, 226). Bancroft goes onto summarize other findings: "A number of studies have now shown that, whereas men tend to respond with more sexual arousal than women to erotic films, when films are used which are designed for women, the difference is less" (2009, 226).[8] We cite these explanations to reinforce the gendered aspects of the erotic motivation for Smith's poetry, but also to problematize those gendered associations at the same time since, for example, Smith is also concerned with creating visual stimuli for her audience. Both male and female arousal are combined in the persona that Smith cultivates throughout her career—and especially in the subject position of "Land."[9]

Patti's androgynous gender performance is rooted in her introduction to rock: she became an avid rock 'n' roller at the same time she discovered her sexual response to the Rolling Stones in 1965. When it came to rock, her favorite performers were males. Mick Jagger, Bob Dylan, Jim Morrison, Jimi Hendrix, and Lou Reed: all were models for her snarling and speech-tending authorial and performing voices. Dylan (with whom Smith has a long personal and professional history) encouraged her tendencies toward myth-imbued surrealism, openness, and intensity. Jagger was a pioneer in rocker androgyny, and another idol, Lou Reed, was openly gay years before Bowie problematized gender in the rock world much more unguardedly than was conceivable in, say, Little Richard's day. Smith performed such Reed songs as "Pale Blue Eyes" (1969)

---

[8] John Bancroft and others have since reevaluated many of Kinsey's observations in this and other studies, critiquing the self-reporting on which Kinsey relied and taking into account changing cultural attitudes that account for gender differences and shifts over time. Bancroft maintains, however, that there are indeed gender differences when it comes to masturbation, concluding that women "who, once they are freed from socio-cultural constraints, use masturbation as a more efficient method of meeting their [. . .] sexual needs" (2009, 186).

[9] Following Butler 1999, M. Lafrance writes that the gay female performance of male-like, hetero-like fantasies of Me'Shell Ndegéocello's "Mary Magdalene" (1996) "must be understood as fundamentally disruptive to heteronormative regimes." In the same source, Burns responds by connecting the subject's desire of her object, the "Other," to the musical setting in ways similar to those we shall demonstrate here (Burns and Lafrance 2002, 144, 149, 152–4). Regarding fantasies as a safe way to negotiate prohibited desires, see also Whiteley and Rycenga 2006, 250.

in early shows and his "[We're Gonna Have a] Real Good Time Together" (also 1969) was long her concert opener.

Performing as another transgressor of boundaries, in the Doors' "The End" (1967), Morrison mixes spoken and sung passages in a myth-and-sex family melodrama that very much prefigures "Land."[10] Smith also revitalizes Jagger's vocal technique, which is often referred to as quintessentially male: note, for instance, the upward-soaring portamento in the word "twist" in "Land" and compare it to the far less energetic "street" in the Rolling Stones' "Rocks Off" (1972).[11] We'll return to Hendrix in discussing the ending of "Land," but we can note here his Dylan-like speech-song and his "Hey Joe" (1967), the vehicle for Smith's inaugural single. As for musical style more generally, Smith was drawn to the three-chord proto-punk garage rock of the mid-1960s, and would often import a classic like "Louie Louie" (1963), "Gloria," or "My Generation" (both 1965) into a song of her own, all to express the power of guitar-driven rock 'n' roll in revolutionizing humanity to achieve a new communal oneness comparable to sexual union.[12] In fact, Smith's cover of Van Morrison's "Gloria" ("G, L, O, R, I, A!"), the opening track on *Horses*, anticipates the radical gender fluidity of "Land," especially as a setting for sexual violence.

As covered in Chapter 2, female pop singers often cover heteronormative songs originally made popular by males without adjusting incidental pronouns; sometimes gender ambiguity is even central to the narrative, as when Joan Baez introduces herself as Virgil Caine in taking over Robbie Robertson's "The Night They Drove Old Dixie Down" (1971). But Smith's "Gloria" is highly unusual in its application of such an androgynous self-characterization to a song so fully based on sexual attraction, even sexual predation, targeting a woman. Smith has corrected many listeners who have taken this as an expression of lesbianism:

> Sexually, I'm really normal.[13] I always enjoyed doing transgendered songs. That's something I learned from Joan Baez, who often sang songs that had a male point of view. No, my work does not reflect my sexual preferences, it reflects the fact

---

[10] Smith made pilgrimages to Morrison's and Rimbaud's graves in her first, pre-fame visits to France in 1972–3.

[11] Links between rock vocal tone and range, a singer's gender, and sexuality have been explored in Reynolds and Press 1995, 239, Hisama 1999, 117, and Cusick 1999b, 34–6.

[12] Smith believed that the aggressive pulsating rhythms of guitars, as in "cock rock" in general and in "My Generation" (her first B-side) in particular, would drive the world's youth to a new level of activism. Hear "Land" on May 11, 1975, and see Smith 1974, 199–200, and 2010, 245. On March 27, 1976, she told her audience, "Rock 'n' roll has come a long way; we're getting people out of prison," likely referring to John Lennon's inspiring the 1972 release of John Sinclair.

[13] Despite the liberated stance of her art and subversive advocacies, Smith personally has a strong socially conservative streak, as when characterizing heterosexuality as "normal." She has attracted

that I feel total freedom as an artist. On *Horses*, that's why the sleevenote has that statement about being "beyond gender." By that, I meant that as an artist, I can take any position, any voice, that I want.[14]

This unbound perspective informs the gender identity queered throughout "Land," which in recent years has closed Smith concerts by segueing directly into her version of "Gloria" (a song by which composer Van Morrison had epitomized the predatory male, according to Whiteley 2000, 101). "Land" would seem to be an early manifestation of what Susan McClary (1991, 33) theorizes about 1980s women artists, who "can *choose* to write music that foregrounds their sexual identities without falling prey to essentialist traps and that departs self-consciously from the assumptions of standard musical procedures." McClary's musicological point of view is echoed in sexologist Bancroft's statement on gender stereotypes. He suggests that the fluidity of gender identity is related to the irrational quality of sexuality—perhaps, then, a corollary of Smith's fantasy realm:

> There is a tension or conflict between our identities as rational, civilized beings and our sexual identities and less rational sexual drives. Our sexuality endows us with an absurd quality which gives some immunity against pomposity and excess dignity. On the other hand, our sexual vulnerabilities have become incorporated into some of our least attractive or most questionable characteristics. Our sex role stereotypes, for example, institutionalise the sexual irresponsibility of the male, whilst assuming sexual responsibility and other less enviable virtues in the female. (1989, 2)

It may also be that Smith is interested in regaining a pre-Fall genderless innocence; as Blake writes in "To Tirzah," "The Sexes sprung from Shame & Pride" (1981, 30). Smith follows Blake, who imagines a genderless life as one recapturing a time without guilt. In this view, we might understand Smith's assertion of "normality" as ironic, especially given her fluid approach to sexuality, evidenced in her Rimbaud fantasies and informed by her exposure to more contemporaneous gay writers.

Young Patti's emerging bohemianism also led her to embrace Beat writers Allen Ginsberg and her fellow Chelsea Hotel lodger William Burroughs, both

criticism for her complete satisfaction over decades with a patriarchal domestic life with husband Fred "Sonic" Smith.

[14] Tarr 2008, 23. Smith's "Notice" at the opening of *Witt* starts, "These ravings, observations, etc. come from one who, beyond vows, is without mother, gender, or country" (1973, 11).

chroniclers of colorful gay sex and both of whom she met soon after her arrival in New York in 1967. Smith invokes the memorable opening line of Ginsberg's *Howl* (1956), "I saw the best minds of my generation destroyed by madness," in such shows as those of February 27, and July 2, 2013. Therein, Smith introduces her indignant protagonist in "Land" by recounting how "Johnny saw the best minds of his generation" destroyed by various nefarious forces, which immediately positions Johnny as a prophetic onlooker akin to Ginsberg's speaker. *Howl* continues with several images Smith often incorporates into "Land" performances. Burroughs' 1969 novel, *The Wild Boys*, explored in more detail in the following pages, is another crucial inspiration for "Land" given the name of its lead character, Johnny, and, as Smith has said of "Land" imagery, "Usually there's Mexican boys and space guys, weird Burroughs stuff like Arab guys and Christian angels fucking in the sand, pulling out each others' entrails."[15] *The Wild Boys*, as a conceit, reads at some times like a screenplay and at others like a stage play, always like a narcotic nightmare or wet dream with hallucinogenic scenes and pungent phrases varied in rhythmic repetition like moments lived and re-lived in emotional and sexual rushes. Burroughs' earlier "cut-up" technique, whereby his prose would be constructed through the chopping up and random splicing together of narrative bits, is approximated in the superimposition of separately recorded, sometimes unrelated, vocals in the studio recording of "Land." Burroughs is the co-dedicatee, along with Rimbaud and Smith's lover Allen Lanier, of *Witt* (1973), Smith's second poetry collection.

Following her literary inspirations, Smith's early artistic preoccupations lay in such dark themes as sin, violence, and mortality. Her first works reacted to the early deaths of Rolling Stone Brian Jones, Jim Morrison, and Jimi Hendrix in odes imbued with a sensibility formed by her Catholic upbringing. Smith's first public performances in 1970–2 set her free Beat-like raps and melic readings of her long balladic poems to the improvisatory guitar accompaniment of Lenny Kaye. Kaye's playing could range from metric repetition of a two- or three-chord vocabulary through feedback and other experimental effects, sometimes organized in what he and Smith referred to as "fields." As he says,

> one of my roots was free jazz and free rock improvisation. We'd just get on these rhythmic moves—we called them fields—where we just kinda rode around in

---

[15] Bockris and Bayley 1999, 127. Smith 1977a contains two key references to *The Wild Boys*: a photo of the composer at the typewriter (p. 13) shows a copy of the book's first edition propped open next to her. Second, the punningly spelled line "wild boys burroughed in the sand in mexico" is seen within the earliest extant draft of "Land," from April 1975 (p. 47).

them. And [with] a lot of our early songs that's all they were. "Free Money" [on *Horses*] was just those [A minor - G - F - G] chords repeated over and over again. . . "Land of a Thousand Dances." "Gloria" certainly, they weren't really songs but over the course of performing them we would get into things that we would come up with and they were incorporated into the song. (Heylin 2005, 113)

Another influence on the improvisational technique that makes her "Land" performances so evocative, Kaye has always been the linchpin of the Patti Smith Group and remains with her to this day.

Patti continued to meditate on desire and death when she fell in with the Velvet Underground, formed by academically trained poet Lou Reed and avant-garde violist John Cale. This band, partly inspired by their impresario Andy Warhol, explored extreme violence reminiscent of Burroughs in tracks like "The Gift" and nonmainstream sexuality in "Sister Ray" and "Venus in Furs." "The Gift" (1968) culminates in the plunging of a blade "right through the center of Waldo Jeffers's head, which split slightly and caused little rhythmic arcs of red to pulsate gently in the morning sun," lines that could have been written for "Land." "Ray" (1968) and "Venus" (1967) merge images of intravenous drug use, oral sex by transvestites, and murder in repetitive three-chord riffs supporting atonal improvisation.[16] The Velvets' "Heroin" (1967) shuttles between two chords and features long and expressive gradual accelerations and retardations, which also characterize the large-scale changes of sexual energy in the similarly economic "Land." Reed would introduce Smith to Clive Davis, who signed her to Arista Records to release *Horses*, which was produced by Cale in Jimi Hendrix's Ladyland Studios.[17]

Interviewed during the recording of *Horses*, Smith spoke about her desire to inject a lusty rock spirit into her poetry:

I'm starting to learn about sound as opposed to linear motion with language. It's like pumping blood into words. Poetry goes hand in hand with anemia. Poets are always anemic looking and I just want to pump a lot of blood into it—I don't want to get away from poetry . . . but there's no reason why the two have to be separated. I think I've proven it with what I do with "Land of a

---

[16] Much more of interest on these tracks is found in Greene 2016, 15, 152, and 164–5.

[17] At Smith's request, *Horses* was recorded in September–October 1975 at Ladyland Studios on West 8th Street, one of her earliest pilgrimage sites in New York. Hendrix is the central figure in the original final section of "Land"; note also that he'd incorporated the name "Dylan," who was a strong influence on his own poetry and singing style, within the name "Ladyland."

1000 Dances" . . . it's totally impossible to distinguish what is poetry from . . . the rock and roll, they're so integrated. (Robinson 1976)

Catholicism, androgyny, sexual desire, death, wordplay, garage rock, and free improvisation all come together in the opening track of *Horses*, which takes the love object of Van Morrison's "Gloria" and merges her with that siren's namesake in the ordinary of the Latin mass. The *Horses* album begins—in "Gloria"—with the line, "Jesus died for somebody's sins, but not mine."

"Land": "Horses"

As outlined in Table 5.2, Smith divides her tableau into three portions, the first of which is subtitled "Horses," for its galloping climax that gives the LP its name. The second is subtitled "Land of 1000 Dances," for the garage-rock cover that dominates the song's middle section. The third subtitle is "La Mer (de)," her pun for the sea as the traditional wet, soft yielding feminine yin as opposed to the land's dry, hard, aggressive masculine yang, for the Horse (mare), and for the excremental waste of death and disintegration (since *merde* is French for "shit"). The recording will here be further divided into eight subsections (two

Table 5.2 Sections and Subsections of Studio Recording of "Land"

Time Stamps	Section	Beginning and Ending Lyrics
	§ 1 *"Horses"*	
0:00–0:19	§§ 1	"The boy was in the hallway"—"the mirror in the hallway"
0:19–1:11	§§ 2	"The boy looked at Johnny"—"horses, horses, horses, horses"
	§2 *"Land of 1000 Dances"*	
1:12–2:14	§§ 3	"Do you know how to pony?"—"yeah, do the watusi"
2:15–3:49	§§ 4	"Life is filled with holes"—"Twistolettes, Twistolettes"
	§3 *"La Mer (de)"*	
3:49–6:01	§§ 5	"Let it calm down"—"and go, Johnny go"
6:02–7:00	§§ 6	"Well, do the watusi"—"like playing in the sea, the sea"
7:01–8:04	§§ 7	"In the sea of possibility"—"That nobody heard, no one heard"
8:04–9:25	§§ 8	"That cry no one heard"—"to the simple rock and roll song"

within "Horses," two within "Dances," and four within "La Mer (de)"), largely marked by contrasting tendencies toward either improvisation or fixedness. We shall take up each subsection in turn, continuing to explore Smith's literary influences and intertextual associations, along with the rhetorical outcomes of her improvised performances, whose nuances add to the interpretation of her representation of sexuality as a process of command and surrender.

Subsection One

Subsection One is spoken, its two unmetered opening lines delivered a cappella:

> The boy was in the hallway drinking a glass of tea.
> From the other end of the hallway a rhythm was generating.

This opening, invariable in every performance, introduces Johnny ("the boy") and his Otherized agent-provocateur counterpart (at first perceived as simply "a rhythm"), calls upon a muse, and initiates action, as will soon be explained. Such initiation is followed by improvised material that in live performance tends to run two minutes or more, different every night. Then the song is gripped by three straight controlling passages, identical in every performance.

The boy, unnamed at first, is Johnny, the name borrowed from a character who participates in frequent gay sex throughout *The Wild Boys*. From Smith's remarks, we surmise that Johnny represents her own psyche as a third-person avatar, her protagonist who reacts in different nightly tellings to various attacks from dark and conformist orthodoxies in the church (e.g., "he was a punk in private school, Catholic school"   March 25, 1976), governments, corporations, militaries, and sociopathic polluters of various stripes.[18] In Subsection Four a "Go, Johnny, go" quote from Chuck Berry's "Johnny B. Goode" (1958) identifies our hero with the trickster rebel who used the weapons of rock 'n' roll twenty years before *Horses*,

---

[18] In the April 1975 draft of "Land" (Smith 1977a, 47), Johnny is identified immediately ("Johnny was waiting in the hallway . . ."); later in this draft, after identifying all other band members with colorful imagery, she writes, "thus set free I am Johnny." Smith discusses Johnny's androgynous identity in the first set of her December 26, 1975, show ("It was 1963; Johnny looked just like me," who at the time cut her hair like a male figure, Keith Richards), and in Smith 1995, 83. Hiss and McClelland 1975 are the first to refer to Johnny as Patti's alter ego. See also Paytress 2011, 172. On March 9, 1976, Smith tells her audience, "I've been to the museum [the Detroit Institute of Art]; love these huge murals of Diego Rivera," during a performance of "I Man a Mafia"; in frequent recent renderings of "Land," it is *Johnny* who walks the streets of each concert's city, tracing steps likely taken by the artist herself earlier that day. The variability of Johnny's story with each telling is linked to Scheherazade in Smith's statement that "People used to come to [the Greenwich Village club] CBGBs night after night to find out what was gonna happen to Johnny next" (Heylin 2005, 192).

but in various interviews Smith also links the given name to others: the witty off-the-cuff monologuist Johnny Carson, an outrageously spontaneous John Cale present in the studio control booth, a cool extemporaneous John Coltrane, and even (in Smith 1995, 83) the cultivator of land, Johnny Appleseed (by which "seed" is made to rhyme with "steed"). The reference to the latter is another reminder of Smith's attention to human sexuality in a Blake-like association between embodied experiences cultivated by the artistic imagination.

In accordance with Smith's logic, literary influences, and attitudes toward sexuality, the hallway of "Land" (at times appearing as a tunnel, cave, aisle, or street) becomes a vagina, sometimes portrayed as connecting two cloaca-like sewer openings that lead to a vulva-like vine-covered cottage (as on December 1, 2012) and other times traversed by an Other, suggesting intercourse. Violent intercourse is often intimated—note the reference above to nuns "burning holes in their groins with a cigarette."[19] Moreover, "carnival! carnival!," a poem in *Babel*—Smith's then-recent third book—contains these lines:

> 36 movements become 36 perfect stills from the same movie. cinema is so exciting, murmur the spectators, caressing their parts. we are the feminine corridors. the hallway of pink gloss. we are the taut lights and the forequarters of a bull. tourists jack-off as the movie keeps moving and carving credentials on the storage bin of stars. (1974, 133)

The references to film media will soon inform our reading of "Land," but we can already understand how Smith shapes a hallway's vaginal meaning. Her very first-composed song, "A Fire of Unknown Origin" (1971, released 1979), encourages us to hear the potential for dangerous, anonymous red-hot sex:

> death comes sweeping
> thru the hallway
> like a ladies dress
> death comes riding
> down the highway
> in its Sunday best.[20]

---

[19] Our earliest draft of "Land" combines the burning image with horses: "Johnny was waiting. he puts down his glass of tea he lights a cigarette. ~~he mounts the pony~~ the hallway goes on forever ~~they fly~~ he mounts his steed and they fly thru the hallway burning etc—" (Smith 1977a, 47). Rock music's associations of burning with sex are summarized in Chapter 4.

[20] Smith 1972, 17. The phrase "fire of unknown origin" first appears on p. 9 of Burroughs 1969 and was taken as the title of a 1981 Blue Öyster Cult LP.

The poem illustrates Smith's tendency to eroticize the everyday while also blurring the gender of the subject (in this case "death"), which is characterized as both a penetrative force and the whispering layers of fabric.

In *The Wild Boys* (Burroughs 1969, 64; see also 19), Johnny drinks yage, a medicinal and spiritual brew ritualized along the Amazon. The narcotics of the Velvet Underground may also be considered in the opening of "Land," wherein a glass of tea begins Johnny's transformation (January 9, 1976: "I was drifting, head on a cloud, dreamin' of a space, anything's allowed, I went into a café, I was drinkin' tea. Tellin' stories; What is the story you wish for me?"). A recurring object throughout Smith's writings, tea is a metamorphic device in Smith's second memoir, *M Train* (e.g., "I got up, boiled a pot of water, drank some powdered tea, and stepped into a cloud of well-being"; Smith 2015, 178). Along these lines, the action that plays out in "Land" may be imagined to occur in Johnny's—Patti's—altered imagination, once the "tea" evokes the muse for her somewhat veiled sex fantasy.

In the studio recording, the narrator presents two (and later, three) separately taped overlapping voices in several passages. The overdubbing technique, pioneered in the Velvet Underground's "The Murder Mystery" (1969) and evocative of young Patti's strabismus, ultimately becomes in "La Mer (de)" a studio compromise that suggests (1) the multiple directions that the song's stories take in live performance, (2) the multivocal confusion of Babel, and (3) Johnny's fragmented psyche. (In "La Mer (de)," at 4:22, a second voice enters once again, evoking a multiplicity of waves in the "sea of possibilities.") An Other is introduced "at the other end of the hallway." This is Not-Johnny, even though it is sometimes the reflection Johnny sees in a mirror, as we are told by Voice One of two simultaneous Smith vocals on the LP:

VOICE ONE	VOICE TWO
Another boy was sliding up the hallway	His golden orbs merged perfectly with the hallway
He merged perfectly with the hallway	A radiant light through the door around the mirror
He merged perfectly with the mirror in the hallway	. . . looked at Johnny and asked him to . . .

Such references to a mirror as a triggering mechanism make a multiple-self yin-yang autoeroticism quite palpable. We are also reminded of Lacan's mirror stage, covered in Chapter 1, which is based on an image of "apparent smoothness and totality [that] is a myth. The image in which we first recognise ourselves is a *mis-recognition*."[21] Sometimes, as on October 20, 2016, the mirror shatters into shards (an image likened to castration in Butler 1993, 83). On May 11, 1975, months before the studio recording took place, Johnny divided into two personages, one of which approaches his self: "something was comin' up the hallway, lookin' to him like a mirror. Came up on little wheels." It advances by varying means: "Wheels" . . . or "beating wings" (December 26, 1975) . . . or takes on its own Hendrix-inspired appearance: "a neon figure at a microphone inside a burning bush" (December 27, 1975) or "two snakes bitin' each others' tails" (March 9, 1976). Whatever its form, Not-Johnny would always set in motion a rhythm, in slow but evenly spaced Stooges-like E5 power chords, one per beat, in Lenny Kaye's guitar, Ivan Kral's bass and Jay Dee Daugherty's drums. On the LP, Kaye enters alone, and then only in Subsection Two does Kral join when the boy takes Johnny, both guitars then augmented by the bass drum for the penetrating line, "he drove it home."

Early performances often employ hallucinatory figures to represent Not-Johnny, such as Burroughs' Mexican boy (who sometimes "has a hard-on": see Smith 1977a, 47; compare Burroughs 1969, 163) or a snowman with a ruby-shaped disc instead of a piece of coal (March 24, 1976). Then action is triggered by a talisman such as a vibrating jewel, crystallizing kryptonite, a rolling stone, a cracking egg (in an extended three-week-early Easter tale, March 27, 1976), a cliff-rushing T-bird, a flowing fountain, a spinning pinwheel, or a heated filament. In live shows, such energies would frequently open into evocative tales. In numerous performances of 2013–17, Johnny extends his arms, engorged with hot blood as the guitar's pulse quickens, accelerating in a gesture that, given what follows (as well as the primordial Mexican boy sporting a hard-on), can be taken for an erection.[22] A finger might be stuck in a hole, at which point it disintegrates (June 25, 2005), signifying a post-coital drooping if not erectile dysfunction. References to negative "forces" can be heard as a rhyme for "Horses," although the similar words are never proximate (see November 10, 2015, or April 9, 2017). In more recent years, rape is generalized through stories of corporations' destruction of nature, thematic material again consistent with Blake's diatribes

---

[21] Lacan et al. 1982, 30. Musician Lawrence Kramer theorizes that in the nineteenth century, the mirror became a woman's source of sex-based subjectivity as opposed to a sign of her vanity: "Before the mirror, women may do for themselves affirmatively what men do to women appropriately: they may gaze with a pleasure that constructs the thing it sees" (1993, 306 and 315). The role of the mirror in fictional characterizations involving gender and sexuality is treated interestingly in Halberstam 1998, 99–101, 104, 106, 195–6, and 219–20.

[22] Increases of blood circulation, warmth, and muscular action in peripheral limbs during sexual excitation is discussed in Kinsey 1953, 594, and Masters and Johnson 1966, 32, 136.

against "dark Satanic mills" and "mind-forg'd manacles," or with Wordsworth's lament over "sordid boon"s. Subsection Two is regularly cued by a strong activist Johnny aggressively commanding the forces of injustice, "Bring it on! Come on!"

Subsection Two

Subsection Two of "Land" returns to constant verses in all performances, which remains the case for Subsections Three and Four as well. In the opening lines of Subsection Two, Johnny and Not-Johnny engage, and Patti's vocals synchronize with each other (on the LP) and with the band's suddenly established and gradually accelerating tempo:

VOICE ONE	VOICE TWO
The boy looked at Johnny,	The boy looked at Johnny,
Johnny wanted to run,	Johnny wanted to run;
but the movie kept moving as planned.	Johnny wanted to run, but the movie kept moving as planned.
The boy took Johnny; he pressed him against the locker;	The boy took Johnny; he pressed him against the locker;
He drove it in, he drove it home, he drove it deep in Johnny.	He drove it in, he drove it home, he drove it deep in Johnny.

As the power chords of "Land" grow louder and pick up speed, vocals in their thrall, we have the same sense of foreboding that had been created in the Velvet Underground's "The Gift" (1968, "He could feel the vibrating footsteps; it would be soon"); the Velvets' "Heroin" (1967) speeds up from 69 to 144 beats per minute (bpm) to convey the promise of a drug rush. An accelerando from 112 to 176 bpm characterizes an Oedipal erotic frenzy in the Doors' "The End" (1967). The onset of sexual desire in Smith's "Gloria" is portrayed by a radical acceleration from 84 to 184 bpm (on February 7, 1976). In "Land," energy emerges as an unstoppable negative force that quickly attacks Johnny.[23] All bars contain four beats with a heartbeat's regularity, but the numbers of bars grouped together into phrases remain irregular until a commanding climax is reached with Subsection Three.

---

[23] The B-side of Smith's first release, "Piss Factory" (recorded in June 1974), contains rhythm that both provides a factory-floor worker's tempo (that of a "Horses"-presaging "Mustang Sally") and cues a premonition of the foreman's approach: "you gotta find the rhythm within. Floor boss slides up to me and he says 'Hey sister, you just movin' too fast. You screwin' up the quota.'" "Mustang Sally" was made a hit by Wilson Pickett, who had released his top-ten version of "Land of 1000 Dances" just four months previously.

Unable to run, a passive Johnny surrenders to the grips of a preordained movie script over which he has no control and is thus feminized by an objectifying peep-show gaze.[24] Like Blake and his illuminated poetry, Smith was just as interested in visual as in verbal relationships; her early dabbling at drawing predated her meeting Mapplethorpe. Her favorite Polaroid Land Camera shots taken over decades have been collected in the book *Land 250*, which—after the home of a thousand dances—is our second source for the title, "Land." The movie that "keeps moving as planned" ("planned" rhymes with "Land") might be reminiscent of the Magic Theater in Hesse's *Steppenwolf*, wherein looking into a mirror results in the "little suicide" of a shattering ego (before the device is sent "rolling down the endless corridor" (Hesse 1963, 203), but Smith's image is actually drawn from Burroughs' *The Wild Boys*, the second chapter of which opens, "Fatima drinking tea with the trade in the kitchen. Here in the middle of a film to find myself one of the actors." In Burroughs's fifth chapter, "The Penny Arcade Peep Show," boys including Johnny, wearing rainbow-colored jock straps, enter the peep show from a long narrow building, four screens surrounding them. One male named Audrey says:

> I am pulled into the film in a stream of yellow light and I can pull people out of the film withdrawal shots pulling the flesh off naked boys. Sequences are linked by the presence of some arbitrary object a pin wheel, a Christmas-tree ornament, a pyramid, an Easter egg, a copper coil going away and coming in always in the same numerical order. Movement in and out of the screen can be very painful like acid in the face and electric sex tingles. . . . The penis spurts again and again as the body twists in the wrenching spasms. Finally the body hangs limp . . . "He dead now."[25] (Burroughs 1969, 38–46)

[24] Burns and Lafrance consider the effect of such a gaze in Tori Amos's "Crucify" (1992) (2002, 77).
[25] Burroughs 1969, 38–46. In an earlier text, *The Ticket That Exploded* (1967), Burroughs conjures similar hallucinogenic film-related orgasmic images that could have caught Smith's thousandfold imagination: "A maze of mirrors and screens reflected sex acts in slow motion to a thousand sound tracks shifted and permutated—slow waves of orgasm in a muttering sea of nitrous film flesh."

> The bronze mold sank into his flesh a black seal—The other moved back seeking some precise coordinate point with the blue wall symbols—The room hummed and vibrated—Pubic hairs of black wire crackled in blue sparks and a quivering blue line divided his body—Bradly felt his own body split down the middle like a cracked egg the two halves rubbing against each other, held together by some sticky gelatinous substance that leaked out the crack and dripped into the obsidian platform where he stood—From the open bronze mold emerged a transparent green shape criss-crossed with pulsing red veins, liquid screen eyes swept by color flashes—a smell of sewage and decay breathing from years of torture films, orgasm death in his black eyes glinting with slow fish lust of the swamp mud. (1967, 70 and 89)

Like *The Wild Boys*, *Ticket* tells the story of a Johnny, here one Johnny Yen, "the Boy-Girl Other Half strip tease God of sexual frustration" (1967, 53); the cut-up novel also relates of tea drinking

Smith's interest in multimedia, trained by her reading of Burroughs and Blake, informs this image of control by outside forces. One "Land" recitation connects this sensation to the numbing power chord as well: "I was a slave to twenty-two minutes of the eternal heartbeat."[26] Smith's reference to the "eternal heartbeat" as an enthralling container is evocative of Blake's memorable opening lines, "To see a World in a Grain of Sand / And a Heaven in a Wild Flower / Hold Infinity in the palm of your hand,/ And Eternity in an hour," in "Auguries of Innocence" (490). This poem is so instructive to Smith that she lifts it for the title of one of her own collections of poetry (2005). Like the Romantic poet, Smith reaches for and acquiesces to a sacred experience in the here and now, a resistant stance to ideologies that promise happiness in a nebulous afterlife.[27]

Smith borrows her literary predecessors' attitudes toward containment and penetration as sources of potential destruction, which is creation-inducing at the same time. Along these lines, the Burroughs passage quoted earlier, which represents sex in the context of everyday objects, is followed by the line, "They know an aphrodisiac so potent that it shatters the body to quivering pieces" (1969, 22–3). In the fantasy of "Land," Johnny is violated—stabbed, raped, and/or given a heroin rush—thus destructively controlled by external forces. One interpretation that follows this reading, especially if we remember Smith's attention to the autoerotic potential of mirrors, is that "Land" represents a masturbatory fantasy, with all characters imagined, all parts of the protagonist's ego. Creative, improvised passages demonstrate a conscious, freely exploring foreplay, but the throes of empowered repetition denote a thrusting, compulsive, and ungovernable uniformity. The middle of Subsection Three contains the commanding rhythmic lines, "Got to lose control. Got to lose control. Got to lose control, and then you take control." Does orgasm come with turns between command and surrender? The aggressor wields a volition not afforded the receiver, who abandons self to the Other; orgasm follows capitulation to the inevitable.

(p. 101), switchblades (p. 152), and other notions that reappear as constants in Smith's "Land." Johnny Yen is also reanimated in Iggy Pop's "Lust for Life" (1977); see Bradley 2017, 288–9.

26 March 28, 1976. Note the parallel images to Subsections One and Two in Smith's poems "notice" and "the stream" (1974, 13–14 and 44–5); celluloid works in many ways throughout *Babel*. Patti's close friend and mentor in the 1970s, poet Jim Carroll, once linked the Polaroid to sex: "I can remember when you had to wait an entire sixty seconds before the Polaroid ejaculated the print" (1987, 32; cf. Smith 2010, 154; see also Smith 2008 and 2010, 257–8). In a spoken interlude within "Space Monkey" (1978), Smith differentiates between a Polaroid shot and a jack-knife (the song dates to February 1975 or earlier).

27 Again, I am indebted to Katie Kapurch for this Blake reference.

Subsection Two culminates in the phallic attack, by what weapon we are not told—a penis? a knife? a hypodermic syringe? The specific violation is unnamed, as is the attacking personage.[28] The striking force is never identified as anything other than "the boy"; a driving phallogocentric testosterone is the sole defining quality. The rape (or at least a highly aggressive sex act) seems to involve two male characters, but Smith has often written about her own desire to flaunt apparent gender characterizations, as when she sings of being sexually attracted to "Gloria," but not because she identifies as a lesbian. As discussed earlier, Smith intends to free any representations within the song from her personal gender.[29] This, along with the nightmarish environment, requires us to step back from literal readings and seek a psychoanalytic understanding that appreciates gender fluidity as symbolic and dreamlike, whether considering the composer-performer's role or whether analyzing the narrative and its characters on their own terms. Recalling how McClary says that in the 1980s, "women can *choose* to write music that foregrounds their sexual identities without falling prey to essentialist traps" (1991, 33), we would say that Smith chooses to interrogate, rather than expose, the nature of sexual identity.

As for the male aggression, at least three of nine possible functions of sexual behavior (other than reproduction) identified by Bancroft and listed early in Chapter 3, are presented: Factors six (reduction of tension) and eight (risk-taking as a source of excitement) may be at work, but certainly numbers one (assertion of masculinity), three (exertion of power or dominance), and seven (expression of hostility) are strongly suggested; ambiguity prevents any more certain an assignment.[30]

For Smith, the surrender of control that is central to improvisation, although it comes from within, is analogous to the fearsome loss resulting from rape: "The concept of improvisation has long repelled and excited me,

---

[28] The composer's ambiguity is intentional; the April 1975 draft of "Land" has this reductive revision: ". . . the movie goes on as planned. He rams ~~his cock up~~ it home" (Smith 1977a, 47).

[29] Smith does not necessarily avoid lesbian themes; her "Redondo Beach," also on *Horses*, is introduced in concert as "a beach where women love other women." The ambiguity is not an instance of male impersonation, as discussed elsewhere in relation to Joan Jett, Suzi Quatro, and PJ Harvey (Reynolds and Press 1995, 243–4); Burns and Lafrance write of the "dissonant juxtaposition" that results from a butch lesbian fantasy in Ndegéocello (2002, 144), and Butler's notion (1993, 62) that the principle of the phallus is not synonymous with the penis and is therefore transferrable to the female (see Pavda 2006, 105). See discussions of the female appropriation of the phallic in rock in McClary 1991, 54, Whiteley 1997, xvii, and Coates 1997, 58.

[30] In defining reaction formation, Bancroft discusses one motivation for sex-based hostility: "Heterosexuals who are unsure of their sexual competence or identity may bolster their self-confidence by attacking homosexuals" (1989, 305).

for it contains the possibilities of humiliation and illumination."[31] "I'll always enjoy putting myself on the spot, always enjoy playing with fire" (Tarr 2008, 30, quoting from Tosches 1976). Such embrace of darkness also speaks to Smith's fixation on death imagery, as her work is often haunted by her memories of the assassinations of Kennedys and King and the deaths of Vladimir Mayakovsky, Johnny Ace, Brian Jones, Jim Morrison, Janis Joplin, Jimi Hendrix, and Edie Sedgwick. The mythic accounts of destruction and loss, particularly the Biblical (and Blakean) accounts of the fall of Man and the death of Christ, also figure throughout her poetry, as in her first collection, *Seventh Heaven* (1972). Smith's romantic view of the darkness that exists on society's margins is also informed by her idealization of outlaws and (some of them short-term) prisoners such as Jesse James, Jean Genet, Arthur Rimbaud, Jackson Pollock, Wilhelm Reich, and Patty Hearst, characters all tied to risky behavior and notably, in Pollock's case, improvisation.[32] Thus, the grim ending of one poem in that group, "fantasy" (p. 31), equates sex and death:

> he says on your back bitch.
> I crouch down.
> he shoves the whole barrel up
> my cunt, cocks the lever
> pulls the trigger.
> blows his load.

Smith's representation is a reminder of the French term for orgasm, "la petite mort," which means the little death, because of its convulsions, momentary loss of consciousness that may come with vasocongestion and hyperventilation, and semblances of pained expression.[33]

As Not-Johnny drives "it" home, the thrice-heard "drove" coming in close succession—each instance stressed on a strong beat—suggests the thrusts leading to an orgasm that Johnny observes but does not feel, as there is no let-up in the overall building of excitement. In concert, Smith often spits immediately after the next line, "the boy disappeared" (see, e.g., January 8, July 1, or October

---

[31] Smith 2006, 32. Her poem "rape" (1972) details the attacks of Richard Speck (Smith 2010, 216).

[32] Psychoanalyst Wilhelm Reich conceived of the "orgone accumulator," a device intended to corral a cosmic libido, which intrigued both Burroughs (see 1967, 69n) and Smith (inspired by him to create the *Horses* track, "Birdland," which she would introduce onstage by saying the song was her interpretation of Reich's son Peter getting picked up by a UFO as a little boy after his daddy's death).

[33] See Masters and Johnson, 1966, 7, re physiologic responses in sex. Note the direct connection between orgasm and death in the Burroughs passage quoted earlier (1969, 45–6). Toril Moi reminds us that for Freud, death "is the ultimate object of desire" (1995, 101, quoted in Burns and Lafrance 2002, 173), which cannot be fully satisfied in life.

20, 2016). Such an onstage act may be a mark of contempt, perhaps for the aggressor—even if a lover—who ejaculates and exits prematurely in a little death (withdrawing the penis, withdrawing emotionally, withdrawing from the scene, or withdrawing from Patti's imagination). Or perhaps the spitting is Smith's own portrayal of ejaculation. Johnny—aroused but unfulfilled—continues to thrash, masturbating to his own climax without the need of any imagined partner, as the charging horses, horses, and horses give way in anticipation to the spasmodic contractions of the pony, a 1960s dervish that follows Patti's performance of the 1970s punk era's up-and-down pogo.[34]

One may wonder why a homosexual rape would induce orgasm in the object (whose sexual preference is not stated). Judith Butler presents a nuanced reading of gay fantasy that is relevant: "Within lesbian contexts, the identification with masculinity that appears as butch identity is not a simple assimilation of lesbianism back into the terms of heterosexuality. . . . It is precisely this dissonant juxtaposition and the sexual tension that its transgression generates that constitute the object of desire" (Butler 1999, quoted in Burns and Lafrance 2002, 144). But the forceful pressure of Johnny being repeatedly pushed against the locker—or his fantasy of such—is enough to arouse him, regardless of the gender of the aggressor. Kinsey writes of the effect of reciprocation of such pressure: "If [an animal] responds [to a stimulating object] by pressing against the object, a considerable series of physiologic events may follow. If the tactile stimulation becomes rhythmic, or the pressure is long-continued, the level of response may increase and build up neuromuscular tensions which become recognizable as sexual responses" (Kinsey 1953, 595). This combination of interpretations leads us to consider the rape, and the existence of Not-Johnny, as fully imaginary, whereby Johnny acts out a masturbatory fantasy of Smith's.[35] In fact, Smith herself says "Land" is "all about embracing your darkest fantasies about murder, rape, and suicide and feeling good about it, masturbating to it" (Tarr 2008, 26).

The interpretation of "Land" as a witnessed masturbatory fantasy is furthermore evidenced when our protagonist is about to reach climax: we hear "Suddenly Johnny gets the feeling. . . ." This sensation of lost control, when male orgasm becomes inevitable, was covered in Chapter 4. While all of these dynamics are expressed in lyrics, rhythm, increasing tempo, and loudness, Smith's pitchwork

---

[34] The horses' noses are in flames, apparently a reference to the fury of Revelation 9:17.

[35] For a reaction against the musical idea of victims of sexual violence outside of fantasy "wanting it," see Burns and Lafrance on Hole's "Violet" (1994) (2002, 108–11).

gains in intensity as well. She leaves behind the spoken word and free verbal exposition of Subsection One, and intones as if by preordained command "the boy looked at Johnny . . . ." all on her low vocal E, the first scale degree. At "he drove it home," she arpeggiates up to ^5, and then up to her higher E at "the boy disappeared." Through the remaining eleven lines of Subsection Two, Smith sings the blues-based (025) trichord (D-E-G), accenting the tension of the upper ^b3 (G) first on weak second halves of second beats and then combining pitch and metric accents by stressing ^b3 on first beats four times in the lines, "When SUD-denly, JOHN-ny gets the FEEL-ing he's being sur-ROUND-ed by." (Continued acceleration is accompanied at this point by the addition of heavy reverb and the convergence of Patti's multiple vocals.) These three pitches anticipate the set of four (still a subset of the bluesy minor-pentatonic scale) that constitutes the entire melody of the "Land of 1000 Dances" that erupts at the outset of Section Two (and continues through Subsection Three). The added fourth pitch, the B (^5) below the upper E, is introduced with "horses, horses, horses, horses," which line mechanically alternates between a metrically accented ^1 and its weak-beat ^5, as every backbeat is struck on the tightly closed hi-hat as well as the guitar, and a bass drone enters, sounding twice in each beat.

From the LP, one can imagine Smith rhythmically posting on her steed, hands grabbing mane and knees gripping flank; in concert, she grabs her mic with both hands and has now racheted up to full pogo, bouncing up and down at double speed against the tightly constrained melody and the crescendo of quickening power chords beneath "horses, horses, horses, horses." This "suddenly" comes off as an involuntary response, as "Johnny gets the feeling," marking the precipitous inevitability of ejaculation at which point—galloping into a frenzied release in the feverish "Land of 1000 Dances"—he/she can only surrender control to the band and the tune. (This point in "Land" could be compared to the agitated orchestral transition in "Brown Shoes" [4:04–4:27].) Orgasm, as in Masters and Johnson's Phase II, comes only with Subsection Three, which introduces bass, full drum set and piano, and brings the anticipated completion of the minor-pentatonic collection when ^4 appears as root within the continually repeated double-plagal field, I - bVII - IV (- I).[36]

---

[36] A horse-related passage in the Patti Smith B-side, "Piss Factory" (1974), uses a similar musical structure: Kaye solos on a minor-pentatonic lead over Richard Sohl's piano chording on a dorian field alternating IV and i, in support of the line, "now you get off your mustang, Sally!"

"Land": "Land of 1000 Dances"

Subsection Three

Subsection Three opens with the structural downbeat of the entire tableau, everything prior functioning as anticipatory foreplay. The gradual preparatory unfolding of "Land of 1000 Dances" throughout Subsection Two is dictated by Smith's handwritten note within what appears to be a study for "Land," appearing as the frontispiece of the *Horses* folio (1977a) and typeset for the LP cover. Here, she recommends to herself "The feel of horses long before horses enter the scene" (presumably foretold by Not-Johnny's rhythm and finally making their appearance with the pony dance, "Do you know how to pony?"). On the LP, a splice joins different mixes of "Horses" and "Land of 1000 Dances," with piano and second guitar now having joined the ensemble and the double-plagal cadence having broken from its reins.[37] The double-plagal field continues through the rest of the track, its instrumental texture varied throughout. It is the same chord loop heard in "Gloria" and in fact supports a transition to that song in live performance.[38]

"Land of 1000 Dances" charted as a hit by five different artists in the 1960s, but Smith follows Chris Kenner's original 1963 version, rhapsodizing by adding several of her own lines that have not varied since its 1975 première. In "Land," the cover song represents Johnny's orgasm and perhaps his joyous rebirth, marked in recent years (as on June 23, 2016) by the onset of a vibrant light show for Smith's gyrations all across the stage. Notable in "1000 Dances" are references to a baby sister who reverberates with the nuns who helped inspire "Land" and who appear in numerous parts of its April 1975 draft, and the sister's rising up from her knees, which connects Johnny's falling to his knees in "Horses" to the sensation of a hand on the singer's knee in "La Mer (de)." (In April 1975, sisters

---

[37] The double-plagal cadence, whereby ♭VII falls contrapuntally to IV in the same way that IV falls contrapuntally to I, represents a directed *voice-leading descent* to tonic, analogously to how V - I represents a *harmonic descent* to tonic. McClary equates tonal pull to libidinal energy: "tonality itself—with its process of instilling expectations and subsequently withholding promised fulfillment until climax—is the principal musical means during the period from 1600 to 1900 for arousing and channeling desire" (1991, 12–13). Popular music, of course, as McClary would likely agree, extends tonal principles far beyond the nineteenth century.

[38] The double-plagal succession also undergirds much of the Doors' "The End" (1967). Hendrix's verses in "The Wind Cries Mary" follow the double-plagal scheme, and his "Hey Joe" (both 1967; covered by Smith, as noted earlier) pre-extends the plagal voice leading by two extra steps, to ♭VI - ♭III - ♭VII - IV - I.

are naked in the sand with their knees open; in the studio recording, the singer, standing, has her "legs spread like a sailor" when the hand is felt on her knee.)

In Subsection Three, Smith's primary addition is the interjection already noted, "got to lose control, got to lose control, got to lose control and then you take control." Losing control is opening oneself to the Other, submitting to orgasm, but also key to improvisation. Smith on the studio recording of "Land":

> I didn't know what direction the song was taking, there was all this strange imagery I didn't understand. . . . On the last take it was obvious that I was being told what I wanted to know about Hendrix's death. The song is like eight or nine minutes long, so it's obvious I'm gonna lose control sometime—but I felt like it was *The Exorcist*, or somebody else talking thru my voice . . . and it ended up with 'in the sheets, there was a man'—it really frightened me. After I was done I felt like all three [vocal] tracks had the total information of his last seconds, so I decided to mix them all together.[39]

While we have argued that Johnny loses control when he "gets the feeling," when ejaculation becomes inevitable, a smaller loss of control had presaged this, when he was unable to run because of the nightmare-like sensation of being in a movie. At the same time as Johnny surrenders, Smith exerts increased control over her audience as she improvises, exercising her authorial sovereignty and commanding them to undergo the masturbatory experience. In ways small and large, the entirety of the performance moves in and out of control for multiple persons, at multiple levels.

Although it appears only once in "Land," the "Land of 1000 Dances" section, attained as the goal of an on-ramp, emerges with the inexorable quality of a song's chorus.[40] This "frenzied release," in which the spoken text has gradually given way to a song originally made popular by an Other in conveying an orgasmic surrender, works exactly like the abandon brought by a chorus that replaces spoken text with song, in connection with Me'Shell Ndegéocello's "Mary Magdalene" (1996) as discussed by Burns and Lafrance:

> It is significant that the chorus is entirely sung: that is, the subject relinquishes the spoken form, which was her self-reflective mode of expression, in favor

---

[39] Heylin 2005, 192. One of the featured lines in "1000 Dances" is "I like it like that" [also a Chris Kenner title], a line borrowed by Hendrix in "Fire" (1967). The loss of control in orgasm leads not only to genital contractions but to somatic experiences comparable in an EEG to grand mal seizures (Bancroft 1989, 80–1, 88–9).

[40] Perhaps "1000 Dances" functions as a metachorus, as it appears only once in the song (unlike the chorus, which by definition recurs), but represents a forceful arrival night after night.

of the vocal style that was associated with the Other (or the subject's desire for the Other). This adoption of the elaborated melodic style signifies in concrete musical terms that the subject's lyrical movement toward the object is complete; she has given herself over to her desire and is in a state of emotional abandon. (2002, 161)

In "Land," Smith's freely improvised spoken text gives way, submits, to Kenner's dictated song; the singer may abandon the work of inventing anew all storytelling foreplay, and revel in the pure joy brought by an adherence to an Other's regularized text. As in good sex, the concepts of command and surrender are interwoven in subtly paradoxical ways.

Subsection Four

Subsection Four is a lengthy interpolation between the "Do the watusi" command that ends Subsection Three, and the same invocation that calls for Subsections Five and Six in "La Mer (de)." Following "1000 Dances," the remainder of "Land" is nearly all delivered in rhythmically declaimed spoken word, with just a few excited outbursts (starting with the knife list) that bring small minor-pentatonic subsets. Here is the opening text:

> Life is filled with holes
> Johnny's laying there in his sperm coffin
> Angel looks down at him and says "Ah pretty boy,
> Can't you show me nothing but surrender?"
> Johnny gets up takes off his leather jacket
> Taped to his chest there's the answer:
> He got pen knives and jack knives and
> Switchblades preferred, switchblades preferred

Johnny having reached his own climax, his "sperm coffin" strengthens the identification of sex with death.[41] The lines contain direct allusions to Smith's literary

---

[41] "The refractory period in the male [following his 'little death'] serves a spacing function—allowing a replenishment of sperm numbers and avoiding excessive sexual activity which could be biologically maladaptive" (Bancroft 1989, 86). Sheila Whiteley finds that Hendrix's "Dolly Dagger" (1971) suggests a fear of castration (2000, 38), which may underlie Johnny's anxiety that produces the angel, and various blades that serve as protestations of virility. Smith holds an amplifier's vacuum tube protruding from her crotch in the photo "EL34" taken by her brother Todd Smith (Smith 1974, 204), as if an instrument of phallic transferal, a strap-on dildo. Hear Smith on the macho quality of leather jackets in the December 1972 interview; two Mapplethorpe

influences, especially her sexual fantasy, from Rimbaud's "A Season in Hell," which includes the line, "The fate of the family's son, a premature coffin covered with limpid tears" (273). A third figure enters as consciousness is lost in the dreamlike denouement that is Subsection Four: an angel appears and demands of a still-kneeling Johnny, "can't you show me nothing but surrender?" He rises again, reborn (literally shedding skin through doffing his leather jacket), himself now the aggressor wielding penknives and jackknives and, best of all, tumescent switchblades.[42]

Again underscoring Smith's erotic treatment of death, the scenario is an allusion to Blake's "The Chimney Sweeper" from *Songs of Innocence* (1789), in which Tom dreams of an angel delivering him from the early death that surely awaits him:

> That thousands of sweepers Dick, Joe, Ned & Jack
> Were all of them lock'd up in coffins of black,
>
> And by came an Angel who had a bright key,
> And he open'd the coffins & set them all free." (10)

This poem concludes with the child speaker determining, "So if all do their duty, they need not fear harm" (10), which shows how these children have internalized the logic of the oppressor, specifically religion, which promises them an afterlife as a reward for an almost assured early death from laboring in dangerous, deathly conditions. The sadomasochistic undertones of this exchange are amplified in Smith's portrayal of Johnny's pleasure in the memory of the violent rape. Thus, in "Land" the knife types are predicted with scratchy guitar timbre and addition of both a second piano and dynamic drum fills, and are each indicated with strong downbeat metallic cymbal crashes.

---

self-portraits showing himself in leather boots and bondage are printed with Smith's broadside, "Dolor Desvelado" ("Pain unveiled") (1977?).

The angel reminds us of the Jungian archetype representing "a doorway to psychic recovery. When the anima reaches such a stage in an individuating male psyche, the next development is the appearance of a new archetype—the Self—which can appear as 'a masculine initiator and guardian (an Indian *guru*), a wise old man, a spirit of nature,' and so forth. In the case of an individuating female psyche, the animus image will give way to 'a superior female figure—a priestess, sorceress, earth mother, or goddess of nature or love'" (Moores 2010, 115–16, quoting von Franz 1995).

[42] In *Psychopathia Sexualis* (1886), pioneering sexologist Richard von Krafft-Ebing recounted this case history: "In the [1860s] the inhabitants of Leipzig were frightened by a man who was accustomed to attack young girls on the street, stabbing them in the upper arm with a dagger. Finally arrested, he was recognized as a sadist, who at the instant of stabbing had an ejaculation, and with whom the wounding of the girls was an equivalent for coitus" (Bergner 2009, 70). A 1974 track by Grand Funk, "Little Johnny Hooker," relates gender to a switchblade: "Little Johnny Hooker was a sissy on the street all his life; . . . Freddy Miller went and got in Johnny's way, boy—he took his knife from his pocket, pushed a button on the side."

Freed from the rape remnants and brandishing his switchblade, Johnny apparently masturbates to further angel-inspired orgasms, which come in waves characteristic of a feminine response, the third climax (following the second, with blades) arriving with the "horses"-like repetition, "go Rimbaud, go Rimbaud, go Rimbaud and go Johnny go and do the watusi," a text once again highlighted by Smith's minor-pentatonic singing. This is not to suggest merely figurative waves; Subsections Five through Seven are populated with roiling "seas of possibilities," multiplicities crashing over each other at 5:10 in the studio recording, "the waves coming in like Arabian stallions coming in like sea horses," a reminder of the wave-like nature of female sexual response as considered in Chapter 4. Smith clears the tension—cymbals out, guitar muted, second piano featured—with a sotto voce setting, "There's a little place, a place called space." Tension builds once again from rest, quickly, as the house band, the Twistolettes, is introduced as they apparently enjoy their own group climax—long repeated syncopated bass glissandi, wah pedal added to Kaye's guitar signal, and more drum fills as the band name is intoned, just about like "horses," seven times (see, e.g., the performances of November 22, 2011, January 26, 2015, and July 21, 2015). This all occurs over the long-continuing double-plagal I - bVII - IV loop for tonal support. In the televised May 11, 1976, show, this is the point at which Smith first plays the guitar she has been holding throughout the song. Reynolds and Press associate surrender and repetition with wave-like feminine sexual response in "Land":

> Patti Smith's most successful attempts to create a non-phallic rock, organised around endless crescendos rather than the tension/explosion structure of male rock, took the form of long pieces like "Land" and "Radio Ethiopia" [1976]. Like "The End" on the Doors' debut, "Land" is the climax and centrepiece of *Horses*. It's a classic example of the Velvet Underground's minimal-is-maximal approach—simplistic rock'n'roll repetition accumulating into an overwhelming gush and rush of sound. The piece is truly "like ocean," wave after wave of noise crashing like breakers, then remounting their assault. Smith is carried along on their crest like a surfer, her delivery veering from classic rock'n'roll urgency ("Go Johnny go") to a giddy stream of mythological imagery. (1995, 356–7)

Reynolds and Press point to nonlinear circularity, which is a mode of discourse often associated with feminine writing and communication (see Chapter 2). But their analysis fails to recognize the genderqueer aspects of Smith's oceanic qualities that present more complexity than the male/female binary: while she does indeed surrender to the waves, she also commands their assault.

"Land": "La Mer (de)"

Subsection Five

Subsection Five opens with Smith calling for a reduction of tension: "Let it calm down," she asks her bandmates twice. All text is spoken, mostly quietly, nearly all improvised against the continued "1000 Dances" plagal field and scratchy guitar. To evoke softness, she sometimes describes or requests "a more gelatal feel"; she will return to a similar "sea of jelly" in Subsection Eight. Without providing any logical context, Smith replies to a question from the audience with this non-sequitur on January 9, 1976, following "Free Money": "Man's best friend is a gelatin cube." One poem in *Babel*, however, "christ! the colors of your energies," suggests that Smith considers gels and jelly to be signs of transformation, as from loud to soft or hard to soft; it opens, "neo boy melts in jelly machine. the whole thing is how he can change the scene or be changeling. transformation is relative says neo boy" (1974, 38). In early shows, this transitional opening of "La Mer (de)," "Let it calm down," marks a crisis point where Smith would have to ask for rebalanced sound levels or a lighting adjustment (January 9 and March 9, 1976), or help from her muse in finding a key, a way out of her confusion (March 9 and 24, 1976). In one such show, Smith suggests that a key will lead to a gelatal feel, perhaps a return to a quieted flaccidity after the climax-marking snakes of entwining Twistolettes: "I want a door opened, the lock, the key to the treasure, it's the key, the one that opens the box, key, key, I want to get into a more gelatal feel so I can be lost in something substantial for a moment, I'm lost, I'm lost, I'm so confused" (March 27, 1976). Liner notes for *Radio Ethiopia* (1976) include a cryptic allusion to "Land," "the sea around me is the jelly in/land." While the gelatal consistency may well suggest a potentially changeable male or female flaccidity, it may also signify the mercurial nature of Smith's own subject gender and even the transitional confusion of which she often speaks or makes demands at this point. Smith regards

> herself as open to both her feminine and masculine instincts. It could be argued that this oceanic attitude enabled her to create a genuinely "feminine" music—songs such as "Birdland" and "Land," that peak and subside repeatedly, like—on a good day—the female orgasm. Freed up from the jackhammer approach of the overtly masculine rock bands, these extended pieces certainly created the conditions to achieve moments "more magical." (Paytress 2011, 184)

At this point in the studio recording, an improvised tale (representing the LP track's first departure from a fixed "score") begins with a horse in a forest and a stair to be climbed, when overdubs produce up to three simultaneous Smith vocals, all swimming in a pregnant "sea of possibilities." As if in answer to the Doors' "Horse Latitudes" (1967), the horse and the sea are joined as "seahorses" on the LP and very differently on January 8, 2016: "Johnny [walks] into the sea of possibilities. He walks those waves; each was like a fine steed. The horses dissipated in clouds."

"Land"'s greatest variabilities in imagery occur throughout "La Mer (de)"; Burroughs-like appearances herein are made, on different nights, by a coral flame, a telescope, a canopy, a mausoleum, a king, an equation, a golden halo, a raft of leather, a cream bomb, a Christmas tree, alchemy, wisdom, a tongue with flowers, eye wax, strawberries, lambskin, and the list goes on. Invariable in every performance, though, is the motherly sea of possibilities from which all notions are born, and suggestions of yet more sex: "it started hardening in my hand and I felt the arrows of desire" (as on the LP), soft undulations then pushed aside by the climax, "we had such a brainiac amour; go Rimbaud, go Rimbaud, go Rimbaud, oh Go Johnny Go!," which leads through another watusi to Subsection Six.[43] The sea—the ocean—presents waves—loud and soft, soft and hard, rising and falling—that continue expressing the feminine sexual response from Subsection Four through succeeding transformations that bring multiple climaxes to contrast the male Land against the female Sea.[44] Smith relates this to her sense of free improvisation: "We're a feminine band, we'll go so far and peak and then we'll start again and peak, over and over. It's like ocean. We leave ourselves wide open for failure, but we also leave ourselves open to achieving a moment more magical" (Rambali 1978, quoted in Tarr 2008, 114). Although Masters and Johnson find only one sexual response pattern in the human male, that of the single orgasm, the female exhibits three: the single orgasm, multiple orgasms, and plateaus marked by numerous small excitements before resolution (1966, 4). Masters and Johnson's findings have since been reevaluated,

---

[43] We saw in Chapter 4 that Hendrix writes of "arrows of desire" in "Voodoo Chile" (1968).
[44] D. J. Moores on "The Rime of the Ancient Mariner": "Water, another emblem of the unconscious in Jungian symbolism, suggests life, and is indeed the basis of human life, which literally evolved from the primordial sea. The body, moreover, consists of 70 percent water and emerges from the mother's amniotic fluid, itself a primordial ocean. The Mariner cannot drink the water all around him, and his thirst signifies his inability to imbibe the living waters of his own unconscious"; Moores on *Moby-Dick*: "The sea itself is the vast unconscious, the 'masterless ocean [that] overruns the globe' (299). If so, then land represents the security of ego, the illusory sense of self that tries to master and subjugate the other energies in the psyche" (Moores 2010, 44, 64).

but "Land" conforms to their explanation, which still has significant traction in 1960s-era social understandings of orgasmic experiences. In "Land," Smith seems to present first Not-Johnny's single orgasm, and then this third pattern of multiple climaxes in "Johnny."

A Johnny who queers Cixous's *l'Écriture feminine* feels the "arrows of desire" as an unspecified something hardens in the singer's hand—his/her penis or clitoris? Hite notes "Masturbation is . . . such an easy source of orgasms for most women. Women in [Hite's] study said they could masturbate and orgasm with ease in just a few minutes" (1976, 3). (On March 25, 1976, the object is identified: a silver corkscrew hardens in Smith's hand.[45]) Scheherazade tells story after story, hoping to keep death at bay, alternatively surrendering and taking control, akin to achieving orgasm after orgasm, getting off on her romance with words night after night.[46]

It was said previously that "Land" moves in and out of control at multiple levels. Most such undulations noted thus far have occurred at a large section-wide frequency, but it might also be said that the song's ubiquitous I - ♭VII - IV loop is like a recurring surface-level wave that tracks motion between the stable I chord and its gentle ♭VII and IV ornaments. The song's lack of a lurching (read "masculine") V chord portrays all climaxes as feminized, and so even Not-Johnny's male orgasm is portrayed as if from a woman's imagination, further supporting the idea that all of "Land" represents a woman's self-oriented, autoerotic fantasy, despite its "male" characters.[47]

---

[45] Two nights later, in a "gelatal feel," Smith says of a baby's face, "she felt it crumble in her hand," reminiscent of the finger that, as noted previously, disintegrates on June 25, 2005. In the spoken interlude of "Space Monkey" (1978) (cited earlier in n. 26), a phallic "Old rusty Polaroid" "starts crumbling in his hands."

[46] Reynolds and Press: "Some feminists have gladly embraced [an] identification of woman-as-nature, despite its hazards, precisely because it's a way of valorising feminine attributes, and because it provides a stable base for a positive female identity. In this vein, Hélène Cixous's 1975 essay 'Sorties' uses the ocean as a metaphor for female subjectivity; unlike the masculine trait of fortifying the self against invasion, female consciousness oozes out beyond the self to embrace the world. Women feel more connected to nature and the cosmos, according to Cixous, since they are part of a continuum, an 'endless body, without "end".' Where masculine sexuality 'gravitate[s] around the penis', feminine sexuality is polymorphous. 'Her libido is cosmic, just as her unconscious is worldwide: her writing also can only go on and on, without ever inscribing or distinguishing contours.' . . . This 'cosmic libido' or oceanic sensibility is intimately connected with *écriture féminine*, writing that privileges flux and fluidity" (1995, 284). (Such flux is key to Smith's improvisatory openness to failure and the magical, noted earlier.) The ocean is the setting for Smith's *Horses* ode to lesbians, "Redondo Beach." Hear John Lennon's ocean imagery in writing of both his lover and his mother in the Beatles' "Julia" (1968) and see Jennifer Rycenga on PJ Harvey's "Water" (*Dry* [1992]) (1997, 219).

[47] As for the remainder of the *Horses* LP, V harmony functions strongly in "Kimberly" and in the twelve-bar blues, "Redondo Beach"; appears in a chordal loop in "Birdland" and in minor form in "Free Money" and "Break It Up"; not at all in "Gloria"; and only as the final chord of "Elegie." The dominant is suppressed just as much or more in *Radio Ethiopia*.

Subsection Six

Subsection Six introduces the land-based Tower of Babel with excited cries of "Build it, build it . . ." that soon capitulate with the rigid towers being replaced by a flowing sea of possibilities. Following is the passage's spoken text, underscored by the continuing "1000 Dances" harmonic loop:

VOICE ONE	VOICE TWO
	Well, do the watusi, yeah, do the watusi; do, do the watusi.
So Johnny opens coiled snakes white and shining, twirling and encircling.	
Our lives are now entwined; we will for years be together twining,	
Your nerves, your mane of the black shining horse,	
And my fingers all entwined through your silky hair.	Build it, build it, build it, build it.
I could feel it; it was the hair going through my fingers.	Build it, build it, build it, build it.
The hairs were like wires going through my body.	Build it, build it, build it, build it.
I, that's how I, that's how I died.	Build it, build it, build it, build it.
	Oh that Tower of Babel, they knew what they were after.
	They knew what they were after.
Everything on the current moved up.	
I tried to stop it but it was too warm.	
Too unbelievably smooth, like playing in the sea,	No possible endings, no possible endings,
The sea.	No possible endings, no possible endings.

The Babel story is of great interest to Smith. In one 1976 photo, she sits on a couch, her newly acquired 1957 Fender Duo-Sonic across her lap, below two wall hangings: one her Grand Prix du Disque award for top pop album of 1976, *Horses*, and the other the front page of a Nation of Islam periodical whose lead story, "The Tower of Babel," bemoans both the global confusion resulting from an undirected accumulation of secular knowledge and the lust born of a towering false pride (Muhammad 1975). In Genesis 11, mankind's transgression by communal overreach led to punishment through linguistic separation. In "Land," Patti's multiple overdubbed vocals exemplify what she calls "Babelogues" (as opposed to her monologues), suggesting a primal pre-Babel tongue of illumination; Arista Records' October 1975 press release for *Horses* cites the artist's search "for a lingual Rosetta Stone by fusing poetry and rock 'n' roll."[48] Man's invasion of the heavens is related to rape in Patti's early poem, "babelfield," in which she writes, "the tower is the symbol of penetration" (1974, 199; see also p. 26 and Smith 2002, 54). The fable's related issues of universal language and an abhorrent censorship of the artist would soon drive Patti to conceive of a *Radio Ethiopia* (the title of her second LP) through which all of humanity could communicate openly about sex and in otherwise taboo speech without interfering censorship, unfiltered, the dirty remaining alongside the clean.[49] In commenting on the reception of music by Janika Vandervelde, Susan McClary relates women's sexual response, indeed a Patti Smith-like nonphysical sexual response, to the act of communication:

> I have had Vandervelde present *Genesis II* to several of my classes. Interestingly, many women students recognize . . . an image of female erotic pleasure—pleasure that is not connected with being somewhere else [as with the male goal of reaching climax], indeed, pleasure that need not even be thought of as tied specifically to sexual encounter, but pleasure that permits confident, free, and open interchange with others. (1991, 124)

Subsections Seven and Eight

Subsection Seven, intoned over the harmonic loop played only by the bass and a scratchy muted guitar, tells of a shiny blade in the sea of possibilities, pressed against a throat, and causing "a scream . . . so high-pitched that nobody heard" it. This gradually moves into the scaled-down Subsection Eight, where the muted lead guitar and repeated ^1 in the bass are joined by a surf backbeat on the snare, which closes the track on its own. The death of Hendrix, asphyxiated and thus mute, is represented by a butterfly silently flapping in the throat and a black tube disintegrating to the whine of a Fender guitar.[50] Hendrix's Fender

---

[48] See Reynolds and Press 1995, 358–9, re Smith's "Babelogue." Smith recounts the Babel tale and her yearning for a rock 'n' roll Rosetta Stone as symbolized in the Stones' "tongue" logo in a February 14, 1976, performance.

[49] In her youth, Patti was put off by religion when "the elders of the church told me that art was a material thing that was not needed in Christ's world" (Tarr 2008, 4). Smith incorporated this story, telling of how "art makes God sick," in stage monologues, as on March 27, 1976. Re her censorship crusade, see Smith 1977b. Ethiopia, then Abyssinia, was Rimbaud's last home, but the "Radio Ethiopia" construct is also informed by Jimi Hendrix's "[Radio Station] EXP" (1968).

[50] Likely Hendrix-inspired images populate Subsection One of "Land" in early back-to-back performances: wings flap noiselessly in lungs on December 26, 1975, and on the next night, Smith speaks, "if you set a bush on fire, it's exactly like, uh, sort of like a neon figure around a microphone." The black tube (which Smith explains symbolizes Hendrix in Brazier 1978, accessed at http://www .oceanstar.com/patti/intervus/7803melo.htm on November 2, 2017) also recalls *The Wild Boys*: "A

Stratocaster—whether or not on fire—was always his sexual locus on stage, so a logical transition emerges when "Land" ends by recapitulating the "humping on the parking meter" of "Gloria," set with the same E - D - A chord changes. The phallic parking meter of course recalls Dylan's "Subterranean Homesick Blues" (1965), but also the composer's more personal memory of Mapplethorpe from 1967: "I do recall peering through one of the [Whitney] museum's unique trapezoidal windows, seeing Robert across the street, leaning against a parking meter, smoking a cigarette."[51] Despite this feint to "Gloria," the LP ends with a full "Elegie" for Hendrix, which quotes his line from "1983 (A Merman I Should Turn to Be)" (1968), "it's too bad that our friends can't be with us today." The reference to this particular song once again reiterates gender fluidity in the context of water as a source of creation and destruction; indeed, the lore of water-folk speaks to a host of transitional experiences. Although they are often mer*maids* given the female body's association with water, mermen embody similarly ambiguous gender roles.

In today's performances, the final subsections of "Land" typically surround Johnny with local topics familiar to her given audience, such as surfers who "rode those waves like Icelandic ponies," in Santa Cruz (January 2, 2016), and with appeals to good stewardship of the natural environment, such as the Great Barrier Reef when she plays Sydney or Melbourne. A party invitation then leads to a space from which a look out the window spies the parking meter that actually does call forth further exhibitions of sex in the concert encore, "Gloria." The evening then ends with the drawn-out return to the fundamental question that drives "Land" by commanding audience reciprocity: "Do you know how to pony?"

Conclusion

"Land" is a marvel of poetic and musical give-and-take: free spoken improvisation of obscure referential images encompassing a given chorus-like sung text; fluidities

Mayan priest is drawing the flesh sap from a bulbous phallic tree. He has inserted an obsidian tube into the soft flesh of the tree and is draining the sap into a stone jar" (75). Perhaps related to the third "Land" subtitle, the "Mer" label had been created by Mapplethorpe for the 1974 release of Smith's cover of Hendrix's 1967 version of "Hey Joe." Like *Horses*, this track was recorded in Hendrix's 8th Street studio, the opening of which Smith attended in August, 1970. See also Hiss and McClelland 1975, 29. Toril Moi reminds us that for Freud, death is "the ultimate object of desire" (1995, 101), a concern that relates to much of "Land."

51 Smith 2010, 48. Smith played The Other End on June 26, 1975; seeing Dylan in the audience, she began to improvise lines about parking meters.

of androgynous identity and novel personal experiences surrounding a preordained outline filled with accepted elements; the shock of rape as opposed to familiar thrusts controlled by an Other; seclusionary and transgressive masturbatory hallucinations yielding multiple involuntarily transcendent resurrections; the breaking of taboos answered by channeling communal desires; multiple instances of foreplay surrendering to climaxes. Patti Smith wishes to inspire listeners to reach their own new heights by sharing her experience of fantasy, that sex is conceptual: a brainiac amour. Got to lose control, and then you take control . . .

Sources Cited

Abbate, Carolyn. 1993. "Opera; Or, the Envoicing of Women." In *Musicology and Difference: Gender and Sexuality in Music Scholarship*, ed. Ruth A. Solie. Berkeley: University of California Press: 225–58.

Adorno, Theodor W. 2002. "On the Social Situation of Music" [1932]. In *Essays on Music*, ed. Richard Leppert, trans. Susan H. Gillespie. Berkeley: University of California Press: 391–436.

Althof, Stanley. 2000. "Erectile Dysfunction: Psychotherapy with Men and Couples." In *Principles and Practice of Sex Therapy*, 3rd ed., ed. Sandra R. Leiblum and Raymond C. Rosen. New York: The Guilford Press: 242–75.

Apolloni, Alexandra. 2016. "Authority, Ability, and the Aging Ingénue's Voice." In *Voicing Girlhood in Popular Music: Performance, Authority, Authenticity*, ed. Jacqueline Warwick and Allison Adrian. New York: Routledge: 143–67.

Arnold, Gina. 2014. *Exile in Guyville*. New York: Bloomsbury Academic.

Askerø, Eirik. 2017. "Spectres of Masculinity: Markers of Vulnerability and Nostalgia in Johnny Cash." In *The Routledge Research Companion to Popular Music and Gender*, ed. Stan Hawkins. London: Routledge: 63–76.

Attig, R. Brian. 1991. "The Gay Voice in Popular Music: A Social Value Model Analysis of 'Don't Leave Me This Way,'" *Journal of Homosexuality* 21/1–2: 185–202.

Auslander, Philip. 2000. "I Wanna Be Your Man: Suzi Quatro's Musical Androgyny," *Popular Music* 19/2: 1–16.

Auslander, Philip. 2006. *Performing Glam Rock: Gender and Theatricality in Popular Music*. Ann Arbor: University of Michigan Press.

Bancroft, John. 1989. *Human Sexuality and Its Problems*, 2nd ed. London: Elsevier Limited.

Bancroft, John. 2009. *Human Sexuality and Its Problems*, 3rd ed. London: Elsevier Limited.

Bannister, Matthew. 2006. *White Boys, White Noise: Masculinities and 1980s Indie Guitar Rock*. Aldershot: Ashgate Press.

Barmak, Sarah. 2016. *Closer: Notes from the Orgasmic Frontier of Female Sexuality*. Toronto: Coach House Books.

Barthes, Roland. 1978. *A Lover's Discourse: Fragments*, trans. Richard Howard. New York: Hill and Wang.

Basler, Roy P. 1970. *Sex, Symbolism, and Psychology in Literature*. New York: Octagon Books.

Bayton, Mavis. 1993. "Feminist Musical Practice: Problems and Contradictions." In *Rock and Popular Music: Politics, Policies, Institutions*, ed. Tony Bennett, Simon Frith, Lawrence Grossberg, John Shepherd, and Graeme Turner. London and New York: Routledge: 177–92.

Bayton, Mavis. 1998. *Frock Rock: Women Performing Popular Music*. New York: Oxford University Press.

The Beatles. 2021a. *The Beatles Get Back*. New York: Callaway Arts & Entertainment.

The Beatles. 2021b. *The Beatles Get Back*. Part 2: Days 8–16. Documentary film directed by Peter Jackson, as streamed from Disney+ in November 2021. Wingnut Films Production.

Becker, Audrey. 1990. "New Lyrics by Women: A Feminist Alternative," *Journal of Popular Culture* 24: 1–22.

Beizer, Janet. 1994. "Rewriting Ophelia: Fluidity, Madness, and Voice in Louise Colet's *La Servante*." In *Embodied Voices: Representing Female Vocality in Western Culture*, ed. Leslie C. Dunn and Nancy A. Jones. Cambridge: Cambridge University Press: 152–65.

Bell, Leslie C. 2018. "Psychoanalytic Theories of Gender." In *Gender, Sex, and Sexualities: Psychological Perspectives*, ed. Nancy K. Dess, Jeanne Marecek, and Leslie Bell. New York: Oxford University Press: 195–217.

Benjamin, Jessica. 1978. "Authority and the Family Revisited: Or, A World Without Fathers?," *New German Critique* 13: 35–57.

Bennett, Andy. 2001. *Cultures of Popular Music*. Buckingham: Open University Press.

Berger, Maurice, Brian Wallis, and Simon Watson, eds. 1996. *Constructing Masculinity*. New York: Routledge.

Bergner, Daniel. 2009. *The Other Side of Desire: Four Journeys into the Far Realms of Lust and Longing*. New York: HarperCollins.

Bergner, Daniel. 2013. *What Do Women Want? Adventures in the Science of Female Desire*. New York: HarperCollins.

Berman, Leslie. 1997. "Charmed Circle: Folksingers and Singer-Songwriters." In *Trouble Girls: The Rolling Stone Book of Women in Rock*, ed. Barbara O'Dair. New York: Random House: 125–35.

Berrios-Miranda, Marisol, Shannon Dudley, and Michelle Habell-Pallán. 2018. *American Sabor: Latinos and Latinas in US Popular Music*. Seattle: University of Washington Press.

Biddle, Ian, and Freya Jarman-Ivens. 2007. "Introduction." In *Oh Boy! Masculinities and Popular Music*. New York: Routledge: 1–17.

Biernat, Monica, and Amanda K. Sesko, 2018. "Gender Stereotypes and Stereotyping: A Cognitive Perspective on Gender Bias." In *Gender, Sex, and Sexualities: Psychological Perspectives*, ed. Nancy K. Dess, Jeanne Marecek, and Leslie C. Bell. New York: Oxford University Press: 171–94.

Blake, William. 1981. *The Complete Poetry and Prose of William Blake*, ed. David V. Erdman. Berkeley: University of California Press.

Bland, Lucy, and Laura Doan. 1998. *Sexology Uncensored: The Documents of Sexual Science*. Cambridge: Polity.

Blecha, Peter. 2004. *Taboo Tunes: A History of Banned Bands & Censored Songs*. San Francisco: Backbeat Books.

Bockris, Victor, and Roberta Bayley. 1999. *Patti Smith: An Unauthorized Biography*. New York: Simon & Schuster.

Bordo, Susan. 1990. "Feminism, Postmodernism, and Gender-Scepticism." In *Feminist/Postmodernism*, ed. Linda J. Nicholson. New York: Routledge, Chapman & Hall: 133–56.

Bornstein, Kate. 2016. *Gender Outlaw: On Men, Women, and the Rest of Us*, rev. ed. New York: Vintage Books.

Brackett, David. 2009. *The Pop, Rock, and Soul Reader: Histories and Debates*, 2nd ed. New York: Oxford University Press.

Bradby, Barbara. 1993. "Sampling Sexuality: Gender, Technology and the Body in Dance Music," *Popular Music* 12/2 (May): 155–76.

Bradley, Adam. 2017. *The Poetry of Pop*. New Haven: Yale University Press.

Braziel, Jana Evans. 2004. "'Bye, Bye Baby': Race, Bisexuality, and the Blues in the Music of Bessie Smith and Janis Joplin," *Popular Music and Society* 27/1: 3–26.

Brazier, Chris. 1978. "The Resurrection of Patti Smith," *Melody Maker* (March 18).

Brown, Lyn Mikel, and Dana Edell. 2016. "I Love Beyoncé, But I Struggle with Beyoncé: Girl Activists Talk Music and Feminism." In *Voicing Girlhood in Popular Music: Performance, Authority, Authenticity*. New York: Routledge: 56–74.

Burns, Lori. 1997. "'Joanie Get Angry': k. d. lang's Feminist Revision." In *Understanding Rock*, ed. John Covach and Graeme M. Boone. New York: Oxford University Press: 93–112.

Burns, Lori. 1999–2000. "Genre, Gender, and Convention Revisited: k.d. lang's Cover of Cole Porter's 'So in Love,'" *Repercussions* 7–8: 299–325.

Burns, Lori, and Mélisse Lafrance. 2002. *Disruptive Divas: Feminism, Identity & Popular Music*. New York: Routledge.

Burns, Lori, and Mark Lafrance. 2014. "Celebrity, Spectacle, and Surveillance: Understanding Lady Gaga's 'Paparazzi' and 'Telephone' through Music, Image, and Movement." In *Lady Gaga and Popular Music: Performing Gender, Fashion, and Culture*, ed. Martin Iddon and Melanie L. Marshall. New York: Routledge: 117–47.

Burns, Lori, Alyssa Woods, and Marc Lafrance. 2016. "Sampling and Storytelling: Kanye West's Vocal and Sonic Narratives." In *The Cambridge Companion to the Singer-Songwriter*, ed. Justin Williams and Katherine Williams. Cambridge University Press: 159–70.

Burroughs, William S. 1967. *The Ticket That Exploded*. New York: Grove Press.

Burroughs, William S. 1969. *The Wild Boys: A Book of the Dead*. New York: Grove Press.

Busse, Kristina. 2006. "'I'm Jealous of the Fake Me': Postmodern Subjectivity and Identity Construction in Boy Band Fan Fiction." In *Framing Celebrity: New*

Directions in Celebrity Culture, ed. Su Holmes and Sean Redmond. London: Routledge: 253–67.

Butler, Jess. 2013. "For White Girls Only?: Postfeminism and the Politics of Inclusion," *Feminist Formations* 25/1 (Spring): 35–58.

Butler, Judith. 1993. *Bodies That Matter: On the Discursive Limits of "Sex."* New York: Routledge.

Butler, Judith. 1999. *Gender Trouble: Feminism and the Subversion of Identity*. New York: Routledge.

Butler, Mark. 2007. "'Some of Us Can Only Live in Songs of Love and Trouble': Voice, Genre/Gender, and Sexuality in the Music of Stephin Merritt." In *Oh Boy! Masculinities and Popular Music*. New York: Routledge: 235–59.

Califia, Pat. 1983. *Sapphistry: The Book of Lesbian Sexuality*, rev. 2nd ed. Tallahassee: The Naiad Press.

Cameron, Deborah, and Don Kulik. 2003. *Language and Sexuality*. Cambridge: Cambridge University Press.

Carbery, Rebecca. 2011. "Queer Genders: Problematising Gender through Contemporary Photography." Ph.D. dissertation, Durham University.

Carby, Hazel V. 2015. "'It Jus' Be's Dat Way Sometime': The Sexual Politics of Women's Blues" [1986]. In *Keeping Time: Readings in Jazz History*, 2nd ed., ed. Robert Walser. New York: Oxford University Press: 33–44.

Carlson, Dennis L. 2012. *The Education of Eros: A History of the Education and the Problem of Adolescent Sexuality*. New York: Routledge.

Carroll, Jim. 1987. *Forced Entries: The Downtown Diaries, 1971–1973*. New York: Penguin Books.

Carson, Mina, Tisa Lewis, and Susan M. Shaw. 2004. *Girls Rock! Fifty Years of Women Making Music*. Lexington: University Press of Kentucky.

Cavicchi, Daniel. 2011. *Listening and Longing: Music Lovers in the Age of Barnum*. Middletown: Wesleyan University Press.

Centawer, Marlie. 2018. "Rock-and-Roll Kinderwhore: Gender, Genre, and 'Girlville' in Liz Phair's *Girly Sound* (1991)," *Rock Music Studies* 5/1: 58–75.

Chion, Michel. 2009. *Film, a Sound Art*, trans. Claudia Gorbman. New York: Columbia University Press.

Cisoux, Hélène. 1997. "Sorties" [1975]. In *The Feminist Reader: Essays in Gender and the Politics of Literary Criticism*, ed. Catherine Belsey and Jane Moore. Malden: Blackwell.

Citron, Marcia J. 1993. *Gender and the Musical Canon*. Cambridge University Press.

Clark, Anna. 2008. *Desire: A History of European Sexuality*. New York: Routledge.

Clarke, Eric, Nicola Dibben, and Stephanie Pitts. 2010. *Music and Mind in Everyday Life*. New York: Oxford University Press.

Clawson, Mary Ann. 1999. "When Women Play the Bass: Instrument Specialization and Gender Interpretation in Alternative Rock Music," *Gender and Society* 13/1: 193–210.

Cloonan, Martin. 1996. *Banned! Censorship of Popular Music in Britain: 1967–92*. Aldershot: Arena.

Coates, Norma. 1997. "(R)evolution Now? Rock and the Political Potential of Gender." In *Sexing the Groove: Popular Music and Gender*, ed. Sheila Whiteley. London: Routledge: 50–64.

Coates, Norma. 1998. "Can't We Just Talk about Music? Rock and Gender on the Internet." In *Mapping the Beat: Popular Music and Contemporary Theory*, ed. Thomas Swiss, John Sloop, and Andrew Herman. Oxford: Blackwell Publishers: 77–99.

Cohen, Nancy L. 2012. *Delirium: How the Sexual Counterrevolution Is Polarizing America*. Berkeley: Counterpoint.

Cohen, Scott. 1976. "How a Little Girl Took Over a Tough Gang: The Hard-Rock Poets," *Oui* (July).

Cohn, Richard. 2006. "Hexatonic Poles and the Uncanny in Parsifal," *The Opera Quarterly* 22/2 (Spring): 230–48.

Colton, Lisa. 2014. "Who's Calling? Telephone Songs, Female Vocal Empowerment and Signification." In *Lady Gaga and Popular Music: Performing Gender, Fashion, and Culture*, ed. Martin Iddon and Melanie L. Marshall. New York: Routledge: 67–81.

Connell, R[aewyn/Bob]. W. 1995. *Masculinities*. Berkeley: University of California Press.

Cook, Susan C. 2005. "The Importance of Gender." In *Music Cultures in the United States: An Introduction*, ed. Ellen Koskoff. New York: Routledge: 81–8.

Coulter, Bridget. 2017. "'Singing from the Heart': Notions of Gendered Authenticity in Pop Music." In *The Routledge Research Companion to Popular Music and Gender*, ed. Stan Hawkins. London: Routledge: 267–80.

Courrier, Kevin. 2002. *Dangerous Kitchen: The Subversive World of Frank Zappa*. Toronto: ECW Press.

Cox, Kathryn B. 2018. "'What Happened to the Post-War Dream?' Nostalgia, Trauma, and Affect in British Rock of the 1960s and 1970s." Ph.D. dissertation, The University of Michigan.

Crafton, Lisa. 2018. "'Tangle of Matter and Ghost': U2, Leonard Cohen, and Blakean Romanticism." In *Rock and Romanticism: Blake, Wordsworth, and Rock from Dylan to U2*. New York: Lexington Books: 65–82.

Crawley, Sara, Lara J. Foley, and Constance L. Shehan. 2008. *Gendering Bodies*. New York: Rowman & Littlefield.

Cusick, Suzanne G. 1999a. "Gender, Musicology, and Feminism." In *Rethinking Music*, ed. Nicholas Cook and Mark Everist. New York: Oxford University Press: 471–98.

Cusick, Suzanne G. 1999b. "On Musical Performances of Gender and Sex." In *Audible Traces: Gender, Identity, and Music*, ed. Elaine Barkin and Lydia Hemessley. Zürich: Carciofoli Verlagshaus: 25–48.

Cusick, Suzanne G. 2006. "On a Lesbian Relationship with Music: A Serious Effort Not to Think Straight." In *Queering the Pitch: The New Gay and Lesbian Musicology*, 2nd

ed., ed. Philip Brett, Elizabeth Wood and Gary C. Thomas. New York: Routledge:
   67–83.

Dabhoiwala, Faramerz. 2012. *The Origins of Sex: A History of the First Sexual
   Revolution*. New York: Oxford University Press.

Davis, Angela. 1999. *Blues Legacies and Black Feminism: Gertrude 'Ma' Rainey, Bessie
   Smith and Billie Holliday*. New York: Vintage.

de Beauvoir, Simone. 1989. *The Second Sex* [1949], trans. H. M. Parshley. New York:
   Vintage Books.

de Berg, Henk. 2003. *Freud's Theory and Its Use in Literary and Cultural Studies*.
   Rochester: Camden House.

de Boise, Sam. 2014. "Cheer Up Emo Kid: Rethinking the 'Crisis of Masculinity' in
   Emo," *Popular Music* 33/2: 225–42.

de Boise, Sam. 2015. *Men, Masculinity, Music and Emotions*. New York: Palgrave
   Macmillan.

de Lauretis, Teresa. 1987. *Technologies of Gender: Essays on Theory, Film, and Fiction*.
   Bloomington: Indiana University Press.

Dean, Carolyn J. 1996. *Sexuality and Modern Western Culture*. New York: Twayne
   Publications.

Deighnan, Alice. 1997. "Metaphors of Desire." In *Language and Desire: Encoding Sex,
   Romance and Intimacy*, ed. Keith Harvey and Celia Shalom. London: Routledge:
   21–42.

Deleuze, Gilles, and Felix Guattari. 1992. *A Thousand Plateaus: Capitalism and
   Schizophrenia*, trans. Brian Massumi. London and New York: Continuum.

D'Emilio, John, and Estelle B. Freedman. 2012. *Intimate Matters: A History of Sexuality
   in America*, 3rd ed. Chicago: The University of Chicago Press.

Dess, Nancy K., Jeanne Marecek, and Leslie C. Bell, eds. 2018. *Gender, Sex, and
   Sexualities: Psychological Perspectives*. New York: Oxford University Press.

Dhaenens, Frederik. 2016. "Reading Gay Music Videos: An Inquiry into the
   Representation of Sexual Diversity in Contemporary Popular Music Videos," *Popular
   Music and Society* 39/5: 532–46.

Diamond, Lisa M. 2008. *Sexual Fluidity: Understanding Women's Love and Desire*.
   Cambridge, MA: Harvard University Press.

Diamond, Lisa M. 2016. "Sexual Fluidity in Males and Females," *Current Sexual Health
   Reports*, 8/4: 249–56.

Diamond, Lisa M. 2017. "Wanting Women: Sex, Gender, and the Specificity of Sexual
   Arousal," *Archives of Sexual Behavior* 46: 1181–5.

Diamond, Lisa M. 2018. "Contemporary Theory in the Study of Intimacy, Desire, and
   Sexuality." In *Gender, Sex, and Sexualities: Psychological Perspectives*, ed. Nancy K.
   Dess, Jeanne Marecek, and Leslie C. Bell. New York: Oxford University Press: 271–94.

Dibben, Nicola. 1999. "Representations of Femininity in Popular Music," *Popular Music*
   18/3: 331–55.

Dickinson, Kay. 2004. "'Believe': Vocoders, Digital Female Identity and Camp." In *Music, Space and Place: Popular Music and Cultural Identity*, ed. Sheila Whiteley, Andy Bennett and Stan Hawkins. Aldershot: Ashgate.

Dinnerstein, Dorothy. 2002. "Higamous-Hogamous" [1999]. In *Sexuality and Gender*, ed. Christine L. Williams and Arlene Stein. Oxford: Blackwell Publishers: 5–19.

Djupvik, Marita B. 2017. "'Working It': Female Masculinity and Missy Elliott." In *The Routledge Research Companion to Popular Music and Gender*, ed. Stan Hawkins. London: Routledge: 117–31.

Donaghue, Ngaire. 2018. "Discursive Psychological Approaches to the (Un)making of Sex/Gender." In *Gender, Sex, and Sexualities: Psychological Perspectives*, ed. Nancy K. Dess, Jeanne Marecek, and Leslie C. Bell. New York: Oxford University Press: 127–48.

Douglas, Susan J. 2010. *Enlightened Sexism: The Seductive Message that Feminism's Work Is Done*. New York: Times Books.

Dryfoos, Joy G., and Carol Barkin. 2006. *Adolescence: Growing Up in America Today*. New York: Oxford University Press.

Durham, Meenakshi Gigi. 2002. "Girls, Media, and the Negotiation of Sexuality: A Study of Race, Class, and Gender in Adolescent Peer Groups." In *Sexuality and Gender*, ed. Christine L. Williams and Arlene Stein. Oxford: Blackwell: 332–48.

Dyhouse, Carol. 2017. *Heartthrobs: A History of Women and Desire*. Oxford: Oxford University Press.

Edwards, Emily D. 1994. "Does Love Really Stink?: The 'Mean World' of Love and Sex in Popular Music of the 1980s." In *Adolescents and Their Music: If It's Too Loud, You're Too Old*, ed. Jonathon S. Epstein. New York: Garland Publishing: 225–49.

Ehrenreich, Barbara, Elizabeth Hess, and Gloria Jacobs. 2009. "Beatlemania: Girls Just Want to Have Fun" [1986]. In *The Pop, Rock, and Soul Reader: Histories and Debates*, 2nd ed., ed. David Brackett. New York: Oxford University Press: 216–20.

Elliott, Beth [as Geri Nettick]. 1996. *Mirrors: Portrait of a Lesbian Transsexual*. New York: Rhinoceros.

Ellwood-Clayton, Bella. 2012. *Sex Drive: In Pursuit of Female Desire*. Sydney: Allen & Unwin.

Epstein, Jonathon S., ed. 1994. *Adolescents and Their Music: If It's Too Loud, You're Too Old*. New York: Garland Publishing.

Epstein, Jonathon S. 1998. *Youth Culture: Identity in a Postmodern World*. Oxford: Blackwell.

Epstein, Julia, and Kristina Straub, eds. 1991. *Body Guards: The Cultural Politics of Gender Ambiguity*. New York: Routledge.

Evans, Liz. 1994. *Women, Sex and Rock'n'Roll: In Their Own Words*. London: Pandora.

Everett, Walter. 1986. "Fantastic Remembrance in John Lennon's 'Strawberry Fields Forever' and 'Julia'," *The Musical Quarterly* 72/3: 360–93.

Everett, Walter. 1999. *The Beatles as Musicians: Revolver through the Anthology*. New York: Oxford University Press.

Everett, Walter. 2004. "A Royal Scam: The Abstruse and Ironic Bop-Rock Harmony of Steely Dan," *Music Theory Spectrum* 26/2 (Fall): 201–35.

Everett, Walter. 2007. "Pitch Down the Middle." In *Expression in Pop/Rock Music: Critical and Analytical Essays*, ed. Walter Everett. New York: Oxford University Press: 111–74.

Everett, Walter. 2009. *The Foundations of Rock: From 'Blue Suede Shoes' to 'Suite: Judy Blue Eyes.'* Oxford: Oxford University Press.

Everett, Walter. 2012. "The Representation of Meaning in Post-Millennial Rock," *Black Box Pop: Beiträge zur Popularmusikforschung* 38: 149–69.

Fanshel, Rosalie Zdzienicka. 2013. "Beyond Blood Brothers: Queer Bruce Springsteen," *Popular Music* 32/3: 359–83.

Fast, Susan. 2001. *In the Houses of the Holy: Led Zeppelin and the Power of Rock Music*. New York: Oxford University Press.

Fast, Susan. 2005. "Led Zeppelin and the Construction of Masculinity." In *Music Cultures in the United States: An Introduction*, ed. Ellen Koskoff. New York: Routledge: 89–91.

Fast, Susan. 2006. "Rethinking Issues of Gender and Sexuality in Led Zeppelin: A Woman's View of Pleasure and Power in Hard Rock." In *The Popular Music Studies Reader*, ed. Andy Bennett, Barry Shank, and Jayson Toynbee. London: Routledge: 362–69.

Fast, Susan. 2009. "Genre, Subjectivity and Back-up Singing in Rock Music." In *The Ashgate Research Companion to Popular Musicology*, ed. Derek Scott. Surrey: Ashgate Press: 171–87.

Fast, Susan. 2010. "Bold Soul Trickster: The 60s Tina Signifies." In *She's So Fine: Reflections on Whiteness, Femininity, Adolescence and Class in 1960s Music*. Surrey: Ashgate Press: 203–34.

Fast, Susan. 2012. "Michael Jackson's Queer Musical Belongings," *Popular Music and Society* 35/2 (May): 281–300.

Fausto-Sterling, Anne. 2002. "The Five Sexes: Why Male and Female Are Not Enough." In *Sexuality and Gender*, ed. Christine L. Williams and Arlene Stein. Oxford: Blackwell: 468–73.

Firestone, Shulamith. 1970. *The Dialectic of Sex*. New York: Morrow.

Flax, Jane. 1990. "Postmodernism and Gender Relations in Feminist Theory." In *Feminism/Postmodernism*, ed. Linda J. Nicholson. New York: Routledge: 39–62.

Foucault, Michel. 1978. *The History of Sexuality, Vol. 1: An Introduction*, trans. Robert Hurley. New York: Pantheon.

Freitas, Donna. 2013. *The End of Sex: How Hookup Culture Is Leaving a Generation Unhappy, Sexually Unfulfilled, and Confused About Intimacy*. New York: Basic Books.

Freud, Sigmund. 1953–74. *The Standard Edition of the Complete Psychological Works of Sigmund Freud*, ed. James Strachey, in collaboration with Anna Freud, assisted by Alix Strachey and Alan Tyson, London: Hogarth.

Friday, Nancy. 1976. *My Secret Garden: Women's Sexual Fantasies*. London: Quarter.

Friedman, Rachel, and Ashley B. Maxwell. 2021. "Transgender and Transracial Identity: A Cultural Examination of 'Passing.'" In *Beyond Binaries: Trans Identities in Contemporary Culture*, ed. Mike Perez, Rachel Friedman, and John C. Lamothe. Lanham: Lexington Books: 125–35.

Friend, David. 2017. *The Naughty Nineties: The Triumph of the American Libido*. New York: Twelve.

Frith, Simon. 1981. *Sound Effects: Youth, Leisure and the Politics of Rock 'n' Roll*. New York: Pantheon.

Frith, Simon. 1990. "Afterthoughts." In *On Record: Rock, Pop, and the Written Word*, ed. Frith and Andrew Goodwin. New York: Pantheon Books: 419–24.

Frith, Simon. 1996. *Performing Rites: On the Value of Popular Music*. Cambridge: Harvard University Press.

Frith, Simon, and Andrew Goodwin. 1990. "Music and Sexuality." In *On Record: Rock, Pop, and the Written Word*, ed. Frith and Goodwin. New York: Pantheon: 369–70.

Frith, Simon, and Angela McRobbie. 1990. "Rock and Sexuality (1978)." In *On Record: Rock, Pop, and the Written Word*, ed. Frith and Andrew Goodwin. New York: Pantheon: 371–89.

Frith, Simon, Will Straw & John Street. 2001. *The Cambridge Companion to Pop and Rock*. Cambridge, UK: Cambridge University Press.

Gaar, Gillian G. 1992. *She's a Rebel: The History of Women in Rock & Roll*, 2nd ed. Seattle: Seal Press.

Gagnon, John H. 1977. *Human Sexualities*. Glenview: Scott, Foresman and Company.

Geller, Theresa L. 2014. "Trans/Affect: Monstrous Masculinities and the Sublime Art of Lady Gaga." In *Lady Gaga and Popular Music: Performing Gender, Fashion, and Culture*, ed. Martin Iddon and Melanie L. Marshall. New York: Routledge: 209–30.

Gendron, Bernard. 2004. "Rock and Roll Mythology: Race and Sex in 'Whole Lotta Shakin' Goin On." In *Popular Music: Critical Concepts in Media and Cultural Studies*, ed. Simon Frith. London: Routledge: 297–310.

Gerard, Kent, and Gert Hekma, eds. 1988. "The Pursuit of Sodomy: Male Homosexuality in Renaissance and Enlightenment Europe," *Journal of Homosexuality* 16/1–2.

Gill, Rosalind. 2007. "Postfeminist Media Culture: Elements of Sensibility," *European Journal of Cultural Studies* 10/2: 147–66.

Gill, Rosalind. 2009. "Supersexualize Me!: Advertising and the 'Midriffs.'" In *Mainstreaming Sex: The Sexualization of Western Culture*, ed. Feona Attwood. London: I.B. Tauris: 93–109.

Ginsberg, Allen. 1956. *Howl*. San Francisco: City Lights.

Gioia, Ted. 2015. *Love Songs: The Hidden History*. New York: Oxford University Press.

Gitlow, Ali. 2018. "Nicki Minaj." In *Women Who Rock: Bessie to Beyoncé: Girl Groups to Riot Grrrl*, ed. Evelyn McDonnell. New York: Black Dog & Leventhal: 383–86.

Goldberg, Emma. 2021. "Salary Transparency Fails to Fix the Gender Pay Gap," *The New York Times*, Business (July 4): 5.

Goldin-Perschbacher, Shana. 2007. "'Not with You But of You': 'Unbearable Intimacy' and Jeff Buckley's Transgendered Vocality." In *Oh Boy! Masculinities and Popular Music*, ed. Freya Jarman-Ivens. New York: Routledge: 213–33.

Goodwin, Sarah Webster. 1994. "Wordsworth and Romantic Voice: The Poet's Song and the Prostitute's Cry." In *Embodied Voices: Representing Female Vocality in Western Culture*, ed. Leslie C. Dunn and Nancy A. Jones. Cambridge: Cambridge University Press.

Gowarty, Patricia Adair. 2018. "On Being and Becoming Female and Male: A Sex-Neutral Evolutionary Perspective." In *Gender, Sex, and Sexualities: Psychological Perspectives*, ed. Nancy K. Dess, Jeanne Marecek, and Leslie C. Bell. New York: Oxford University Press: 77–102.

Gracyk, Theodore. 2001. *I Wanna Be Me: Rock Music and the Politics of Identity*. Philadelphia: Temple University Press.

Graddol, David, and Joan Swann. 1989. *Gender Voices*. Cambridge: Basil Blackwell.

Grajeda, Tony. 2002. "The Feminization of Rock." In *Rock Over the Edge: Transformations in Popular Music Culture*, ed. Roger Beebe, Denise Fulbrook, and Ben Saunders. Durham: Duke University Press.

Green, Abel. 2009. "A Warning to the Music Business" [1955]. In *The Pop, Rock, and Soul Reader: Histories and Debates*, 2nd ed., ed. David Brackett. New York: Oxford University Press: 102–03.

Green, Lucy. 1997. *Music, Gender, Education*. Cambridge: Cambridge University Press.

Greene, Doyle. 2016. *Rock, Counterculture and the Avant-Garde, 1966–1970*. Jefferson: McFarland & Company, Inc.

Griffiths, Dai. 2002. "Cover Versions and the Sound of Identity in Motion." In *Popular Music Studies*, ed. David Hesmondhalgh and Keith Negus. London: Arnold: 51–64.

Hajdu, David. 2016. *Love for Sale: Pop Music in America*. New York: Farrar, Straus and Giroux.

Halberstam, Judith/J. Jack. 1998. *Female Masculinity*. London and Durham: Duke University Press.

Halberstam, Judith/J. Jack. 2007. "Queer Voices and Musical Genders." In *Oh Boy! Masculinities and Popular Music*, ed. Freya Jarman-Ivens. New York: Routledge: 183–95.

Halberstam, Judith/J. Jack. 2012. *Gaga Feminism: Sex, Gender, and the End of Normal*. Boston: Beacon Press.

Halberstam, Judith/J. Jack. 2018. *Trans*: A Quick and Quirky Account of Gender Variability*. Berkeley: University of California Press.

Hamm, Charles. 1983. *Yesterdays: Popular Song in America*. New York: W. W. Norton & Co.

Hansen, Kai Arne. 2017. "Holding On for Dear Life: Gender, Celebrity Status, and Vulnerability-on-Display in Sia's 'Chandelier.'" In *The Routledge Research Companion to Popular Music and Gender*, ed. Stan Hawkins. London: Routledge: 89–101.

Haraway, Donna. 2003. "A Manifesto for Cyborgs: Science, Technology, and Socialist Feminism in the 1980s." In *The Haraway Reader*, comp. Donna Haraway. New York: Routledge: 7–45.

Harper-Scott, J. P. E. 2013. "Britten and the Deadlock of Identity Politics." In *Masculinity in Opera: Gender, History, and New Musicology*, ed. Philip Purvis. New York: Routledge: 144–66.

Harris, Anita. 2004. *Future Girl: Young Women in the Twenty-First Century*. New York: Routledge.

Harvey, Keith, and Celia Shalom, 1997. "Introduction." In *Language and Desire: Encoding Sex, Romance and Intimacy*, ed. Harvey and Shalom. London: Routledge: 1–17.

Hawkes, Gail. 2004. *Sex & Pleasure in Western Culture*. Cambridge: Polity Press Ltd.

Hawkins, Stan. 2002. *Settling the Pop Score: Pop Texts and Identity Politics*. Aldershot: Ashgate Press.

Hawkins, Stan. 2009. *The British Pop Dandy: Masculinity, Popular Music and Culture*. Farnham: Ashgate Press.

Hawkins, Stan. 2014. "'I'll Bring You Down, Down, Down': Lady Gaga's Performance in 'Judas.'" In *Lady Gaga and Popular Music: Performing Gender, Fashion, and Culture*, ed. Martin Iddon and Melanie L. Marshall. New York: Routledge: 9–26.

Hawkins, Stan. 2016. *Queerness in Pop Music: Aesthetics, Gender Norms, and Temporality*. New York: Routledge.

Hawkins, Stan. 2017. *The Routledge Research Companion to Popular Music and Gender*. London: Routledge.

Hebdige, Dick. 1988. *Hiding in the Light: On Images and Things*. London: Routledge.

Heetderks, David. 2020. "Play with Closing Markers: Cadential Multivalence in 1960s Prechoruses and Related Schemas," *Music Theory Spectrum* 42/1 (Spring): 1–23.

Hegarty, Peter, Y. Gavriel Ansara, and Meg-John Barker. 2018. "Nonbinary Gender Identities." In *Gender, Sex, and Sexualities: Psychological Perspectives*, ed. Nancy K. Dess, Jeanne Marecek, and Leslie C. Bell. New York: Oxford University Press: 53–76.

Hekma, Gert. 1989. "A History of Sexology: Social and Historical Aspects of Sexuality." In *From Sappho to De Sade: Moments in the History of Sexuality*, ed. Jan N. Bremmer. New York: Routledge: 178–81.

Henry, George W. 1948. *Sex Variants: A Study of Homosexual Patterns*. New York: Paul B. Hoeber, Inc.

Hesse, Hermann. 1963. *Steppenwolf* [1927]. trans. Basil Creighton. New York: Bantam Books.

Hewitt, Nancy A. 2000. "Beyond the Search for Sisterhood: American Women's History in the 1990s." In *Unequal Sisters: A Multi-Cultural Reader in U.S. Women's History*, ed. Vicki L. Ruiz and Carol DuBois. New York: Routledge: 1–19.

Heylin, Clinton. 2005. *From the Velvets to the Voidoids: The Birth of American Punk Rock*. Chicago: A Cappella Books.

Heywood, Leslie L., and Justin R. Garcia. 2018. "Integrating Evolutionary Affective Neuroscience and Feminism in Gender Research." In *Gender, Sex, and Sexualities: Psychological Perspectives*, ed. Nancy K. Dess, Jeanne Marecek, and Leslie C. Bell. New York: Oxford University Press: 295–317.

Hines, Melissa. 2018. "The Integrative Psychology of Early Gender Development." In *Gender, Sex, and Sexualities: Psychological Perspectives*, ed. Nancy K. Dess, Jeanne Marecek, and Leslie C. Bell. New York: Oxford University Press: 247–70.

Hisama, Ellie M. 1993. "Postcolonialism on the Make: The Music of John Mellencamp, David Bowie and John Zorn," *Popular Music* 12/1 (May): 91–104.

Hisama, Ellie M. 1999. "Voice, Race, and Sexuality in the Music of Joan Armatrading." In *Audible Traces: Gender, Identity, and Music*, ed. Elaine Barkin and Lydia Hamessley. Zürich: Carciofoli Verlangshaus: 115–31.

Hiss, Tony, and David McClelland. 1975. "Gonna Be So Big, Gonna Be a Star, Watch Me Now!," *The New York Times Magazine* (December 21): 25–31.

Hite, Shere. 1976. *The Hite Report*. New York: Macmillan Publishing Company.

Høge-Olesen, Henrik, 2019. *The Aesthetic Animal*. New York: Oxford University Press.

Hoke, S. Kay. 2001. "American Popular Music." In *Women & Music: A History*, 2nd ed., ed. Karin Pendle. Bloomington: Indiana University Press: 387–416.

hooks, bell. 1994. "Feminism Inside: Toward a Black Body Politic." In *Black male: Representations of Masculinity in Contemporary American Art*, ed. Thelma Golden. New York: Whitney Museum of American Art: 127–40.

hooks, bell. 2004. *We Real Cool: Black Men and Masculinity*. London: Routledge.

Horton, Donald. 1990. "The Dialogue of Courtship in Popular Song." In *On Record: Rock, Pop, and the Written Word*, ed. Simon Frith and Andrew Goodwin. New York: Pantheon Books.

Householder, April Kalogeropoulos. 2015. "Girls, Grrrls, *Girls*: Lena Dunham, *Girls* and the Contradictions of Fourth-Wave Feminism." In *Feminist Theory and Pop Culture*, ed. Adrienne Trier-Bieniek. Rotterdam: Sense Publishers: 19–33.

Hubbs, Nadine. 1996. "Music of the 'Fourth Gender': Morrissey and the Sexual Politics of Melodic Contour," *Genders* 23 (June 30): 266–96.

Hubbs, Nadine. 2014. *Rednecks, Queers, & Country Music*. Berkeley: University of California Press.

Iddon, Martin, and Melanie L. Marshall. 2014. "Introduction." In *Lady Gaga and Popular Music: Performing Gender, Fashion, and Culture*. New York: Routledge.

Jameson, Frederic. 1983. "Postmodern and Consumer Society." In *The Anti-Aesthetic: Essays on Postmodern Culture*, ed. Hal Roster. Port Townshend: Bay Press: 111–25.

Jasmine, Lucretia Tye. 2018a. "Courtney Love." In *Women Who Rock: Bessie to Beyoncé: Girl Groups to Riot Grrrl*, ed. Evelyn McDonnell. New York: Black Dog & Leventhal: 270–73.

Jasmine, Lucretia Tye. 2018b. "k.d. lang." In *Women Who Rock: Bessie to Beyoncé: Girl Groups to Riot Grrrl*, ed. Evelyn McDonnell. New York: Black Dog & Leventhal: 235–37.

Jeffrey-Poulter, Stephen. 1991. *Peers, Queers, and Commons: The Struggle for Gay Law Reform from 1950 to the Present.* London: Routledge.

Julian, Kate. 2018. "Sex Recession," *The Atlantic* (December). https://www.theatlantic .com/ magazine/archive/2018/12/the-sex-recession/573949/ (accessed 21 December 2018).

Kajikawa, Loren. 2015. *Sounding Race in Rap Songs.* Berkeley: University of California Press.

Kandel, Eric R. 2012. *The Age of Insight: The Quest to Understand the Unconscious in Art, Mind, and Brain, from Vienna 1900 to the Present.* New York: Random House.

Kaplan, E. Ann. 1987. *Rocking Around the Clock: Music Television, Postmodernism, and Consumer Culture.* New York: Methuen.

Kearney, Mary Celeste. 1998. "'Don't Need You': Rethinking Identity Politics and Separatism from a Grrrl Perspective." In *Youth Culture: Identity in a Postmodern World*, ed. Jonathon S. Epstein. Oxford: Blackwell: 148–88.

Kearney, Mary Celeste. 2017. *Gender and Rock.* New York: Oxford University Press.

Kelly, Gary F. 2012. *America's Sexual Transformation: How the Sexual Revolution's Legacy Is Shaping Our Society, Our Youth, and Our Future.* Santa Barbara: Praeger.

Kessler, Suzanne J., and Wendy McKenna. 1978. *Gender: An Ethnomethodological Approach.* Chicago: University of Chicago Press.

Khazan, Olga. 2016. "How Older Brothers Influence Homosexuality," *The Atlantic* (April 27).

Kimmel, Michael. 1996. *Manhood in America: A Cultural History.* New York: The Free Press.

Kimmel, Michael. 2008. *Guyland: The Perilous World Where Boys Become Men.* New York: Harper.

King, Martin. 2013. *Men, Masculinity and the Beatles.* Burlington: Ashgate.

Kinsey, Alfred C., et al. 1948. *Sexual Behavior in the Human Male.* Philadelphia: W. B. Saunders Co.

Kinsey, Alfred C. 1953. *Sexual Behavior in the Human Female.* Bloomington: Indiana University Press.

Kleinberg, S. J. 1999. *Women in the United States, 1830–1945.* New Brunswick: Rutgers University Press.

Koedt, Anne. 1973. "The Myth of the Vaginal Orgasm" [1968]. In *Radical Feminism: A Documentary Reader*, ed. Koedt, Ellen Levine and Anita Rapone. New York: Quadrangle Books: 198–207.

Kopkind, Andrew. 2009. "The Dialectics of Disco: Gay Music Goes Straight" [1979]. In *The Pop, Rock, and Soul Reader: Histories and Debates*, 2nd ed., ed. David Brackett. New York: Oxford University Press: 352–60.

Kosnick, Kira. 2011. "Sexuality and Migration Studies: The Invisible, the Oxymoronic and Heteronormative Othering." In *Framing Intersectionality: Debates on a Multi-Faceted Concept in Gender Studies*, ed. Helma Lutz, Maria Teresa Herrera Vivar, and Linda Supik. Farnham, Surrey: Ashgate: 121–35.

Kramer, Lawrence. 1984. *Music and Poetry: The Nineteenth Century and After*. Berkeley: University of California Press.

Kramer, Lawrence. 1993. "*Carnaval*, Cross-Dressing, and the Woman in the Mirror." In *Musicology and Difference: Gender and Sexuality in Music Scholarship*, ed. Ruth A. Solie. Berkeley: University of California Press: 305–25.

Krell, Elias. 2013. "Contours through Covers: Voice and Affect in the Music of Lucas Silveira," *Journal of Popular Music Studies* 25/4: 476–503.

Kurtis, Tuğçe, and Glenn Adams. 2018. "Gender and Sex(ualities): A Cultural Psychology Approach." In *Gender, Sex, and Sexualities: Psychological Perspectives*, ed. Nancy K. Dess, Jeanne Marecek, and Leslie C. Bell. New York: Oxford University Press: 105–25.

Lacan, Jacques. 1977. *Écrits: A Selection*, trans. Alan Sheridan. London: Routledge.

Lacan, Jacques, and the *école freudienne*. 1982. *Feminine Sexuality*, ed. Juliet Mitchell and Jacqueline Rose, trans J. Rose. New York: W. W. Norton & Company.

Lafrance, Marc, Lori Burns, and Alyssa Woods. 2017. "Doing Hip-Hop Masculinity Differently: Exploring Kanye Wet's *808s & Heartbreak* through word, sound, and image." In *The Routledge Research Companion to Popular Music and Gender*, ed. Stan Hawkins. London: Routledge: 285–99.

Lakoff, George. 1987. *Women, Fire, and Dangerous Things: What Categories Reveal about the Mind*. Chicago: The University of Chicago Press.

Lakoff, George, and Mark Johnson. 1980. *Metaphors We Live By*. Chicago: The University of Chicago Press.

Lakoff, Robin Tolmach. 2004. *Language and Women's Place: Text and Commentaries*, rev. ed. Oxford: Oxford University Press.

Lambert, Charles. 1997. "Speaking Its Name: The Poetic Expression of Gay Male Desire." In *Language and Desire: Encoding Sex, Romance and Intimacy*, ed. Keith Harvey and Celia Shalom. London: Routledge: 204–21.

Lankford, Jr., Ronald D. 2010. *Women Singer-Songwriters in Rock: A Populist Rebellion in the 1990s*. Lanham: Scarecrow Press.

Laqueur, Thomas. 1990. *Making Sex: Body and Gender from the Greeks to Freud*. Cambridge, MA: Harvard University Press.

Leaper, "Gender, Dispositions, Peer Relations, and Identity." In *Gender, Sex, and Sexualities: Psychological Perspectives*, ed. Nancy K. Dess, Jeanne Marecek, and Leslie C. Bell. New York: Oxford University Press: 219–45.

Lee, Gavin. 2018a. "Introduction: From Difference to Ambiguity." In *Rethinking Difference in Gender, Sexuality, and Popular Music*, ed. Lee. London: Routledge: 1–11.

Lee, Gavin. 2018b. "Queer Desire is Not Gay, Gender Is a Fantasy: Ways of Loving Britney." In *Rethinking Difference in Gender, Sexuality, and Popular Music*, ed. Lee. London: Routledge: 150–67.

Lee, Summer Kim. 2013. "Alive with You: Blood Orange's Sense of Distance in Resonant Love," *Journal of Popular Music Studies* 25/4: 459–75.

Lefkowitz, Eva S., and Sara A. Vasilenko. 2014. "Healthy Sex and Sexual Health: New Directions for Studying Outcomes of Sexual Health," *New Directions for Child and Adolescent Development* 144 (Summer): 87–98.

Leibetseder, Doris. 2012. *Queer Tracks: Subversive Strategies in Rock and Pop Music*, ed. and trans. Rebecca Carbery. Surrey: Ashgate.

Leiblum, Sandra R., and Raymond C. Rosen, eds. 2000. *Principles and Practice of Sex Therapy*, 3rd ed. New York: Guilford.

Lester, C. N. 2017. *Trans Like Me: Conversations for All of Us*. New York: Seal Press.

Leonard, Marion. 2007. *Gender in the Music Industry: Rock, Discourse and Girl Power*. Aldershot: Ashgate.

Lieb, Kristin J. 2013. *Gender, Branding, and the Modern Music Industry: The Social Construction of Female Popular Music Stars*. New York: Routledge.

Longhurst, Brian. 1995. *Popular Music & Society*. Cambridge: Polity Press.

Lorraine, Renée Cox. 2001. "Recovering Jouissance: Feminist Aesthetics and Music." In *Women & Music: A History*, 3rd ed. Bloomington: Indiana University Press: 3–18.

Lowe, Kelly Fisher. 2006. *The Words and Music of Frank Zappa*. Westport: Praeger.

Lutz, Helma, Maria Teresa Herrera Vivar, and Linda Supik, eds. 2011. *Framing Intersectionality: Debates on a Multi-Faceted Concept in Gender Studies*. Farnham, Surrey: Ashgate.

Lykke, Nina. 2011. "Intersectional Analysis: Black Box or Useful Critical Feminist Thinking Technology." In *Framing Intersectionality: Debates on a Multi-Faceted Concept in Gender Studies*, ed. Helma Lutz, Maria Teresa Herrera Vivar, and Linda Supik. Farnham, Surrey: Ashgate.

Macarthur, Sally. 2002. *Feminist Aesthetics in Music*. Westport: Greenwood Press.

MacKinnon, Catherine. 1982. "Feminism, Marxism, Method and the State: An Agenda for Theory," *Signs* 7/3: 515–44.

Magnusson, Eva, and Jeanne Marecek. 2018. "Setting the Stage: Gender, Sex, and Sexualities in Psychology." In *Gender, Sex, and Sexualities: Psychological Perspectives*, ed. Nancy K. Dess, Jeanne Marecek, and Leslie C. Bell. New York: Oxford University Press: 3–28.

Mahon, Maureen. 2004. *Right to Rock: The Black Rock Coalition and the Cultural Politics of Race*. Durham: Duke University Press.

Manalansan, Martin F. 2006. "Queer Intersections: Sexuality and Gender in Migration Studies," *International Migration Review* 40/1 (Spring): 224–49.

Manzarek, Ray. 1999. *Light My Fire: My Life with The Doors*. London: Arrow Books.

Marcuse, Herbert. 1956. *Eros and Civilisation: A Philosophical Inquiry into Freud*. London: Ark Paperbacks.

Martin, Karin A. 1996. *Puberty, Sexuality, and the Self: Boys and Girls at Adolescence*. London: Routledge.

Martin, Karin A. 2002. "'I Couldn't Ever Picture Myself Having Sex. . . .': Gender Differences in Sex and Sexual Subjectivity" [1996]. In *Sexuality and Gender*, ed. Christine L. Williams and Arlene Stein. Oxford: Blackwell Publishers: 142–66.

Masters, William H., and Virginia E. Johnson. 1966. *Human Sexual Response*. Boston: Little, Brown.

Maus, Fred E. 2001. "Glamour and Evasion: The Fabulous Ambivalence of the Pet Shop Boys," *Popular Music* 20/3 (October): 379–93.

Maus, Fred E. 2006. "Intimacy and Distance: On Stipe's Queerness," *Journal of Popular Music Studies* 18/2: 191–214.

McClary, Susan. 1991. *Feminine Endings: Music, Gender, and Sexuality*. Minneapolis: University of Minnesota Press.

McClary, Susan. 2006. "Constructions of Subjectivity in Schubert's Music." In *Queering the Pitch: The New Gay and Lesbian Musicology*, 2nd ed., ed. Philip Brett, Elizabeth Wood, and Gary C. Thomas. New York: Routledge: 205–33.

McClary, Susan. 2013. "Soprano Masculinities." In *Masculinity in Opera: Gender, History, and New Musicology*, ed. Philip Purvis. New York: Routledge: 33–50.

McCracken, Allison. 2015. *Real Men Don't Sing: Crooning in American Culture*. Durham: Duke University Press.

McDonnell, Evelyn. 1997. "Rebel Grrrls." In *Trouble Girls: The Rolling Stone Book of Women in Rock*, ed. Barbara O'Dair. New York: Random House: 453–63.

McDonnell, Evelyn, ed. 2018. *Women Who Rock: Bessie Smith to Beyoncé: Girl Groups to Riot Grrrl*. New York: Black Dog & Leventhal.

McGoldrick, Monic, Robbin Loonan, and David Wohlsifer. 2007. "Sexuality and Culture." In *Principles and Practice of Sex Therapy*, 4th ed., ed. Sandra R. Leiblum. New York: The Guilford Press: 416–41.

McRobbie, Angela. 1994. *Postmodernism and Popular Culture*. London: Routledge.

McRobbie, Angela. 1997. "*More!* New Sexualities in Girls' and Women's Magazines." In *Back to Reality? Social Experience and Cultural Studies*, ed. McRobbie. Manchester: Manchester University Press: 190–209.

Michael, Robert T., John H. Gagnon, Edward O. Laumann, and Gina Kolata. 1994. *Sex in America: A Definitive Survey*. Boston: Little, Broan and Company.

Middleton, Richard. 1990. *Studying Popular Music*. Philadelphia: Open University Press.

Middleton, Richard. 2007. "Mum's the Word: Men's Singing and Maternal Law." In *Oh Boy! Masculinities and Popular Music*, ed. Freya Jarman-Ivens. New York: Routledge: 103–24.

Miles, Barry. 2004. *Zappa*. New York: Grove Press.

Miller, Edward D. 2003. "The Nonsensical Truth of the Falsetto Voice: Listening to Sigur Rós," *Popular Musicology Online* 2, http://www.popular-musicology-online.com/issues/02/miller.html.

Moi, Toril. 1995. *Sexual/Textual Politics: Feminist Literary Theory*. London: Methuen.

Moore, Allan F. 2012. *Song Means: Analysing and Interpreting Recorded Popular Song*. Surrey: Ashgate.

Moores, D. J. 2010. *The Dark Enlightenment: Jung, Romanticism, and the Repressed Other*. Madison: Fairleigh Dickinson Press.

Mozer, G. M. 2021. "Popular vs. Personal: *Transgender Narratives in Public Media Culture*." In *Beyond Binaries: Trans Identities in Contemporary Culture*, ed. Mike Perez, Rachel Friedman, and John C. Lamothe. Lanham: Lexington Books: 17–31.

Muhammad, W. Dean. 1975. "The Tower of Babel," *Bilalian News* (Chicago, 7 November).

Mulvey, Laura. 1975. "Visual Pleasure and Narrative Cinema," *Screen* 16/3 (Autumn).

Mulvey, Laura. 2009. *Visual and Other Pleasures*, 2nd ed. Basingstoke: Palgrave Macmillan.

Murray, Stephen O. 1988. "Homosexual Acts and Selves in Early Modern Europe," *Journal of Homosexuality* 16/1–2: 457–77.

Muto, Jan. 1995. "He Was the Woman of His Dreams: Identity, Gender, and Kurt Cobain." *Popular Music and Society* 19/2 (Summer): 69–85.

Nagel, Joane. 2003. *Race, Ethnicity and Sexuality*. New York: Oxford University Press.

Nicholson, Linda J., ed. 1990. *Feminism/Postmodernism*. New York: Routledge, Chapman & Hall.

Nobile, Drew. 2020. *Form as Harmony in Rock Music*. New York: Oxford University Press.

Nyong'o, Tavia, and Francesca Royster. 2013. "'Different Love?': Introducing the Trans/Queer Issue," *Journal of Popular Music Studies* 25/4: 411–14.

Oakes, Jason Lee. 2009. "'I'm a Man': Masculinities in Popular Music." In *The Ashgate Research Companion to Popular Musicology*, ed. Derek Scott. Surrey: Ashgate: 221–39.

O'Brien, Lucy. 2002. *She Bop II: The Definitive History of Women in Rock, Pop and Soul*. New York: Penguin.

O'Brien, Lucy. 2014. "Not a Piece of Meat: Lady Gaga and *that* Dress. Has Radical Feminism Survived the Journey?" In *Lady Gaga and Popular Music: Performing Gender, Fashion, and Culture*, ed. Martin Iddon and Melanie L. Marshall. New York: Routledge: 27–43.

O'Dair, Barbara. 1997. "Polly Jean Harvey." In *Trouble Girls: The Rolling Stone Book of Women in Rock*, ed. O'Dair. New York: Random House: 543–49.

O'Meara, Caroline. 2004. "The Raincoats: Breaking Down Punk Rock's Masculinities," *Popular Music* 23/1: 299–313.

Orejuela, Fernando. 2015. *Rap and Hip Hop Culture*. New York: Oxford University Press.

Orenstein, Peggy. 2016. *Girls & Sex: Navigating the Complicated New Landscape*. New York: HarperCollins.

Orenstein, Peggy. 2020. *Boys and Sex: Young Men on Hookups, Love, Porn, Consent, and Navigating the New Masculinity*. New York: HarperCollins.

Otis, Johnny. 2009. "Upside Your Head! Rhythm and Blues on Central Avenue." In *The Pop, Rock, and Soul Reader: Histories and Debates*, 2nd ed., ed. David Brackett. New York: Oxford University Press: 60–1.

Owens, Craig N. 2014. "Celebrity without Organs." In *Lady Gaga and Popular Music: Performing Gender, Fashion, and Culture*, ed. Martin Iddon and Melanie L. Marshall. New York: Routledge: 94–113.

Padgug, Robert A. 1999. "Sexual Matters: On Conceptualizing Sexuality in History." In *Culture, Society and Sexuality: A Reader*, 2nd ed., ed. Richard Parker and Peter Aggleton. London: Routledge: 17–30.

Paglia, Camille. 1993. "Madonna II: Venus of the Radio Waves." In *Sex, Art and American Culture: Essays*. London: Penguin: 3–13.

Papayanis, Marilyn Adler. 2010. "Feeling Free and Female Sexuality: The Aesthetics of Joni Mitchell," *Popular Music and Society* 33/5 (December): 641–56.

Pavda, Gilad. 2006. "Hey, Man, You're My Girlfriend!" In *Queering the Popular Pitch*, ed. Sheila Whiteley and Jennifer Rycenga. London: Routledge: 101–13.

Paytress, Mark. 2011. *Patti Smith's Horses and the Remaking of Rock 'n' Roll*. Boston: Little, Brown.

Pecknold, Diane. 2016. "'These Stupid Little Sounds in Her Voice.'" In *Voicing Girlhood in Popular Music: Performance, Authority, Authenticity*, ed. Jacqueline Warwick and Allison Adrian. New York: Routledge: 77–98.

Pelly, Liz. 2018. "Sleater-Kinney." In *Women Who Rock: Bessie to Beyoncé: Girl Groups to Riot Grrrl*, ed. Evelyn McDonnell. New York: Black Dog & Leventhal: 306–8.

Peoples, Whitney A. 2007. "Under construction: Identifying Foundations of Hip-Hop Feminism and Exploring Bridges between Black Second-Wave and Hip-Hop Feminisms," *Meridians: Feminism, Race, Transnationalism* 8/1: 19–52.

Peraino, Judith. 2015. "Synthesizing Difference: The Queer Circuits of Early Synthpop." In *Rethinking Difference in Music Scholarship*, ed. Olivia Bloechl, Melanie Lowe, and Jeffrey Kallberg. Cambridge: Cambridge University Press: 287–314.

Perez, Mike. 2021. "A Nonbinary Letter: From Camp Epicene." In *Beyond Binaries: Trans Identities in Contemporary Culture*, ed. Mike Perez, Rachel Friedman, and John C. Lamothe. Lanham: Lexington Books: 177–207.

Perez, Mike, Rachel Friedman, and John C. Lamothe, eds. 2021. *Beyond Binaries: Trans Identities in Contemporary Culture*. Lanham: Lexington Books.

Perry, Imani. 2004. *Prophets of the Hood: Politics and Poetics in Hip-Hop*. Durham: Duke University Press.

Perry, Mary Elizabeth. 1988. "The 'Nefarious Sin' in Early Modern Seville," *Journal of Homosexuality* 16/1–2: 67–89.

Person, Ethel Spector. 1988. *Dreams of Love and Fateful Encounters*. New York: Penguin.

Petersen, Karen E. 1987. "An Investigation into Women-Identified Music in the United States." In *Women and Music in Cross-Cultural Perspective*, ed. Ellen Koskoff. New York: Greenwood Press: 203–12.

Phillips, Stephanie. 2018. "Dusty Springfield." In *Women Who Rock: Bessie to Beyoncé: Girl Groups to Riot Grrrl*, ed. Evelyn McDonnell. New York: Black Dog & Leventhal: 70–3.

Pini, Maria. 1997. "Women and the Early British Rave Scene." In *Back to Reality? Social Experience and Cultural Studies*, ed. Angela McRobbie. Manchester: Manchester University Press: 152–69.

Plummer, Ken. 2002. "Symbolic Interactionism and Sexual Conduct: An Emergent Perspective" [1982]. In *Sexuality and Gender*, ed. Christine L. Williams and Arlene Stein. Oxford: Blackwell Publishers: 20–32.

Powell, Anastasia. 2010. *Sex, Power and Consent: Youth Culture and the Unwritten Rules*. Cambridge: Cambridge University Press.

Powers, Ann. 2017. *Good Booty: Love and Sex, Black & White, Body and Soul in American Music*. New York: Dey St.

Purvis, Philip. 2013. "The 'Crisis' of Masculinity in Poulenc's *Les Mamelles*." In *Masculinity in Opera: Gender, History, and New Musicology*, ed. Purvis. New York: Routledge: 236–53.

Rabaté, Jean-Michel. 2014. *The Cambridge Introduction to Literature and Psychoanalysis*. New York: Cambridge University Press.

Rambali, Paul. 1978. "Breaking the Shackles of Original Sin," *New Musical Express* (16 September).

Reddington, Helen. 2007. *The Lost Women of Rock Music: Female Musicians of the Punk Era*. Aldershot: Ashgate.

Rey, Mario. 2018. "When the Bearded Lady Sings: Ambiguity Aesthetics, Queer Identity, and the Gendering of the Presentational Voice." In *Rethinking Difference in Gender, Sexuality, and Popular Music*, ed. Gavin Lee. London: Routledge: 15–33.

Reynolds, Simon, and Joy Press. 1995. *The Sex Revolts: Gender, Rebellion and Rock 'n' Roll*. London: Serpent's Tail.

Rich, Adrienne. 1980. "Compulsory Heterosexuality and Lesbian Experience," *Signs* 5/4: 631–61.

Riley, Tim. 2004. *Fever: How Rock 'n' Roll Transformed Gender in America*. New York: Picador.

Rimbaud, Arthur. 2005. *Rimbaud: Complete Works, Selected Letters, a Bilingual Edition*, trans. Wallace Fowlie, rev. ed. University of Chicago Press.

Robinson, Lisa. 1976. "Patti Smith: The High Priestess of Rock and Roll," *Hit Parader* (January).

Rodger, Gillian M. 2018. "What Counts as 'Queer' in an Historical Context? Cross Dressing in Nineteenth-Century Theater." In *Rethinking Difference in Gender, Sexuality, and Popular Music*, ed. Gavin Lee. London: Routledge: 89–110.

Rose, Phil. 2015. *Roger Waters and Pink Floyd: The Concept Albums*. Madison: Fairleigh Dickinson University Press.

Rosen, David. 2009. *Sex Scandal America: Politics & the Ritual of Public Shaming.* Toronto: Key Publishing House.

Ross, Alex. 2010. *Listen to This.* New York: Farrar, Straus and Giroux.

Roszak, Theodore. 1970. *The Making of a Counter Culture: Reflections on the Technocratic Society and its Youthful Opposition.* London: Faber & Faber.

Rubin, Gayle. 1984. "Thinking Sex: Notes for a Radical Theory of the Politics of Sexuality." In *The Lesbian and Gay Studies Reader,* ed. Henry Abelove, Michèle Aina Barale, and David M. Halperin. New York: Routledge: 3–44.

Rubin, Gayle. 1992. "Of Calamities and Kings: Reflections on Butch, Gender, and Boundaries." In *The Persistent Desire: A Femme-Butch Reader,* ed. Joan Nestle. Boston: Alyson Publications.

Rutter, Virginia, and Pepper Schwartz. 2012. *The Gender of Sexuality: Exploring Sexual Possibilities,* 2nd ed. Lanham: Rowman & Littlefield.

Rycenga, Jennifer. 1997. "Sisterhood: A Loving Lesbian Ear Listens to Progressive Heterosexual Women's Rock Music." In *Keeping Score: Music, Disciplinarity, Culture,* ed. David Schwarz, Anahid Kassabian, and Lawrence Siegel. Charlottesville: University of Virginia Press: 204–28.

Rycenga, Jennifer. 2006a. "Endless Caresses: Queer Exuberance in Large-Scale Form in Rock." In *Queering the Popular Pitch,* ed. Sheila Whiteley and Rycenga. London: Routledge: 235–47.

Rycenga, Jennifer. 2006b. "Lesbian Compositional Process: One Lover-Composer's Perspective." In *Queering the Pitch: The New Gay and Lesbian Musicology,* ed. Philip Brett, Elizabeth Wood, and Gary C. Thomas. New York: Routledge: 275–96.

Samuel, Lawrence R. 2013. *Sexidemic: A Cultural History of Sex in America.* Lanham: Rowman & Littlefield Publishers, Inc.

Sanday, Peggy Reeves. 1990. *Fraternity Gang Rape: Sex, Brotherhood, and Privilege on Campus.* New York: New York University Press.

Sayrs, Elizabeth. 1993–94. "Deconstructing McClary: Narrative, Feminine Sexuality, and Feminism in Susan McClary's *Feminine Endings,*" *College Music Symposium* 33–4: 41–55.

Schippers, Mimi. 2002. *Rockin' Out of the Box: Gender Maneuvering in Alternative Hard Rock.* New Brunswick: Rutgers University Press.

Schmalenberger, Sarah. 2018. "'Dirty Love': Frank Zappa and the Antithetical Love Song," *Rock Music Studies* 5/1: 20–8.

Scholnick, Ellin K., and Patricia H. Miller. 2018. "Categories, Gender, and Development: A Feminist Perspective." In *Gender, Sex, and Sexualities: Psychological Perspectives,* ed. Nancy K. Dess, Jeanne Marecek, and Leslie C. Bell. New York: Oxford University Press: 319–41.

Sciortino, Karley. 2018. *Slutever: Dispatches from a Sexually Autonomous Woman in a Post-Shame World.* New York: Grand Central Publishing.

Scott, Derek B. 1994. "The Sexual Politics of Victorian Musical Aesthetics," *Journal of the Royal Musical Association* 199/1: 91–114.

Sedgwick, Eve Kosovsky. 2008. *Epistemology of the Closet*. Berkeley: University of California Press.

Segal, Lynne. 1990. *Slow Motion: Changing Masculinities, Changing Men*, New Brunswick: Rutgers University Press.

Seidman, Steven. 2015. *The Social Construction of Sexuality*, 3rd ed. New York: Norton.

Serano, Julia. 2010. "Performance Piece." In *Gender Outlaws: The Next Generation*, ed. Kate Bornstein and S. Bear Bergman. New York: Seal Press: 85–8.

Serano, Julia. 2016. *Whipping Girl: A Transsexual Woman on Sexism and the Scapegoating of Femininity*, 2nd ed. New York: Seal Press.

Shapiro, Judith. 1991. "Transsexualism: Reflections on the Persistence of Gender and the Mutability of Sex." In *Body Guards: The Cultural Politics of Gender Ambiguity*, ed. Julia Epstein and Kristina Straub. New York: Routledge: 248–79.

Shapiro, Susan. 1975. "Patti Smith: Somewhere, Over the Rimbaud," *Crawdaddy* (December).

Shepherd, John. 1991. "Music and Male Hegemony." In *Music as Social Text*. Cambridge: Polity Press: 152–73.

Siegel, Carol. 2018. "Ambiguities of S/M and Goth Cultures' Sex/Gender Identity Politics." In *Rethinking Difference in Gender, Sexuality, and Popular Music*, ed. Gavin Lee. London: Routledge: 52–67.

Smith, Erin Sweeney. 2017. "Post-imperialism, Imaginary Geography and the Women of Led Zeppelin's *IV*," *Popular Music* 36/3: 410–26.

Smith, Marquita R. 2014. "'Or a Real, Real Bad Lesbian': Nicki Minaj and the Acknowledgement of Queer Desire in Hip-Hop Culture," *Popular Music and Society* 37/3: 360–70.

Smith, Patti. 1972. *Seventh Heaven*. Philadelphia: Telegraph Books.

Smith, Patti. 1973. *Witt*. New York: Gotham Book Mart & Gallery, Inc.

Smith, Patti. 1974. *Babel*. New York: G. P. Putnam's Sons.

Smith, Patti. 1977a. *Horses* [piano-vocal folio]. Warner Bros. Publications.

Smith, Patti. 1977b. "You Can't Say 'Fuck' in Radio Free America," *The Yipster Times* (March–April).

Smith, Patti. 1977? "Dolor Desvelado" single-sheet broadside.

Smith, Patti. 1995. *Early Work: 1970–1979*. New York: W. W. Norton & Company.

Smith, Patti. 2002. *Strange Messenger: The Work of Patti Smith*. New York: The Andy Warhol Museum.

Smith, Patti. 2005. *Auguries of Innocence: Poems*. New York: Ecco.

Smith, Patti. 2006. *Patti Smith Complete, 1975–2006: Lyrics, Reflections & Notes for the Future*. New York: Harper Collins.

Smith, Patti. 2008. *Land 250*. Paris: Fondation Cartier.

Smith, Patti. 2010. *Just Kids*. New York: Harper Collins.

Smith, Patti. 2015. *M Train*. New York: Alfred A. Knopf.

Smith-Rosenberg, Carroll. 1975. "The Female World of Love and Ritual," *Signs* 1: 1–29.

Solie, Ruth A. 1993. "Introduction." In *Musicology and Difference: Gender and Sexuality in Music Scholarship*, ed. Solie. Berkeley: University of California Press: 1–20.

Soling, Cevin. 2019. "'Maxwell's Silver Hammer': The Beatles' Neglected Dark Masterpiece." Paper presented to conference, "Come Together: Fifty Years of *Abbey Road*." Rochester (September).

Spicer, Mark. 2017. "Fragile, Emergent, and Absent Tonics in Pop and Rock Songs," *Music Theory Online* 23/2. mtosmt.org/issues/mto.17.23.2/mto.17.23.2.spicer.html

Stein, Arlene. 1999. "Rock Against Romance: Gender, Rock 'n' Roll, and Resistance." In *Stars Don't Stand Still in the Sky: Music and Myth*, ed. Karen Kelly and Evelyn McDonnell. New York: New York University Press: 214–27.

Stephens, Dionne P., and Layli D. Phillips. 2003. "Freaks, Gold Diggers, Divas, and Dykes: The Sociohistorical Development of Adolescent African American Women's Sexual Scripts," *Sexuality and Culture* 7/1 (March): 3–47.

Stephens, Vincent. 2005. "Pop Goes the Rapper: A Close Reading of Eminem's Genderphobia," *Popular Music* 24/1: 21–36.

Steptoe, Tyina. 2018. "Big Mama Thornton, Little Richard, and the Queer Roots of Rock 'n' Roll," *American Quarterly* 70/1 (March): 55–77.

Stilwell, Robynn J. 2010. "Vocal Decorum: Voice, Body, and Knowledge in the Prodigious Singer, Brenda Lee." In *She's So Fine: Reflections on Whiteness, Femininity, Adolescence and Class in 1960s Music*, ed. Laurie Stras. Surrey: Ashgate Press: 57–87.

Stone, Allucquère Rosanne (= Sandy Stone, q.v.). 1995. *The War of Desire and Technology at the Close of the Mechanical Age*. Cambridge, MA: MIT Press.

Stone, Sandy. 1991. "The Empire Strikes Back: A Posttranssexual Manifesto." In *Body Guards: The Cultural Politics of Gender Ambiguity*, ed. Julia Epstein and Kristina Straub. New York: Routledge: 280–304.

Street, John. 1986. *Rebel Rock: The Politics of Popular Music*, Oxford and New York: Blackwell.

Stryker, Susan. 2017. *Transgender History: The Roots of Today's Revolution*, 2nd ed. New York: Seal Press.

Summach, Jay. 2011. "The Structure, Function, and Genesis of the Prechorus," *Music Theory Online* 17/3. mtosmt.org/issues/mto.11.17.3/mto.11.17.3.summach.html

Sutton, Terri. 1997. "The Soft Boys: The New Man in Rock." In *Trouble Girls: The Rolling Stone Book of Women in Rock*, ed. Barbara O'Dair. New York: Random House: 527–35.

Talbot, Mary M. 1997. "'An Explosion Deep Inside Her': Women's Desire and Popular Romance Fiction." In *Language and Desire: Encoding Sex, Romance and Intimacy*, ed. Keith Harvey and Celia Shalom. London: Routledge: 106–22.

Tarr, Joe. 2008. *The Words and Music of Patti Smith*. London: Praeger.

Taylor, Ian, and David Wall. 1976. "Beyond the Skinheads: Comments on the Emergence and Significance of the Glamrock Cult." In *Working Class Youth Culture*, ed. Geoff Mungham and Geoff Pearson. London: Routledge and Kegan Paul: 105–23.

Taylor, Jenny, and Dave Laing. 1979. "'Disco-Pleasure-Discourse': On 'Rock and Sexuality'," *Screen Education* 31 (Summer): 43–8.

Taylor, Jodie. 2012. *Playing It Queer: Popular Music, Identity and Queer World-making*. Bern: Peter Lang.

Temperley, David. 2018. *The Musical Language of Rock*. New York: Oxford University Press.

Thiel-Stern, Shayla. 2014. *From the Dance Hall to Facebook*. Amherst: University of Massachusetts Press.

Tomlinson, Lori. 1998. "'This Ain't No Disco' . . . or Is It? Youth Culture and the Rave Phenomenon." In *Youth Culture: Identity in a Postmodern World*, ed. Jonathon S. Epstein. Oxford: Blackwell: 195–211.

Tosches, Nick. 1976. "A Baby Wolf with Neon Bones," *Penthouse* (April).

Traub, Valerie. 1991. "The Ambiguities of 'Lesbian' Viewing Pleasure: The (Dis)-Articulations of *Black Widow*." In *Body Guards: The Cultural Politics of Gender Ambiguity*, ed. Julia Epstein and Kristina Straub. New York: Routledge: 305–28.

Trier-Bieniek, Adrienne. 2015. "Introduction." In *Feminist Theory and Pop Culture*, ed. Trier-Bieniek. Rotterdam: Sense Publishers: xiii–xxvi.

Tropiano, Stephen. 2002. *The Prime Time Closet: A History of Gays and Lesbians on TV*. New York: Applause.

Trumbach, Randolph. 1991. "London's Sapphists: From Three Sexes to Four Genders in the Making of Modern Culture." In *Body Guards: The Cultural Politics of Gender Ambiguity*, ed. Julia Epstein and Kristina Straub. New York: Routledge: 112–41.

Turman, Katherine. 2018. "Suzi Quatro." In *Women Who Rock: Bessie to Beyoncé: Girl Groups to Riot Grrrl*, ed. Evelyn McDonnell. New York: Black Dog & Leventhal: 138–40.

Twenge, Jean M. 2017. *iGen: Why Today's Super-Connected Kids Are Growing Up Less Rebellious, More Tolerant, Less Happy—and Completely Unprepared for Adulthood*. New York: Atria Books.

Vance, Carole S. 1999. "Anthropology Rediscovers Sexuality: A Theoretical Comment" [1991]. In *Culture, Society and Sexuality: A Reader*, 2nd ed., ed. Richard Parker and Peter Aggleton. London: Routledge: 41–57.

van der Meer, Theo. 1988. "The Persecutions of Sodomites in Eighteenth-Century Amsterdam: Changing Perceptions of Sodomy," *Journal of Homosexuality* 16/1–2: 263–307.

Van der Merwe, Peter. 1989. *Origins of the Popular Style: The Antecedents of Twentieth-Century Popular Music*. Oxford: Clearendon Press.

Vargas, Deborah R. 2012. *Dissonant Divas in Chicana Music: The Limits of La Onda*. Minneapolis: University of Minnesota Press.

von Franz, Marie-Louise. 1995. *Shadow and Evil in Fairy Tales*, rev. ed. Boston and London: Shambhala Press.

Waksman, Steve. 1996. "Every Inch of My Love: Led Zeppelin and the Problem of Cock Rock," *Journal of Popular Music Studies* 8: 5–25.

Waksman, Steve. 1999. *Instruments of Desire: The Electric Guitar and the Shaping of Musical Experience*. Cambridge, MA: Harvard University Press.

Wald, Gayle. 2016. "Afterword: 'The Art of Yearning.'" In *Voicing Girlhood in Popular Music: Performance, Authority, Authenticity*, ed. Jacqueline Warwick and Allison Adrian. New York: Routledge: 281–85.

Walser, Robert. 1993. *Running with the Devil: Power, Gender, and Madness in Heavy Metal Music*. Middletown: Wesleyan University Press/New England.

Walser, Robert. 2004. "Forging Masculinity: Heavy Metal Sounds and Images of Gender." In *Popular Music: Critical Concepts in Media and Cultural Studies*, ed. Simon Frith. London: Routledge: 343–72.

Ware, Vron. 1997. "Purity and Danger: Race, Gender and Tales of Sex Tourism." In *Back to Reality? Social Experience and Cultural Studies*, ed. Angela McRobbie. Manchester: Manchester University Press: 133–51.

Warwick, Jacqueline. 2004. "'He's Got the Power': The Politics of Production in Girl Group Music." In *Music, Space and Place: Popular Music and Cultural Identity*, ed. Sheila Whiteley, Andy Bennett, and Stan Hawkins. Aldershot: Ashgate Press: 191–200.

Warwick, Jacqueline. 2007. *Girl Groups, Girl Culture: Popular Music and Identity in the 1960s*. New York: Routledge.

Warwick, Jacqueline. 2009. "Singing Style and White Masculinity." In *The Ashgate Research Companion to Popular Musicology*, ed. Derek Scott. Surrey: Ashgate Press: 349–64.

Warwick, Jacqueline, and Allison Adrian, eds. 2016. *Voicing Girlhood in Popular Music: Performance, Authority, Authenticity*. New York: Routledge.

Watson, Ben. 1994. *Frank Zappa: The Negative Dialectics of Poodle Play*. London: Quartet Books.

Weatherall, Ann. 2002. *Gender, Language, Discourse*. New York: Routledge.

Weeks, Jeffrey. 2000. *Making Sexual History*. Cambridge: Polity Press.

Weeks, Jeffrey. 2010. *Sexuality*, 3rd ed. London: Routledge.

Weeks, Jeffrey. 2011. *The Languages of Sexuality*. London: Routledge.

Weinstein, Deena. 1994. "Rock: Youth and Its Music." In *Adolescents and Their Music: If It's Too Loud, You're Too Old*, ed. Jonathon S. Epstein. New York: Garland Publishing: 3–23.

Weinstein, Deena. 2000. *Heavy Metal: The Music and Its Culture*, rev. ed. New York: Da Capo Press.

West, Cornell. 1993. *Race Matters*. Boston: Beacon Press.

Weston, Kath. 2002. "Copycat" [1996]. In *Sexuality and Gender,* ed. Christine L. Williams and Arlene Stein. Oxford: Blackwell Publishers: 100–12.

Whiteley, Sheila. 1992. *The Space Between the Notes: Rock and the Counter-Culture.* London: Routledge.

Whiteley, Sheila, ed. 1997. *Sexing the Groove: Popular Music and Gender.* London: Routledge.

Whiteley, Sheila. 2000. *Women and Popular Music: Sexuality, Identity, and Subjectivity.* New York: Routledge.

Whiteley, Sheila. 2005. *Too Much Too Young: Popular Music, Age and Gender.* New York: Routledge.

Whiteley, Sheila. 2006. "Love, Love, Love: Representations of Gender and Sexuality in Selected Songs by the Beatles." In *Reading the Beatles: Cultural Studies, Literary Criticism, and the Fab Four,* ed. Kenneth Womack and Todd F. Davis. Albany: State University of New York Press: 55–69.

Whiteley, Sheila. 2007. "Which Freddie? Constructions of Masculinity in Freddie Mercury and Justin Hawkins." In *Oh Boy! Masculinities and Popular Music,* ed. Freya Jarman-Ivens. New York: Routledge: 21–37.

Whiteley, Sheila. 2009. "Who Are You? Research Strategies of the Unruly Feminine." In *The Ashgate Research Companion to Popular Musicology,* ed. Derek Scott. Surrey: Ashgate Press: 205–20.

Whiteley, Sheila, and Jennifer Rycenga, eds. 2006. *Queering the Popular Pitch.* London: Routledge.

Williams, Christine L., and Arlene Stein. 2002. *Sexuality and Gender.* Oxford: Blackwell Publishers.

Williams, Melvin L., and Tia C. M. Tyree. 2015. "The Un-Quiet Queen: An Analysis of Rapper Nicki Minaj in the *Fame* Comic Book." In *Feminist Theory and Pop Culture,* ed. Adrienne Trier-Bieniek. Rotterdam: Sense Publishers: 49–64.

Williams, Sarah. 2007. "'A Walking Open Wound': Emo Rock and the 'Crisis' of Masculinity in America." In *Oh Boy! Masculinities and Popular Music.* New York: Routledge: 145–60.

Wincze, John P. 2000. "Assessment and Treatment of Atypical Sexual Behavior." In *Principles and Practice of Sex Therapy,* 3rd ed., ed. Sandra R. Leiblum and Raymond C. Rosen. New York: The Guilford Press: 449–70.

Wise, Sue. 1990. "Sexing Elvis." In *On Record: Rock, Pop, and the Written Word,* ed. Simon Frith and Andrew Goodwin, New York: Pantheon Books: 390–98.

Witt, Emily. 2016. *Future Sex.* New York: Farrar, Straus and Giroux.

Wood, Elizabeth. 2006. "Sapphonics." In *Queering the Pitch: The New Gay and Lesbian Musicology,* 2nd ed., ed. Philip Brett, Wood and Gary C. Thomas. New York: Routledge: 27–66.

Woods, Alyssa. 2011. "Vocal Practices and Constructions of Identity in Rap: A Case Study of Young Jeezy's 'Soul Survivor.'" In *Pop-Culture Pedagogy in the Music Classroom*, ed. Nicole Biamonte. Plymouth: Scarecrow Press: 265–80.

Zaleski, Annie. 2018. "Lady Gaga." In *Women Who Rock: Bessie to Beyoncé: Girl Groups to Riot Grrrl*, ed. Evelyn McDonnell. New York: Black Dog & Leventhal: 369–71.

Zappa, Frank, with Peter Occhiogrosso. 1989. *The Real Frank Zappa Book*. New York: Poseidon Press.

Zemke, Kirsten, and Jared Mackley-Crump. 2018. "'I'ma School That Bitch': Gay Rappers Defying Binaries and Expressing Fierceness." In *Rethinking Difference in Gender, Sexuality, and Popular Music*, ed. Gavin Lee. London: Routledge: 131–49.

Žižek, Slavoj. 1991. *Looking Awry: An Introduction to Jacques Lacan through Popular Culture*. Cambridge, MA: MIT Press.

Subject Index

Index of Names and Titles

Page numbers in *italics* denotes tables.

https://www.bloomsbury.com/us/sex-and-gender-in-poprock-music-9781501345951/

Printed in Great Britain
by Amazon

Sex and Gender in Pop/Rock Music